Faithful to the Future

Faithful to the Future

Listening to Yves Congar

Brother Émile of Taizé
Translated by Karen Scott and Br. Émile

With a Foreword by Charles Taylor

BLOOMSBURY
LONDON • NEW DELHI • NEW YORK • SYDNEY

Bloomsbury T&T Clark

An imprint of Bloomsbury Publishing Plc

50 Bedford Square
London
WC1B 3DP
UK

1385 Broadway
New York
NY 10018
USA

www.bloomsbury.com

Bloomsbury is a registered trade mark of Bloomsbury Publishing Plc

First published 2013

British Library Cataloguing-in-Publication Data
A catalogue record for this book is available from the British Library.

ISBN: PB: 978-0-5670-2548-7
ePDF: 978-0-5674-2560-7
ePub: 978-0-5675-1830-9

Library of Congress Cataloging-in-Publication Data
Faithful to the Future/ Brother Émile of Taizé p.cm
Includes bibliographic references and index.
ISBN 978–0–5670–2548–7 (pbk.)

Typeset by Fakenham Prepress Solutions, Fakenham, Norfolk NR21 8NN
Printed and bound in Great Britain

'The Church is its future as much as its past'.

YVES CONGAR, *Église Catholique et France moderne*
(Paris: Hachette, 1978), p. 10

*'Fidelity to Christian reality can be a fidelity to the present
state of things, to forms presently expressing this reality,
that is, a fidelity to what is at present achieved. It can
also be a fidelity to its future development or a fidelity to
its principle. The two expressions come to the same thing
[…]. A profound, not shallow, fidelity to this dimension
of Christianity is at once a fidelity to principle, to the
tradition, and to the future, that is, to what Christianity can
and ought to become in order to arrive at the truth given
at the beginning, in substance, in its principle. Catholic
(=embracing the whole) fidelity will have to embrace the
two aspects.'*

YVES CONGAR, *True and False Reform in the Church*, trans. Paul Philibert, O.P.
(Collegeville, MN: Liturgical Press, 2011), pp. 366–7

CONTENTS

ACKNOWLEDGEMENTS

A few months spent in Chicago in the spring of 2012 helped me to find many of the English translations of Congar's works. I wish to thank the efficient staff at DePaul University for their assistance. When I returned to Taizé, friends in the UK, Ireland, Canada and the United States were helpful in tracking down a number of texts not available to me in France. I am grateful for their help.

I am especially grateful to Karen Scott, who offered to translate the book in spite of an already heavy workload. She made a first translation of all the chapters, except for Chapter 5 and the Conclusion, which I translated. I carefully went over Karen's translations, made changes when I found them to be necessary and sent them along to Melanie Baffes and David Ash, who patiently re-read them. Often their suggestions very much helped to improve our translations. My deepest thanks to Melanie and David. Gilles Mongeau translated the glossary. My thanks to him as well. Karen Scott and I later reviewed the entire book together.

FOREWORD

by *Charles Taylor*

I am very glad to see this book by Brother Émile coming out in English translation. Yves Congar was one of the small group of theologians – which also included the Jesuit Henri de Lubac – whose thought was foundational to the turn the Church took in Vatican II. Fifty years after the Council is a good point at which to take stock of the achievements of the Council, and also of what it failed to change in the Church.

Brother Émile sets out clearly and eloquently what were the main themes of Congar's work. I should like to mention just three of these here.

The first was his understanding of the Church in history. The Church brings the message of Christ into many societies, many civilizations and many epochs. It has to be able to speak to these epochs. On one level, this has always been recognized. The Bible has been translated into a long and ever-growing list of languages. But just translating the Gospel into the different languages is not enough. The message has to be able to speak to people of different epochs in terms that they can understand. Or otherwise put, the Church must identify the authentic human aspirations of each civilization and epoch, which can serve as the ante-chamber, the taking-off point, to the transformation the Gospel calls us to. In the language of Vatican II, we have to read the 'signs of the times'.

Congar grasped our time, from very early on in his life. As Brother Émile says, he saw that ours is the era of the 'subject'; the era where self-determination, both individual and collective, comes into its own. As we now might put it, it is an epoch of the search for authenticity, of respect for human rights, and of the aspiration to democracy. We can see how Vatican II made it possible for the Catholic Church really to speak to this era for the first time.

The second major theme I want to mention is that of Christian unity. Congar suffered from the sight of a fragmented Church, from the way we too comfortably settle into accepting this as an inevitable, even acceptable, state of affairs. He had a passion for reconstituting the Church in all its width and breadth, for overcoming the schism of 1054, as well as all the other breaks which have afflicted us. We can see how this concern too emerges in Vatican II in its new emphasis on ecumenicism, which then extends even beyond the boundaries of Christianity.

The third major theme was that of the authority of the Church. Of course, the era of the subject was bound to call into question authority in all its forms. But what is the Church's form? For Congar, this had inescapably two poles. There is the pole we are all familiar with, that of the hierarchy, the magisterium, which issues definitions of the faith. But this must always be in balance, in living contact, with the second pole, the community of the faithful, which lives the life of the Church and its sacraments (see page 106).

This is perhaps the aspect of Congar's work that we most urgently need to remember today. Vatican II took some steps down the road this indicated, in stressing the role of the laity in pastoral councils, for instance, and in re-asserting the collegiality of the bishops. But in the last decade we have slid backwards, so that one can say that in its whole history the Catholic church has never been as closely ruled from the centre as it is today; certainly not in the Middle Ages, where the Pope had to take account of local authorities, Cathedral chapters, and the like. We have a hierarchy and a Curia in which some members seem to have lost the will and perhaps the ability to listen to the faithful. The tragic scandal of clerical paedophilia revealed that for the world to see.

We need to take up again the task of *aggiornamento*, of recovering contact with our age which Vatican II started. In this task Congar's life and writings can be a great source of inspiration. His work is not just a footnote to the history of the twentieth century, but is full of urgent messages for our time. We are all in Brother Émile's debt for this limpid and moving description of the life work of this great theologian.

NOTE ON THE ENGLISH EDITION

My intention in preparing this English edition was to make it as useful as possible to readers who do not have access to the original writings of Congar in French. So, instead of referring the reader to the original French sources, I have given references to the English translations of his works whenever possible. In 'Works Quoted' in the last section of this book, the reader will find a complete list of the English translations I have used, as well as information on the French originals.

The English translations of Congar's works are generally good, even excellent. However, on several occasions, I have used translations by Karen Scott. In some cases, we worked together to try to improve an existing translation. In these instances, the words 'tr. modified' appear after the reference.

In the footnotes, the works of Yves Congar are referred to with the initials Y. C., followed by the title appearing in italics for his books and in inverted commas for his articles and contributions.

For books and articles that are quoted infrequently, the full reference appears in the footnotes. For works that are frequently quoted, the full reference can be found in the bibliography.

I have quoted extensively from Paul Philibert's recent translation of Congar's *True and False Reform in the Church* (Copyright 2011 by Order of Saint Benedict. Published by Liturgical Press, Collegeville, Minnesota. Reprinted with permission).

Words followed by an asterisk (*) are explained in the glossary.

Brother Émile

PREFACE

'*You are going to break my wheelchair! And it is not even mine. It belongs to my confrère.*' I can still hear the harsh voice of Father Congar. It was my second year at Taizé, and I had been given the job of accompanying him from place to place during his week-long stay with us. Illness[1] had confined him to a wheelchair, and the pebbles on the unpaved path between the house where he was staying and the church where we were going were giving him a bumpy ride. I had been warned that he could be difficult. This was in 1977. He had also come to Taizé the year before, but another young brother had cared for him then, one who was far more interested in Congar's writings than I was at the time.

I remember the day the community received his registration form. The brother who was opening the mail showed it to me. His shaky handwriting was not easy to read. Could the great theologian Yves Congar be signing up for a visit to Taizé in such an ordinary way?

What did I know of Yves Congar at the time? That he had been one of the greatest theologians at the Second Vatican Council,* that he had been ahead of his time, that he had suffered for his ideas. But his books seemed old, and at that time, quite wrongly, I was interested only in biblical exegesis. He arrived as announced. I heard him speak to the young people at Taizé. He introduced himself as an 'ecclesiologist', but he made fun of this slightly pompous word, which I had never heard before. He spoke of the great river of Tradition that transports the water necessary for life, and which can carry many other things as well: as he put it, '*tree trunks, dead rats …*' He congratulated one of our brothers on the accuracy with which he had translated his talk into English. The brother was slightly embarrassed and did not acknowledge the compliment; Congar, true to form, promptly upbraided him: '*I do not offer praise unless it is warranted!*'

Like many others, I still remember the homily he offered in the church at Taizé. He spoke on 'the geography of salvation' – about how there are places where God is pleased to show his mercy. He mentioned a number of places, spoke of how he saw Taizé's place on this map, and then cited the marvelous cry of St. Catherine of Siena: 'Mercy to Catherine, mercy to the Church, mercy to the world.'

During this visit he mentioned the book he wanted to publish some day on the Holy Spirit – I suspect he had already researched and written a substantial portion of it. He insisted that 'The Spirit is not just a force, not just a power'. At the time I did not quite understand what he meant.

The older brothers, and first of all Brother Roger, were already well acquainted with him. He first visited Taizé in 1960, and gave an account of his stay in an unpublished document. Dialogue Between Christians mentions this visit as well.[2] Other visits followed on the hill of Taizé in Burgundy. And then during Vatican II in Rome, there were meals[3] and long conversations in our apartment on the Via del Plebiscito, followed by more visits to Burgundy, and exchanges of books. In the personally signed books he sent to the community, he would sometimes indicate to us the pages that mentioned Taizé, as a sign of his friendship and trust.

In the 1980s, during one of our first European meetings of young adults, he could be seen in the choir of Notre Dame of Paris together with Marie-Dominique Chenu, O.P., surrounded by thousands of young people who had come that day to fill the cathedral. Brother Roger had strongly insisted that the two Dominicans come to Notre Dame, and their presence among all the young people seemed entirely natural.

When he became ill and entered the Invalides Hospital, Brother Roger visited him on Ash Wednesday. An amusing exchange occurred on that occasion:

Brother Roger: *Father Congar, will you give us ashes?*
Fr. Congar: *You don't need any ashes.*
Brother Roger with insistence: *Oh but yes, we do!*

This went on for several minutes, until Congar gave way to Brother Roger's insistence. And as he marked Brother Roger's forehead

with ashes according to the Lenten practice, he spoke words that
were perhaps not traditional for the occasion ...

There was a world of difference between Brother Roger's
gentleness and Father Congar's abruptness. These two men could
not have been more dissimilar. And yet the same passion burned in
them both: the *ecclesia*. One hesitates to translate this as 'Church',
because the word is so often misunderstood. The *ecclesia* was their
life, the unique communion that exists in Christ. They yearned to
dispel the misunderstandings about this communion and to help
many others discover it. They devoted their existence to this end.
While Congar hid his sensitivity, which in actual fact was quite
acute, behind a somewhat abrupt manner, Brother Roger showed
it freely, though some underestimated the unflinching courage that
went along with it. In rereading Congar's *Power and Poverty in the
Church*, I was struck to find one of Brother Roger's preoccupations
– the importance of the first impression one receives upon entering
a church.

> It is by the outward signs of the Church, by what it is seen to
> be, that human beings know it and through it are, or should be,
> brought to the Gospel, led to God; or else they are estranged
> from it, repelled or even turned towards some sort of religion of
> material things, a system where sociological conduct predomi-
> nates, rather than towards a personal religion with its inherent
> spiritual demands. From this point of view, then, the greatest
> importance attaches to everything that makes the Church
> visible, everything by which it comes into contact with people's
> lives, as their faces, looks, shape, and outwards trappings give
> us contact with our fellows; it may be the wording of a poster,
> a notice, a parish magazine, or more likely a form of ornamen-
> tation or celebration ... the look of the priest, his manner or turn
> of speech, the way he lives – and the same applies to a nun or
> any cleric. These are minor everyday elements in the Church's
> visible form, in its role as the parable of the kingdom of God
> or the sacrament of the Gospel, but they have their significance
> none the less and it may be decisive.[4]

Brother Roger shared the same concern. He knew that what
seems like a minor detail can be upsetting and may become an
obstacle. Like Father Congar, he stressed how important it is that

all participate in the liturgy, and he found new paths to make that possible.

As I look for other things that brought these two men together, an expression used by Yves Congar comes to mind: 'spiritual anthropology',[5] without which it is impossible to enter into the mystery of the Church. Father Congar wrote a great deal on this theme, and his views on this subject, as on many others, were not based exclusively on an intellectual approach. Brother Roger did not theorize much on this topic, but he knew that it is through our life, through our transfigured existence, that Christ becomes accessible in the communion of his Church.

In 1994, the year before his death, I visited Father Congar at the Invalides Hospital. I was astounded by how keen his memory was, and he spoke words to me that I will never forget. He told me how sad he was at not being able to read any more. The following year, Brother Roger sent me to his funeral at Notre Dame. I remember the warm welcome of Father Gy, and the sermon of Timothy Radcliffe who was still Master General of the Dominicans at that time. He was accompanied by Daniel Cadrin, who had been one of the first to speak to me about Taizé in my faraway native province in Canada.

It is not, however, these few personal memories of Yves Congar's long friendship with the Taizé community that have led me to write this book. Some might imagine that it was Congar's pioneering contribution to the ecumenical movement that prompted a Taizé brother to publish on his writings. There would be many reasons to express gratitude to Congar for his courageous and innovative ecumenical work. But other, more compelling reasons have guided me.

The Church is not a system. Inscribing such a negative title on a book cover did not seem like a good idea to me. Yet, this is the title that would convey with the least inaccuracy the content of this book. It is not an introduction to the entirety of Yves Congar's thought and life. Such books have already been written, and I do not see how I could improve on the one recently published by Joseph Famerée and Gilles Routhier.[6] My project here is more modest and more focused, and it is meant to address a difficulty that can be seen at every turn. It is not rare these days to meet young people, and also women and men of all ages, who do not hide their interest in 'spirituality', but immediately turn away as soon as faith is linked with an institution. How can we explain this kind of reaction? Their repugnance for what they perceive as a 'system' appears to be the deciding factor. In reading the work of Yves Congar, this man who identified so deeply with the Church and whose sense of belonging to it was so profound, this man who was so convinced that the institution was necessary, I have been struck by his rejection of a certain kind of 'system'. For Congar, the system is not what characterizes the Church – I mean here the Church when it is true to itself. No, for Congar the 'system' is what distorts the Church; it is a betrayal of its true nature.

It is heartening to realize that the author of such a thought was made a cardinal. The key role that Congar played at Vatican II is well known and is illustrated by Cardinal Avery Dulles' quip: 'The Second Vatican Council? – Ah! You mean Congar's council!' Of course this is an exaggeration: no council is ever the brain-child of one person, but Dulles' comment shows how much Vatican II owed to Yves Congar. Is not Congar the theologian that those who fear systems need to discover? Is he not best placed to help our contemporaries see that the Church is something other than a system? This is the hope that guides me here.

One can learn a great deal by reading the work of such a thinker. To study Tradition under his guidance is to discover a reality that is alive and to hear a call to be faithful not only to the past, but also, and just as much, to the future. To read the author of *True and False Reform in the Church*[7] is to encounter a Christianity that deals with what is real, with the novel questions that arise over time. This is a Christianity in which 'there really can be something new', and where novelty calls for reform. To listen to Congar reflect on the catholicity[8] of the Church is to escape from a sectarian mentality characterized by a lack of reference to the whole. But it is also to come face to face with the eminently personal quality of Christian faith. Readers of Congar discover a way of approaching the notion of authority in the Church that is able to assuage many of their fears. For Congar, genuine authority is not a power that is in thrall to an outdated world, or that is obsessed with the desire to perpetuate itself. In the exercise of this kind of authority, authority the Christian way, the liberty of the individual is not in danger. This authority[9] is at the service not of a closed system, but of 'growth' where the closest attention is paid to what is unknown and unpredictable.

These four themes that I have just referred to – *tradition, reform, catholicity,* and *authority* – are at the heart of this book. The reader will find here some analysis of each of these themes, but my intention is less to dissect Congar's thought than to make his voice heard. The decision to listen to Congar is not fortuitous. The man whose voice we are about to hear examined Christian tradition with great care and patience. 'Encyclopedic' is perhaps not the best word to describe his knowledge of it: his learning, vast as it was, went far deeper. His knowledge, as others have commented, was that of a 'water diviner' [Fr.: *'un sourcier'*]. In reality, very few people have understood the history of Christianity in as much breadth and depth. Few voices are as qualified to attempt to express what the Church is.

There is another reason behind my desire to recall the person and thought of Yves Congar. The challenges we face today, those that are emerging and those that will arise in the future and that remain unknown to us, will no doubt require creative responses from Christians. It is likely that in many areas we will have to do things differently than we have in the past. On certain topics we may have to speak in new ways. We are already being faced with unprecedented situations and, in the future, this is likely to occur with increasing frequency. In this context it seems to me that it is helpful to listen to Yves Congar, for his writings and his thought invite us to mobilize all the resources that the Christian faith has at its disposal, and not to be content with *one* historical expression of it that may have been useful in its own time but which is not the last word on Christianity. Both Congar's audacity and his sense of continuity seem more necessary than ever. On the occasion of the centenary of his birth, Cardinal Walter Kasper said of Congar: 'We are still far from having explored all the perspectives he has opened up for us'. There is surely much to learn from a man who knew that 'Tradition is alive', and that 'the only way to say the same thing in a context that has changed is to say it differently'.[10]

* * *

Towards the end of his visit to Taizé, after the Evening Prayer, I accompanied Father Congar to his room in the guest house. It was a beautiful summer evening. Great purple stripes still stretched across the sky. Congar confided to me how much he loved the peace evening brings. Then, as I was about to leave him, and as he was still sitting in his wheelchair, apparently ready to return to the book that had occupied him for part of the day, he turned to me and said in an almost tender tone of voice: 'Go on a walk for me'. I don't remember if I followed his suggestion, but the journey I have undertaken through his work has convinced me that it deserves to be more widely known.

INTRODUCTION

Yves Congar had a strong aversion to the word 'system'.[1] When he used this word – and this happened frequently – it was always to lament what it has represented in the history of the Church. All those who were acquainted with Father Congar knew that he excelled in the art of expressing displeasure. Although one can imagine him scowling at the system, nothing would be further from the truth than to conclude that his thought lacked rigour. Congar was the epitome of the relentless, precise, and exacting intellectual. Without being blind to the limitations of his training, until the end of his long life he remained grateful for how it structured his mind[2] and instilled in him an appreciation for precision and exact expression.[3] He was keenly interested in the correlation between ideas. If he complained, it was rather because he thought that many of his contemporaries did not perceive these connections clearly enough. For Congar, there was an obvious interdependence among the articles of faith, where he saw, as the Church Fathers did, the presence of the whole in every part of theological discourse. And the same interdependence existed between real life – the life of societies that are continually evolving – and the faith of the Church, whose expression must be constantly renewed. Congar was convinced of this: 'It is through the world's contributions that the Church grows and can give shape to the Body of Christ.'[4] He knew that a religion without the world leads to a world without religion.[5] As a historian, Congar was able, as few other theologians were, to research the origin of an idea, to trace it back to its source, to locate the beginning of a distressing distortion – as he did for the notion of authority in a brilliant lecture during a Franco-English colloquium in 1961. If there was anyone capable of understanding how *everything holds together* and of proving this through historical analysis, it was Congar. More than anyone else, he deplored the atomization of theology.

The system is not the institution

Congar's rejection of the system was in no way a rejection of 'structure'. For this great artisan of Vatican II, structure has its place in the life of Christians, and he did not wish either to minimize it unduly or to overstate its importance. He supported the need for ecclesial structure, just as he saw the need for church hierarchy.[6] If he rejected the system so forcefully, it was because, for him, it disfigured the mystery of the living God, a God who is free and infinitely respectful of persons, of liberties, and of the rich contributions of every time and of every culture. The system also disfigures the project of Christ. For Congar, the Son comes forward to meet human beings and makes himself their contemporary. Christ did not want to call his disciples 'servants', but 'friends', and he wished with an ardent desire to found a community of brothers and sisters. As the witness of an entrenched legalism among Christians, Congar saw how reductionist the system could be, excluding vast portions of reality. The system does not exist 'according to the whole', it empties the word 'catholic' of its meaning, and it does not take into account what is specific to each particular situation.[7] It proposes a straight-jacket, while the founder of Christianity wanted to bring forth the fullness of life. Especially when it feels threatened, the system's main concern is its own self-preservation, and it can become oblivious of reality. Closed in on itself, it rejects the contributions of new life, running the risk of alienating those who are attentive to unprecedented expressions of life and culture. Fostering distrust, the system leads to a general dismissal of the institution, whereas Congar, while rejecting the system, was convinced of the institution's necessity.

His incessant study of the mystery of the Church – his area of expertise – gave him an extremely refined understanding of its history. Among the 1,790 works listed in his bibliography there are not only thick and erudite tomes, but also a good number of shorter and incisive texts, and even these reflect his nuanced understanding. This author abhorred those who make generalizations.

He found the Church that he loved not only among the Fathers of the early Christian centuries, but also in the early Middle Ages, a period he continued to admire. For Congar, the system came into being at a specific point in history and, as we shall see, it was consolidated later in various ways for various reasons.

The Gregorian Reform

In Congar's books, lectures and essays it is always the same event that constitutes the 'turning point',[8] 'the most important turning point that Catholic ecclesiology has ever known'[9]: the Gregorian Reform. For him this determined everything that followed. The Church's situation at the beginning of the eleventh century was muddled:

> Churches remained the property of the lords who had founded and endowed them and who consequently selected the priest they wanted [...]; as a result, simony thrived. The clergy often lacked any real calling, lived with wives and children (Nicolaism), and shrugged off the authority of their bishops. The feudal system further aggravated these problems, not only by subdividing authority, but also by binding the spiritual function so closely to the temporal function connected to it that the two became confused.[10]

There was a clearly felt need for reform. Gregory VII (elected Pope in 1073) had the merit of leading the energetic struggle that led to the confrontation with temporal power. This was 'a very necessary step', said Congar,[11] to keep the temporal power from controlling the Church, but it had the serious disadvantage of bringing the Church to see itself as a power in its own right.[12] In order to avoid being taken over by the temporal powers, the Church defined its own powers, claimed its own rights, and insisted on its prerogatives. And it did all of this by relying on the Papacy to an unprecedented degree, so that the entire Church became dependent on the Papal monarchy. One power confronted the other. What set Gregory VII apart was the way he founded his reform on *juridical* principles.[13] The Gregorian Reform 'set in motion a powerful

wave of canonical studies. Schools were founded, among them the
school at Bologna [...]. The science of Canon law had well and
truly begun'.[14] Gregory's immediate successors were all eminent
canonists, that is, legal specialists. All of this came at a high price:
legalism entered the life of the Church.[15] This emphasis continued
until it distorted realities that were foundational to the life of the
Church – not to mention the chasm between the Western and
Eastern churches, which was further aggravated by this same
juridical focus:

> Perhaps the greatest difference between ancient or patristic ecclesi-
> ology and modern ecclesiology[16] is that the former embodied an
> anthropology while the latter is merely the theory of a system,
> a book of public law – does the system require a certain kind of
> men or does it consider them to be interchangeable?[17]

It did not take long for the consequences of this situation to
become manifest.

Tridentinism

Although the Council of Trent* did not address the ecclesiological issues directly,[18] the period that followed immediately
afterwards interested Congar in a special way, for it set up an
apparatus and marked the beginning of a centralizing regime.[19]
The Curia was organized by Paul III (Pope from 1534 to 1549)
and his successors, and the Holy Office was created in 1542.
Congar recognized the positive achievements of the Council of
Trent (1545–63), which he did not confuse with 'Tridentinism'*.[20]
This Council 'did a very beautiful and deep work'.[21] But the facts
obliged Congar to recognize that, in the wake of Trent, a new
juridical era in theoretical ecclesiology had begun.[22] He focused
less on the Council itself than on its implementation, especially
under Pope Paul IV (who died in 1559): this was 'a Catholic
and Roman *system*, dynamic and gaining ground externally, but
closed in on itself on the inside, living as if in a state of siege'.[23]
Congar continued: 'The ecclesiology that described and justified
the system was that of a society organized like a state, with at the

top of the pyramid, the Pope, assisted by the Roman congregations made up of cardinals and bureaucratic offices. The idea that monarchy is the best form of government is found in almost all the authors of the time'.[24] Undoubtedly, no other theologian has so convincingly traced the ways in which our understanding of the Church's identity has become distorted over time.[25] No one worked harder than Congar to bring that distortion to an end, particularly through his exceptional contribution to the Second Vatican Council. During the period when the system prevailed, 'the Church was seen and defined not as an organism animated by the Holy Spirit, but as a society or rather an organization in which Christ intervened at the beginning as its founder, and the Holy Spirit is confined to the role of legitimizing authority'.[26] Johann Adam Möhler, one of the scholars who inspired Congar's thought, had summarized this misconception with a touch of irony by characterizing the naturalist ecclesiology of the Enlightenment in this way: 'God created the hierarchy and thereby more than sufficiently provided for the needs of the Church until the end of the world.'[27] The word 'Church' started to signify not the 'we' of Christian believers, but a legal person, that is, the institution. A significant example of this shift in meaning, which Congar called 'serious',[28] is found in the writings of Mauro Capellari, the future Pope Gregory XVI: 'The Church is given the task of feeding the flock of Jesus Christ.'[29] Congar asks: 'But is not the Church the flock itself?' The expression *societas perfecta*[30] [perfect society] is the one that dominated nineteenth-century ecclesiological discourse and categories.[31] To unpack this concept, Congar spoke of the 'Church's self-sufficiency'.[32] That Church did not see itself as part of the unfolding of history. It expected nothing from the world, and expected nearly nothing from its members.

> The Church was considered primarily as a ready-made framework, in which all we had to do was to enter it and receive; hardly at all as a community in which all have something to do, something to share with one another, in which the Holy Spirit is supremely active and where, quite apart from our hierarchical positions, we all are transmitters for one another of the *agape* of God: that *agape* which has been poured into our hearts by the Holy Spirit who has been given to us.[33]

WHAT IS TRIDENTINISM?

' '' "Tridentinism" involved the establishment of a complete, coherent, and very strict system, with an internal structure, and also very narrow limits. This system absolutely controlled every aspect of Church life. Its intellectual life was dominated by a kind of scholasticism. Some have called this a 'scholasticism gone to seed' – there is a point when plants are doing nothing but reproducing themselves: this is similar to what happened to scholasticism in the theological manuals – which were obviously not all bad [...]. If something significant happened at Vatican II, it was the dismantling of this system as a system. [...] The system as such was called into question. Its absolute and unconditional side was suppressed. One could say that previously there had been a kind of unconditionality in the system; since then, many things have been called into question because, at the Council, people came to the realization that the Church does not have an answer to everything, and that in the Church there can be more than one opinion [...].'

Yves Congar, *Essais œcuméniques* (Paris: Centurion, 1984), pp. 11–12

Rediscovering the *Ecclesia**

Congar's contribution to what has been called the *ressourcement* effort consisted in rediscovering the meaning that the Church Fathers had given to the word *ecclesia:*

By 'ecclesiology of the *Ecclesia*' I mean the ecclesiology of the Church Fathers, especially St. Augustine and the most ancient liturgical texts. This ecclesiology has two main characteristics: 1) The word *ecclesia* means the community of the faithful, or rather, in the liturgy, a concrete assembly of the faithful; 2) Though the hierarchical powers of the priesthood are very clearly seen as coming from above, they are never separated from the body: they are considered to be powers given to the

Church that have validity only within her unity. So the priest-hood's powers (for example, the forgiveness of sins) are not envisaged as coming only from the hierarchy that mediates between Christ and the body of the faithful, but rather they come from Christ, who is present in this body and is acting here below through ecclesiastical forms and through the ministry of priests, but in the unity of the *ecclesia*, with the entire body being interested and engaged.[34]

Therefore, for the Fathers 'the first and decisive reality of ecclesiology was still the *ecclesia* itself, that is, the totality, the community, the unity of faithful'. Is that not a truism? Congar answered: 'Ten years of study and reflection on the history of ecclesiological doctrines have convinced me that it is not.'[35] Congar came to these views by drawing on the best biblical, patristic, and theological studies. Alongside other theologians, he reinserted history into theology, and this kept him from taking as absolute what is only relative. His theological work has a preeminent place in what has become our common Christian heritage.

In appointing him a cardinal of the Catholic Church, Pope John Paul II recognized and wanted the universal Church to recognize the vast theological contribution of Congar and his decisive influence on Vatican II.[36] Hervé Legrand is right to say: 'It is extremely rare for the personal destiny of any one theologian to prefigure and influence the course of the life of the entire Church to such an extent.'[37] On the occasion of the 20th anniversary of the announcement of Vatican II, Father Congar gave a lecture in Fribourg in which he quoted a text by Pope John XXIII that set out one of the objectives of the Council:

The idea of the Council is not the fruit of lengthy reflection. It is rather the spontaneous flower of an unexpected springtime [...]. With the grace of God, we are convening the Council. And we are intending to prepare it bearing in mind all that is most essential to bring strength and new vigour in the union of the Catholic family, in conformity with Our Lord's plan. Then, as soon as we have accomplished this formidable task, of eliminating everything that may at the human level be an obstacle to more rapid progress, we shall present the Church in all of its splendor *sine macula et sine ruga* [without spot or wrinkle] and we shall say to all the others who are separated from us, Orthodox, Protestants, and other Christians [...]: 'Look, brethren, this is the Church of Christ. We have tried to be faithful to it' [...].[38]

We can understand why the Pope's speech touched Yves Congar, for it expressed his own deep concerns. The many critical-sounding pages that punctuate his writings should not be misinterpreted. It was his fidelity to the Church that led him to critique, sometimes bluntly, all that disfigured it. And it was this same fidelity that motivated his desire to purge the Church of anything coming from human sinfulness that might act as an obstacle for his contemporaries. Congar was, in a profound sense, a man of the Church. He was neither a maverick nor a rebel. It is the voice of the great Tradition that he wanted people to hear. He was animated by the will to call his contemporaries, as Charles Péguy expressed it, 'from a less profound tradition to a more profound one', and this desire penetrated all his theology.[39] This was how he reconnected with the Church as the Fathers had conceived of it. They 'did not deny the juridical structure of the Church', but they 'do not make ecclesiology consist only in the defence and illustration of that structure, as was customary following the controversies of the sixteenth century'.[40] The institution is there, of course, but this 'is not a pure "system"'; it is 'a source of grace', a 'Communion', 'the space for humanity to be for God, a place of spiritual freedom, interiority, peace [...]'. For Congar, the Church

> is, above all, the setting for a spiritual experience by which this institution learns continually about the content and meaning of the heritage by which it lives. As such it is also a fraternity, a family: the communion of saints, dare we say, in which nothing is lost, but each benefiting from all the others and from a wealth of experience amassed through the centuries by the active contribution of all [...].[41]

It is this same kind of Church that Congar found in the writings of St. Bernard of Clairvaux:

> Bernard sees the economy of human salvation as assured by a kind of cascade of love and service: the Church, within

which this salvation is realized (in the nuptial union of the bride and the bridegroom), is constructed from above by a succession of services characterized by love: Christ, who is her head, serves her; the angels, who are above us, serve Christ in us and serve us. Everything here is *ministratio, ministerium* [service, the function of the servant]. The angels do not go about *their own* business; they are pure ministers, as they offer God our work, not their own. Bernard adds that Christ, supreme minister and the humblest of all, serves us by giving himself [...].[42]

This is not a Church whose banner is first and foremost the affirmation of authority, but the Church of St. Augustine, who said to his people: 'I am a bishop for you, but first a Christian with you.' That which concerns the hierarchy is not overlooked, 'but it is seen and presented within the context of the Christian life, which remains first and most important'.[43]

The suspicions that fell for so long on Yves Congar, from his first publications in the 1930s until Vatican II, along with the restraints imposed on the publication and translation of his books and the marginalization he experienced, wounded him deeply. In this regard it is poignant to read his *Journal d'un théologien* (1946–56),[44] which covers the darkest period of his life. His journal reveals the suffering of a man who has been wounded in his vocation as a servant of the Church and as a servant of truth. The right to tell the truth was a right he claimed as a true son of St. Dominic.[45] He refused all 'tampering with the truth', and he noted in his *Journal*: 'I cannot not say what I believe to be true.'[46]

When Jean Puyo asked Father Congar, in a series of conversations published as a book significantly entitled *Une vie pour la vérité*[47] [*A Life for Truth*], what it was about his writings that had caused the greatest adverse reaction, he answered without hesitation:

My vision of the Church. It questioned the pyramidal system, hierarchical and juridical, that had been put in place during the Counter-Reformation. My ecclesiology was that of the 'People of God'; not a kind of democracy or a Soviet, but the active participation of all Christians in the life of the Church.[48]

Such a vision got him into trouble. The return to the sources was also considered problematic by influential members of the Curia. Jean Puyo asked him: 'I don't see how Rome could object to the fact that you were highlighting the thought of the Church Fathers.' Congar answered: 'This called into question a certain system, because it allowed for the rediscovery of aspects of the Church's deep Tradition which had been suppressed.'

What did Yves Congar propose in place of this *system*? Before we answer this question by studying four themes that played an important role in his work, let us try to identify the influences that contributed to the making of the man and theologian named Yves Congar.

1

Seeds and a receptive soil

Part of this chapter deals with Yves Congar's childhood and youth up to the time of his first years with the Dominicans. Although some biographical elements appear here, my aim is not to give an account of Congar's life, but to show what contributed to the making of Yves Congar, the man. He himself seems to have believed that his early years were important, for on more than one occasion he chose to tell his story. The second part of this chapter will name three nineteenth-century thinkers whose influence on Congar's life was significant: Kierkegaard, Newman and Möhler. Congar felt that it was urgent for the Church to rediscover a theological anthropology. I want to show how this awareness prepared him to develop an ecclesiology that steered clear of legalism. We shall see that he avoided this legalism for yet other reasons, notably because of his deep knowledge of history. This will provide me with the opportunity to recall the influence of his contemporary and Dominican confrère, Marie-Dominique Chenu, who, more than anyone else, was responsible for his 'awakening'. Finally, I shall underline the importance of Congar's life experience during World War II, and conclude with a few remarks about his spiritual life.

Childhood

Yves Congar's childhood, which he described as 'happy',[1] 'was spent for the most part in the atmosphere of a "great estate", with something enchanted about it', 'in a human milieu that was simple, real and healthy'.[2] In his memoirs, Congar recalled that, as a child, he had 'a rather difficult personality'. He told this story: 'On one occasion, when I did not want to go out for a walk, I sat down in the street on the streetcar tracks, and the streetcar had to stop in front of me and sound its horn.'[3] Even as a child, Congar's strong, unyielding personality was already evident, a fact that all those who had to deal with him later would come to be familiar with, sometimes at their expense! But it was probably also due to this personality and uncommon stubbornness that he was able, decades later, to open up new paths where others would most likely have thrown in the towel. Reflecting on his childhood, he also wrote that he had the good fortune to have Protestant and Jewish friends. 'They were mostly the children of my parents' Protestant and Jewish friends.' 'These friendships', he wrote, 'taught me to feel comfortable in the presence of "others".'[4] Of his youth, he also said: 'I had a liking for relationships, and I would even have loved "the world": that world where you entertain guests, invite one another [...].'[5] World War I had a profound impact on his childhood. Congar was born in 1904 in the Ardennes, a few kilometers away from the Belgian border.[6] The devastation of war brought him into a more mystical contact with Protestantism, as he recounted in *Dialogue Between Christians* in a section entitled 'Callings and Paths':

> Our parish church, which was situated in a suburb of our little town of Sedan, had been deliberately set on fire by the Uhlans when they entered Sedan on 25 August 1914. The pastor, M. Cosson, offered our parish priest a little Protestant chapel right next to my parents' garden and for the next six years this served as our parish church. It was in this chapel that my religious conscience was awakened during the hard and fervent years of the war and the occupation. If I neither received nor recognized my priestly vocation there, at least I was strengthened in my prayer as a child in which I sought light and assurance from God.

He concluded: 'I have often thought about it since then and I cannot believe that my vocation to ecumenism has no connection with these circumstances.'[7] I will take up Congar's immense contribution to ecumenism when I discuss the theme of catholicity, but we can already see here that rarely was Congar's approach to anything exclusively bookish: he always needed contact with human beings. In 1932, as a young Dominican,[8] he asked his provincial for permission to study for a year at the Protestant Faculty of Theology in Paris. At that time such a request was uncommon, and his provincial answered: 'This is not worth the trouble. Whatever they might say that is interesting, you will find it in their books.' And here is Congar's revealing response: 'I answered that I was going there precisely to find what is not available in books. I quickly understood, and did so increasingly, that in all areas of life nothing can take the place of a direct, concrete, living contact with other people.'[9]

In the early 1930s he took several trips to Germany.[10] Later on, in England, his rather rudimentary English did not keep him from enjoying the beauty of the Anglican liturgy. He also had numerous contacts with the Eastern Orthodox faith, particularly with Russian thinkers such as Nicolas Berdyaev and Sergei Bulgakov, thanks to the Franco-Russian circle around Jacques Maritain and an ecumenical discussion group that met on the second floor of a Parisian café, on rue du Moulin-Vert. Both Congar and Berdyaev took part.[11] In later years, he was led to be self-critical of his own ecumenical writings. Commenting on his books *Divided Christendom* and *Dialogue Between Christians*, he wrote: 'At that time I was still too close to scholastic Thomism and to my study of Schleiermacher and Protestant liberalism. Sometimes I was too ready to classify, to categorize, and pass judgment.'[12]

Birth of a vocation

'It was while meditating upon the seventeenth chapter of St. John's Gospel,' during his ordination retreat, as he wrote later, 'that I clearly recognized my vocation to work for the unity of all who believe in Jesus Christ.'[13] But before that, during his three years at the Carmelites' seminary and during the years that followed, every day when he recited the *Benedictus* at Lauds, 'one versicle of the canticle was less said *by* me than said *within* me by Another: "And you, little child, will be called the prophet of the Most High: for you will go before the Lord to prepare his ways"'.[14] This strong feeling about a particular vocation to which he was being called in order 'to prepare his ways', became a reality for him as early as 1929–30,[15] when he became engaged in the search for Christian unity. We should not underestimate the importance of ecumenism for him even at this early date. As one of his fellow Dominicans put it, one most qualified to comment on his work, 'This is an exceptional key to understanding Congar's vocation: it is not the ecclesiologist who discovered ecumenism; it was the ecumenist who became an ecclesiologist, at one and the same time.'[16]

Love of life

Let us take a step back. Congar is about 14 years old. It is summer 1918. In the spring of that year the idea of becoming a priest had crossed the young man's mind. In that same year he met Father Daniel Lallement, who was also from Sedan.[17] This austere man became his spiritual director and suggested that he attend the minor seminary. They met again in Paris after Congar had entered the Carmelite seminary, for Lallement had become a professor and joined the philosophy department at the Institut Catholique of Paris. They saw each other on a regular basis. In the document that Congar wrote about this time in his life, he devoted several pages to how Father Lallement's spirituality made him feel ill at ease. It is worth reading at length a number of passages from his *Journal d'un théologien* to see how this period was a turning point in the young Congar's life:

> I was both subjugated and repulsed, attracted and recalcitrant. I felt the power and the beauty of what he was telling me, but I did not surrender to it 100 percent. He spoke to me about mortification, about defeating nature, about the Christian and priestly ideal [...]. In all that he said there was a strongly marked opposition between the world and nature, on the one hand, and the spiritual life, on the other. As for me, I desired the spiritual life, and I have often been generous, but I was never able to enter into his sort of aversion for the world, for the world of human beings, for the earth of human beings. I would have loved life, but I knew little of it because between the ages of 10 and 14 I

had been shut inside my little town by the war, without going out, without seeing anything, living in a narrow circle of family and friends; and because after that I immediately left to go to the minor seminary.[18]

Congar continued:

> In 1918 or 1919 I would have liked to become a boy scout, and the same desire returned again later. But Father Lallement would not allow it. He associated the scouts with naturalism. He was horrified by the simple fact of naked knees. I never totally surrendered, I never consented 100 percent, even in the moments when I was living most in unison with the interior piety of this very holy priest, which was fervent, but also somewhat primitive and harsh.[19]

'I would have preferred to study for the Baccalauréat exams at a high school', Congar explained, but Lallement made him enter the minor seminary: 'There was always, for him, this same focus on separation from the world; and for me, the same instinct […].' Congar noted again: 'Father Lallement had from that moment a strong influence on me, even though once again I never consented 100 percent to his ideal, which involved separation from the world; the negation of nature; cloistering within an ecclesial or clerical life defined by renunciation; harsh and irrevocable consecration; the severing of ties with the lives of other human beings.' All of these excerpts were written over 25 years after the fact. One senses here an almost obsessive need for Congar, a man far more sensitive than appearances would make one believe, to clarify the reasons for a fundamental disagreement. One last time, in this same text, he made an analysis of the reasons that had led him to break with Lallement. Rejecting the ideal of 'supernaturalism' or 'antinaturalism', Congar said: 'I have *always* had the feeling that these ideals did not take into account what is *true*, which is that to which I felt an irrepressible attraction. Even as a child I always resisted on this point, and I think I always had that feeling. Today, I cannot conclude that I was wrong.'[20]

But there was another thing that the young Congar did not accept: 'I very quickly felt that he [Lallement] was distrustful of history, and I also refused to accept that.'[21] For Congar, the root cause of their disagreement was the same: 'to trust or not to trust what the subject, the human person has to offer, to reject or to be interested in human creation and aspirations.'[22]

Irrepressible openness to life; rejection of a theology that would ignore history; attention given to human creation and aspirations; the disposition 'to welcome life's needs and developments'[23] – undoubtedly all this was still rather nebulous in the mind of the young Congar. It was through contact with Marie-Dominique Chenu, his Dominican confrère, 'the perfect brother', 'the awakener', 'the catalyst', that Congar moved to a new stage and saw his path more clearly. But this attachment to life and to history was already present in him, latent, waiting.[24]

Kierkegaard (1813–55)

By 1932[25] the theme of 'the subject' had already caught Congar's attention. He even made it into one of the characteristics of the modern world: 'The more I reflect, the more I see that the modern world as a total fact can be characterized by what I would call the discovery of the subject [...].'[26]

A significant sign of this interest is Congar's 1934 article entitled 'The Actuality of Kierkegaard'.[27] More than Kierkegaard's philosophy in and of itself, what Congar wanted to understand was why he had become a reference point for thinkers as different from one another as Karl Barth, Nicolas Berdyaev and Erik Peterson. When asked to name a thinker whose influence on their intellectual development had been decisive, all of them indeed mentioned Kierkegaard. This article, which is rarely cited in studies of Congar, explained his interest in the father of existentialism: 'The approach which the contemporary situation demands of us can find in him [Kierkegaard] some elements of edification; not to be totally ignorant about one of our time's esteemed thinkers can improve our understanding of the present.'[28] What he wanted was not to be ignorant about a thinker with whom our time identifies. Congar set this objective for himself as his duty. He examined Kierkegaard's thought in 25 crisp and succinct pages. The close reading of this article leads us to conclude that perhaps there was more complicity between Congar and Kierkegaard than Congar wanted, or could, admit to – after all, this was 1934.[29] And in these few pages the word 'system' appears no less than nineteen times, not to mention three instances of the word 'systematic'.

Congar saw in Kierkegaard an emblematic figure for our time because he rejected the totalizing system, gave value to subjectivity, and had 'a taste for the concrete' and for 'irreducible heterogeneities'. He was the embodiment of the reaction against the 'great systems' of the nineteenth century, of which Hegel was the main representative, 'where everything is explained and reduced to antecedents or wholes' which 'drown the singular in the general'.

Hegel's mental universe rejected by Kierkegaard, according to Congar, was 'an easy universe, homogeneous and perfectly accessible to a systematic representation; human beings were enmeshed in great collective categories which revealed to them the profound meaning of existence; life is penetrated by spirit, and every finite phenomenon has its place and impact in the general evolutionary process, in which it appears only as a moment'. Congar summarized it in this way: 'Romantic themes, romantic ideal of existence which has become a *system*.'[30] Of course, one could debate whether this is a fair characterization of Hegel's thinking. However that may be, Congar saw in Kierkegaard the perfect opposite of this system. For him, Kierkegaard's approach was not one system opposed to another system, but 'a living attitude, lived as well as thought; before thought there was a spiritual labor, which was all the more poignant because in all of his spontaneous gifts, Kierkegaard was offering a choice instrument to romanticism's aesthetic inspiration'. For Congar, who was explaining his approach, without necessarily agreeing with it, Kierkegaard represented the primacy of subjectivity in thought.

'Instead of losing the self in the timeless realm of objective thought, Kierkegaard wants to bring our real self into being in time. That is his "existential" point of view.' For Congar, there is existential thinking 'when instead of engaging in an impersonal speculation, one's thinking turns to the subject and becomes focused on bringing into being, in temporal existence, the real and eternal self as it appears in God's sight'.[31] This is not about speculating on the subject, Congar specified, but about responding to God.

We will find traces of this focus on the subject and the singularity of beings at all the successive stages of Congar's life. Other

twentieth-century theologians were better equipped[32] than he to give
to the subject its proper place in theological discourse. One thinks,
of course, of Karl Rahner, who sought 'a systematic reconceptual-
ization of Roman Catholic theological anthropology in light of the
modern turn to the subject'.[33] Yves Congar knew that he was no
Karl Rahner.[34] But in the field of ecclesiology, he made an original
contribution by attempting to make room for 'the discovery of the
subject', and more broadly for 'theological anthropology'.

If it does not pay attention to persons, Congar believed,
ecclesiology is in danger of sliding into forms of legalism and self-
sufficiency that exclude the subject. Two other nineteenth-century
thinkers closely studied by Congar had attempted to restore the
subject to its proper place: John Henry Newman and Johann Adam
Möhler. We turn to them now.

THE REAL

'I am very fond of Péguy's saying, "Not the true, but the real",
provided that it is properly understood. I have devoted my
life to the truth [...]. I hold to the truth, but the real, that is to
say, truth with historicity, with its concrete state in becoming, in
time, is something else.'

Yves Congar, *Fifty Years of Catholic Theology, Conversations
with Yves Congar*, edited and introduced by Bernard Lauret,
trans. John Bowden (Philadelphia: Fortress Press, 1988), p. 71

Newman (1801–90)

A few lines by Bernard Dupuy, Congar's fellow Dominican and
another highly respected ecclesiologist, are sufficient to help
us understand why Newman's thought exerted such power of
attraction over Congar. 'Newman's work was the first theology to
take into account the historicity of the Church and to study it in all
of its dimensions.' Dupuy says that in his famous book, *An Essay
on the Development of Christian Doctrine*, Newman showed that

'the hallmark of Catholicism is its historicity. This is a religion that is real, historical, and not a theory or a *system*. "The world is its [Catholicism's] homeland; to know what it is we must look for it in the world and listen to the world's testimony about it".'[35] Hence, Congar could say of the Church: 'We can learn more about it by watching it live than by studying its formula [or theory]; we will not understand well the meaning and richness of the formula unless we look at it in the light of facts and realities, through the life of the institution.'[36] Gustave Martelet echoed this conviction when he wrote of the Church: 'Since it is not the product of a system, it is by watching it unfold in life that we discover its truth.'[37] Or, to put it in yet another way: 'Historicity turns out to be essential for the Church.'[38] For Congar, who was interested in the real and not in the 'system', which for him functioned in a vacuum and in a timeless manner, protected from all surprises, Newman's thought was particularly appealing.[39]

What is more, for Congar, Newman was one of those 'level-headed minds' who 'have thought that there is a certain truth in the subject's point of view, and particularly in the idea that knowledge and assent are conditioned by the dispositions of the subject'.[40] Congar noted: 'It is remarkable that the same men who made room for this point of view applied the idea of development to Christianity, gaining greater acceptance within Catholicism for the psychological and historical.'[41]

Maurice Nédoncelle, one of personalism's key figures who translated and commented on Newman, helps us understand what inspired Newman. He writes that Newman's starting point was the thesis that 'each person is an idea, and each one of us not only is called to speak the truth, but is a constitutive principle of truth'.[42] Congar, who emphasized so well that the Church is a Church of *persons*, and that in entering into the Church these persons do not enter a prefabricated reality, a predetermined framework designed without them, found powerful inspiration in Newman's work.

Johann Adam Möhler (1796–1838)

Congar often reiterated the debt he owed to Möhler, whose great work *Unity in the Church*[43] had a decisive influence on him. In his capacity as director of the *Unam Sanctam* collection, Congar decided to open the series by publishing Möhler's book in French translation, to indicate the spirit of the collection.[44]

Möhler's work is best understood in the context of German Romanticism. According to Congar, it was Romanticism that allowed Möhler 'to break out of individualism – because of its predilection for the communitarian, its recognition of the unity of human achievement over time, and finally and above all, its sense for the living organism. But undoubtedly the most common and certain characteristic of German Romanticism's complex reality is the idea of *life* as a total movement uniting diversity in unity.'[45] Congar went on to explain this further: 'The importance of Möhler and the Tübingen school [...] is that they opened or reopened the topic of a truly *theo*-logical and supernatural understanding of the Church. The Church had been viewed in a relatively external way, either through the category of Papal *potestas* in the textbooks produced by the Counter-Reformation, or in works of apologetics, which were only intended to justify its magisterial authority, or in the very human presentations of the Englightenment.'[46] The distance between the legalistic vision of the Church, which was common in his day, and the one proposed by Möhler is evident in these few words: 'The Church is, above all, an effect of Christian faith, the result of the living love of the faithful brought together by the Holy Spirit.'[47] As a result, 'its external constitution is just the manifestation of its essence, which is "love made flesh"'.[48] Möhler's contribution, according to Congar, was to have reestablished 'the action of the Holy Spirit and the communion of the faithful in a context in which the pure juridical structure of authority had been affirmed exclusively'.[49]

The rediscovery of theological anthropology

The entire work of Yves Congar is marked by his attention to the subject, to persons, and to the action of the Holy Spirit within persons, all held in a remarkable balance with other components of the Church. This led him in 1965 to write a preface and publish in the *Unam Sanctam* series a work entitled *The Christian Lives by the Spirit.*[50] Though initially its connection with ecclesiology may not seem obvious, in reality this collection of essays sheds a bright light on ecclesiology as Congar conceived of it. The authors were two well-known Biblical scholars, both of them Jesuits and professors at the Pontifical Biblical Institute in Rome: Stanislas Lyonnet, who was the rector of the Institute at that time, and Ignace de la Potterie.

In reading Congar's preface, one can measure the distance between Christianity, as he conceived of it, and the 'system' or the 'mold'. At the beginning of the preface, Congar recalled the place of St. Paul in these two studies devoted to Christian life in the Spirit:

> The passages from St. Paul are so emphatic in this connection that we are reluctant to believe they are meant for us, and fear that they may lead to illuminism and anarchy: the Christian is free of the law inasmuch as it is a law, that is, an external restraint in comparison to the demands of love placed in the heart by the Holy Spirit.[51]

To buttress these views and probably to show that they rest on solid doctrine, Congar quoted a text by St. Thomas: 'It is the Holy Spirit himself who is the New Testament, in generating within us the love that is the fullness of the law.'[52]

Congar was proud to publish this book in the series that he directed. 'In reading these penetrating chapters, we have personally experienced in a new and intense way the immense spiritual joy that comes from an intimate contact with Holy Scripture. What power! What expansion and exultation of the soul!' And again: 'We had the feeling not only that this book would come in its own time, but also that it would become one of the most decisive contributions to this renewal of ecclesiology which the *Unam Sanctam* series wants to serve.'[53] He moved straight on to give the reason for his conviction:

> It seems increasingly clear that the ecclesiology of the Apostles, that of the Fathers and that of the liturgy – our prime sources – encompass a certain anthropology. For the Fathers, the Church is not first of all a social structure of which the faithful would be but subjects: it is all the baptized living in communion with each

other, through the Holy Spirit, and by means of the sacraments
and discipline of the Christian life.[54]

Congar then noted a fact that reappears elsewhere in his writings:
'The Fathers speak of the Church in commenting upon the life
of the people of biblical history and in exposing the reality of
the Christian life on the basis of the psalms, parables, baptismal
initiation, and Eucharistic celebration. The Church and the baptized
bring to reality the same mystery: in speaking of one, we speak of
the other.'[55]

In another preface, wary of those who might misinterpret his
intentions, Congar explained more precisely how to understand the
astonishing fact that ecclesiology is also a kind of anthropology:

> Obviously, we do not want to deny or underestimate the impor-
> tance of the hierarchical structure of the Church or the objective
> character of the means of grace, the ministry which has been
> given to the Church. Rather, we want to give it its rightful
> place. For this to happen, instead of assuming the hierarchical
> structure first, and for its own sake, it is simply necessary first of
> all to consider Christian existence, what one might call Christian
> ontology* or anthropology. Next, one should situate the hierar-
> chical structure within this Christian ontology or anthropology,
> as a service to it. Is that not what St. Paul did?[56]

For whoever follows this path, there will be endless discoveries. 'As
one advances, through various occasions or encounters as much as
by any progress brought by methodical effort, the entire landscape
is illuminated by a new light.'[57] At the Second Vatican Council
this kind of ecclesiology reclaimed its proper place. 'Reclaimed',
because Congar, as we know, was painfully aware of the distortions
that occurred following the Gregorian Reform, particularly 'a
growing and invasive legalism'. When *Lumen Gentium** was
published, Congar liked to quote the following passage, which he
saw as a step along the path towards 'the recovery by ecclesiology
of its inalienable anthropological thrust'[58]: 'The state of this people
is that of the dignity and freedom of the sons of God, in whose
hearts the Holy Spirit dwells as in a temple. Its law is the new
commandment to love as Christ loved us (cf. John 13:34).'[59]

Marie-Dominique Chenu (1895–1990)

If Congar was able to avoid being a man of the system, it was undoubtedly in part because of his vast knowledge of history, his 'irresistible liking for history'.[60] In speaking with Jean Puyo about its importance, Congar said that paying attention to history keeps one from 'confusing all the levels and absolutizing what is relative, which in the end is a form of idolatry and not the announcement of the Truth'.[61] In another text devoted to historical theology, he wrote: 'The one who knows the past and is a practitioner of history replaces the special effects, tricks and camouflages of apologetics with the unconditional cult of what is true.'[62] It is not surprising that he also said to Jean Puyo: 'I think that everything needs to be approached historically. In trying to approach theology historically I do not believe that I turned away from theology, as I was tempted to think at the time.'[63] This is because 'many questions and misunderstandings come from the ignorance of history and the lack of a historical sense'.[64]

GOD IS NOT IN COMPETITION WITH HUMAN BEINGS

'Revelation came in and through history, in and through a fully human history. What makes revelation divine is not that it is not human. God is not in competition with human beings; he does not affirm himself by eclipsing his partner.'

Yves Congar, 'L'influence de la société et de l'histoire sur le développement de l'homme chrétien', *Nouvelle Revue Théologique*, 96 (1974), p. 676

It is well known that Newman and his sense of history played an important role in Congar's evolution. But it is Marie-Dominique Chenu, O.P. whose influence on Congar we must discuss here. According to Congar, Chenu was his 'awakener', his 'catalyst', 'the incomparable brother without whom we would not have reached the decisive awakening of those wonderful years'.[65] Congar also said that 'there are human beings who have the gift of stirring up life'.[66] Chenu was that kind of person.

In volume II of *Bilan de la théologie du XXe siècle*,[67] Congar himself wrote the article about M.-D. Chenu. A Dominican who was nine years older than Congar, Chenu became a professor of the history of doctrine at the Saulchoir in 1920. It was mainly because of Chenu that 'the house became a centre of intense intellectual and religious life'. Congar was his student in the late 1920s, and shortly after they became colleagues. 'Father Chenu's teaching was powerfully stirring for the intellect,' Congar remembered. And as for his historical approach to questions: 'The most technical history and the explication of Aristotle's texts were opportunities for him to bring back to life the problems that the human mind had approached, to see what had been missing in their perception and had prevented them from being worked out [...]. What an intellectual lesson!' Chenu was a medievalist who practiced 'the humble virtue of indignation'[68] by pillorying 'textbook scholasticism' and 'Baroque theology', which Chenu, Congar and Feret would later on vow to 'liquidate'. 'Baroque theology' was accused of cutting 'theology off from its divine source, which is faith, a supernatural communication from God to us and the principle of living experience.' When faith 'is emptied of its most mystical values and vitality', it is then reduced to obedience. 'This opened the door to legalism and extrinsicism*.'

Faithful to the legacy of St. Thomas, the master of realism, Chenu wanted to recognize the consistency of the *real*.[69] This insight led Congar to draw a parallel with Teilhard de Chardin's approach:

> Teilhard notes that many people find it impossible to believe because for them the evidence of the world is stronger than the light of Christ. It is only by completely accepting the evidence of the world, its dimensions, its unity, its history, it is only by completely believing in the world that one might, from within, resituate God and Christ and have them come into view. What Father Teilhard perceived for the entirety of the cosmos and the totality of its history, Father Chenu perceived for the historical and social dimension of human life.[70]

Congar thus described one of the causes of modern atheism: it 'feeds for a great part on the opposition that we have allowed it to set up or to imagine between the absoluteness of God and the human person; as if the movements and achievements of our history could only bring distress to people of faith and could only be set victoriously outside of the territory covered by Jesus Christ and faith.'[71]

In 1932, Chenu was named Regent of Studies and, five years later, he published a booklet, which was not intended for sale, entitled *Une école de théologie. Le Saulchoir*. The role he gave to history in the study of theology was central, based on solid conceptual foundations: 'If Christianity thus draws its reality from history and not from metaphysics, then the theologian must set as his first concern – first in dignity and in chronological order – to know this history and to become well-equipped to study it.'[72]

Among other reasons, it was because of his sense of history that Chenu appreciated Möhler (and introduced Congar to his work) as well as other theologians of the Tübingen school: 'With them, it is the abstract intellectualism of the Enlightenment and its indifference to history that we reject.'[73] With Chenu there emerges 'an intelligibility of things that is not purely speculative or dialectic'.[74]

Chenu's concept of Tradition also had its impact on Congar. Tradition, for Chenu, opens one up to life and the future, because it 'is not only the conservation of elaborated dogmas, of established results or decisions taken in the past; but it is also a principle that creates intelligibility and is an endless source of new life'. We can understand what Chenu meant, then, when he wrote the following sentence, and why some people must have been shocked: 'There was no worse disgrace for Thomism, whose original effort was directed towards the foundation in Christendom of a status for human intelligence, than to be treated as a kind of "orthodoxy".'[75] Chenu felt 'the kind of resistance to systematization that prevented him as a theologian from "settling into" the results of his dialectic, and instead compelled him constantly to control his thinking with fear and humility'.[76] As a result, there emerges a particular conception of theology: 'For some thinkers theology looks like a closed science, but that gives a false impression of what theology is; there is no science that is more open, more concerned with progress, more tormented by the need for spiritual purification.'[77]

Any close reader of Congar can easily recognize how Chenu's intuitions bore fruit in Congar's work. The following text, amongst many others, illustrates this new way of doing theology:

> Instead of starting only from what is given in Revelation and Tradition, as classical theology has generally done, we must start from facts and questions received from the world and from history. This is much less comfortable. We cannot be content any more to repeat what is old by starting from the ideas or problems of the thirteenth or sixteenth centuries. We must start from the problems, if not the ideas, of today and take them as a new 'given'. The unchanging 'given' of the Gospel must then shed its light on this new given without the support of the elaborations achieved in the past and possessed in the calm of an assured tradition.[78]

Congar continued: 'All that has been given is unveiled and deployed not only *in* the history of the world, but also *by* that history.'[79] And elsewhere, he wrote: 'The fact that the Church exists and lives within a real history means also that it cannot be liberated from time, from time's weight and depth, or from the delays that it imposes. It is not *in spite of* time and its flow, it is *within them* that the Church brings God's gifts and puts them to work.'[80] Of course this presupposes a conception of history that is not 'just the indefinite alteration of the identical, which is repeated even as it is transformed'.[81] The truly new is possible. For Congar, the action of Christ with and by the Spirit is a source of genuine newness in history: 'It is in this sense that somehow God has said and given everything to us in Jesus Christ, and at the same time there is novelty; there is something truly real happening in history.'[82]

The influence of Chenu, who refused to 'disconnect the search for God from the historically minded attention that needs to be paid to the needs of human beings', led Congar to make of the very life of the Church a locus for theology.[83] The originality that many have noted in his theological method[84] owed a great deal to Chenu. Each of these two theologians spent generous amounts of time with Christians who were having to deal with the harsh realities of the world. Congar confided to Jean Puyo how much he learned from meeting with Christians who were in active service out in the field, so to speak. The titles of two books focused on Congar's contribution to theology are eloquent in this regard. The first one, by Jean-Pierre Jossua, is entitled *Yves Congar, Theology in the Service of God's People*;[85] the second one, a *festschrift* honouring his entire work on the occasion of his 70th birthday, is entitled *Théologie – Le service théologique dans l'Église.*[86] Jean-Jacques von Allmen, who contributed to the second volume, wrote that Congar 'reminded our generation that the theologian's ministry as Doctor deteriorates and is falsified when it is not first and foremost a pastoral ministry'.[87]

Congar said of Chenu that he had the gift 'of discerning in those he met what was still in the bud and of bringing about its flowering. He is a revealer.'[88] Quite obviously Congar was not speaking in the abstract and when he used the metaphor of flowering he was thinking of the effects of his own contact with Chenu.

The experience of captivity

If Congar was a theologian of the real – someone who wanted to take into account the real life of his contemporaries and was inhabited by 'a desire to be faithful to the real'[89] – it was also due to what he had learned about the human condition during his long captivity in Germany during World War II.[90] He was kept prisoner for five years, and his full and stubborn character, and 'repeated attempts to escape'[91] were met with harsh punishment. Yet, it is also during his time in captivity that he forged strong friendships.

'Eighteen months in the fortress, and two years in the camp', we read on a biographical page inserted into the first volume of the French edition of *Tradition and Traditions.*[92] The fortress was at Colditz in Saxony, south-east of Leipzig. The camp was Lübeck, 'where the trouble-makers were assembled'.[93] This experience transformed Congar:

> I have changed quite a bit since 1939, both in good and in bad. My time at Colditz and Lübeck, with life spent 24–7 in a total 'community of destiny', with two hundred wonderful, manly, realistic, and courageous companions, changed my behavior quite profoundly.[94]

He went on to confide to Jean Puyo:

> I owe many friendships to that captivity – wonderful companions;
> I am still in contact with some of them [...]. I owe a certain
> realism to this experience. We met at the shower in our birthday
> suits, we cooked noodles, we did the same jobs ... and then,
> come Sunday, I preached on the Word of God. Still today, when
> I preach, I think of these concrete men whom I got to approach
> so closely. That was a great gift. I say to myself: hey, old chap,
> you're speaking for this or that one – not that I specify the
> particular individual, but a certain kind of man who earns his
> keep, who is married, who is good at sports, who has responsi-
> bilities ... in short, someone who is not a choir boy.[95]

A book soberly entitled *Leur résistance* [*Their Resistance*][96]
written by Congar at Easter 1947 gives a more precise idea of the
men whom he befriended. At the request of several of them he took
up his pen and drew the portrait of those who had not survived the
camps. The book is presented as a 'Memorial to former escapees
from Colditz and Lübeck who died for France'. But let me quote
from a passage in 'Callings and Paths' that is reproduced in
Dialogue Between Christians. He drew these other lessons from his
experience of captivity:

> In captivity, I adopted a militant anti-Nazi attitude which had
> its own consequences and inconveniences. However, it admitted
> me to the fellowship of courageous men in an atmosphere of
> resistance which was a great tonic. I then began to realize that
> one of the most important things in life, particularly in difficult
> times – and what times are not? – is to seek out perceptive and
> courageous men with whom one can associate and keep faith. In
> this respect I was overwhelmed for I had some wonderful friends
> and comrades.[97]

A letter written by Congar at the prison camp confirms that the
theologian had changed: 'I will never again be able to work as if
men were not suffering, and certain academic kinds of work will
now be impossible for me.'[98] He also wrote that his experience of
captivity rid him of all timidity.[99]

To live the questions is a source of fruitfulness

The last lines of *Jean Puyo interroge le Père Congar*[100] reveal how receptive Congar could be and bear witness to his capacity for dialogue, qualities that are present in his entire life and work.

> I say to myself sometimes: I have too many certainties. Having too many certainties may stop questions from emerging before they are even formulated whereas to live the questions is a source of fruitfulness. Rilke wrote to a young poet: 'For now, only live your questions. Perhaps simply by living them you will find yourself entering imperceptibly, some day, into the answers.' I reproach myself sometimes for not sufficiently living the questions, for cutting them off too quickly with answers. Under these conditions, they might only be the answers to the questions of the day before yesterday, or yesterday, but maybe not answers to the questions of today or tomorrow.[101]

Only a man who was totally immune to the spirit of the system could have spoken in this way. His capacity to live the questions and to enter into dialogue was a real one, and so was his capacity to evolve. 'One enters into dialogue when one is disposed to change something in one's own thoughts because of what the other is saying.' Yves Congar was that kind of man. In 1970 he wrote a self-critique and clarification describing his 'path-findings in the theology of laity and ministries': 'I now see many things differently and, I hope, better in comparison with forty years ago. I have not ceased learning and still learn new things each day, beginning afresh to glimpse or lay hold of the most elementary matters. This happens truly every day.'[102]

The message that Congar sent in 1971 to the Catholic intellectuals taking part in a colloquium in Strasbourg is noteworthy. Several of them were worried about the evolution of the Church in the years following the Second Vatican Council. In the message that we are going to read, Congar showed himself to be full of respect and understanding for his interlocutors. He did not deny the abuses that he himself had witnessed, but he tried to communicate his trust – which was surely the secret of his openness to the unknown:

I want to be open even to the problems, to the facts, to the experiences which start out by being jarring to me. For what is new is always jarring at first. We are most aware of this when, for example, we are placed in front of an entirely new form of art or expression. In such circumstances, I try to resist every temptation to panic; and then, without losing my criteria and certainties, but rather by applying them to the new facts or questions, I try to practice the necessary discernment. I have absolutely no doubt that one should not accept everything that comes one's way every day. Many things make me suffer and even worry. But in practicing this discernment that I have mentioned, I try not to allow my unease to make me feel tense. If I were to do so, it would be very difficult, almost impossible for me to be at ease again in a Church that presents many worrisome elements, but also displays extraordinary evangelical resources and a generosity in the search. We find ourselves facing totally new problems, problems that are monumental, world-wide, that arise at an exhausting pace.[103]

A theologian who listened to the Holy Spirit

To this sense of dialogue, to this capacity to live the questions without rushing to answer them, and to this openness to what is new and unknown, we should add Congar's ever-growing attention to the person and the role of the Holy Spirit in the Church. Congar was already elderly when he set out to write a major book on the Spirit. The three volumes that were published between January 1979 and September 1980 were the fulfillment of a project he had cherished for a long time.[104] If Congar was, as one of our best historians put it, 'one of the greatest minds that France produced in the twentieth century',[105] how do we explain his capacity to learn new things every day, to evolve, to welcome his contemporaries' questions and not to be overly attached to the past? We can confidently say that his achievements cannot be explained solely by his outstanding intellect. His deep spiritual life – a true life in the Spirit – and his attention to the person and to the role of the Holy Spirit in the life of the Church were determining factors. Until the end of his life Congar remained a man of prayer. His theological œuvre is that of an apostle. It was towards One greater than himself that he was drawn upwards, so to speak. And the One whom he contemplated, whom he called 'the living God',[106] shaped him, preserved him from the spirit of the system, made him open, and oriented him toward the great open sea. The Spirit of truth, particularly in his later works, is really the Spirit of freedom who guides toward the unknown, the has-not-yet-happened of history, but also nourishes an immense respect for people and for diversity. I would like to end this presentation with a text taken from Yves Congar's great work on the Holy Spirit:

> The Church is in no sense a great system in which, as Arthur Koestler said of another system, the individual is simply the sum of a million divided by a million. It is a communion, a fraternity of persons. This is why a personal principle and a principle of unity are united in the Church. These two principles are brought into harmony by the Holy Spirit. Persons are the great wealth of the Church. Each one is an original and autonomous principle of sensitivity, experience, relationships and initiatives. What an infinite variety of possibilities is contained in each individual![107]

2

Tradition and the future

To propose a study on Tradition[1] in all of its components in Yves Congar's thought[2] is not the objective of this chapter. I shall limit myself here to showing how his way of viewing Tradition welcomes life in its new expressions, and history as it actually happens; how it relates to the people who welcome it; how it never functions as a self-sufficient system, closed in on itself, but, on the contrary, is capable at every moment of being enriched. We shall see how being faithful to Tradition is, despite the spontaneous inclination of our mind to forget this too easily, being faithful to the future as much as being faithful to the past. For Congar, Tradition is inseparable from the mission given to the Church, which is 'to deploy the Gospel as extensively as possible to a humanity that is growing ceaselessly, not only externally and numerically, but also internally.'[3]

What Tradition is not

Let us first counter a misunderstanding. Congar himself encourages us to do this. On the first page of his book, *The Meaning of Tradition*,[4] he told this story: in 1956, during a trip to Moscow, an Anglican theologian entrusted with the mission of making a theological contact with the Orthodox Church was speaking about Tradition and its relationship with Scripture. His Soviet interpreter, who was unfamiliar with theological vocabulary, spontaneously translated the word 'Tradition' with 'old customs'. With a lucid

sense for how his contemporaries, not only those in Russia, understood this concept, Congar commented:

> For many, tradition is simply a collection of time-honored
> customs, accepted, not on critical grounds, but merely because
> things have always been so, because 'it has always been done'.
> [...] Tradition is favored because it prevents change.[5]

Congar was happy to describe himself as a 'man of Tradition',[6]
but his conception of Tradition was the opposite of the Russian
interpreter's approach – he devoted an entire historical study[7] to
showing how his conception of it was 'traditional'. It is not certain
whether he would have agreed with Jean-Georges Boeglin's abrupt
formulation 'Christianity is [...] an anti-traditionalism',[8] but he
would undoubtedly have defended the same living and creative
conception of Tradition. Congar was not the author of the phrase
that caused scandal in the 1940s: 'A theology which is not for the
present time is a false theology.'[9] But his reflection was in the same
spirit when he said:

> Tradition is living because it is carried by living minds – minds
> living in time. These minds meet with problems or acquire
> resources, in time, which lead them to endow tradition, or
> the truth it contains, with the reactions and characteristics of
> a living thing: adaptation, reaction, growth and fruitfulness.
> Tradition is living because it resides in minds that live by it, in
> a history that comprises activity, problems, doubts, opposition,
> new contributions and questions that need answering.[10]

An entire conception of theology flows from such an understanding.

Tradition and traditions

To understand the foundation of this way of thinking, we must
start with Congar's fundamental distinction between 'Tradition'
and 'traditions'. By 'traditions' in the plural, Congar meant 'ways
of living and expressing the faith: customs, rites, practical methods
and all kinds of concrete details, which have also been passed on,

forming a certain discipline for the Christian life'.[11] He did not underestimate their value or their role: 'In their small way these traditions also lend a certain warmth, without which our Church would be more like an old-fashioned classroom than a home.' Still, Congar wrote, 'they have not the same absolute value as the Tradition of the faith; they are rather Tradition's external form'.[12]

By 'Tradition', Congar understood 'that which underlies all this: the reality of God's gift to the world, of Jesus Christ "delivered unto us" – in short, Christianity and the essentials of the Christian message'.[13] In relation to the Church, Tradition 'in a sense [...] is its life, or, if you prefer, the nourishment of that life. [...] Everything in the Church comes from elsewhere, from certain sources that are the fountainheads of the history of salvation. Christianity is essentially an inheritance,[14] passed down by our Fathers in the faith. But Tradition is also present today. Age-old, it is ever fresh and alive; using its inherited riches, it answers the unexpected questions of today.'[15] In commenting further on the 'instituted' character of Christianity, Congar stated: 'This does not mean that we just repeat; there are many examples of this in history and there will be more in the future. This means that all novelty and all repetition must be referred back, as to their norm, to this "faith that was once and for all handed down to the holy ones" (as the Epistle of Jude puts it in verse 3).'[16] Congar belonged to a generation for whom the instituted character of Christianity was undoubtedly more inscribed on people's minds than it is today. This is what brought him to emphasize its corollary, creativity – the inventiveness that is needed to determine what historical forms Christianity must take if it is going to respond to new times. In examining what he wrote on this latter theme, it is necessary to keep the first one in mind at all times. He never forgot that we draw from that 'unique source, the Passover of Christ mediated through the sacraments'.[17]

Another text, which came later in Congar's career, also sheds light on what he meant by 'Tradition'. He sent it as a message to Christian intellectuals who were meeting in Strasbourg in November 1971. To these believers who were worried about certain developments in the Church, Congar wrote: 'Tradition is not fixism; to reproduce the past materially would not transmit the heritage; there are some ways of transmitting that harm true transmission. As for me, *Tradition is the permanence of a principle at all the moments of its history*.'[18]

It is with almost identical words that he ended his book of dialogues with Jean Puyo, allowing us, moreover, to see how Congar understood his vocation ten years after the end of the Council: 'My role, if any, is most likely to be a witness to Tradition in the midst of change; Tradition being something quite different from the mechanical and repetitive affirmation of the past: it is a principle's active presence in all of its history.'[19]

According to François Bousquet, Yves Congar 'brought Tradition back to what is essential in its act, which is *transmission*'.[20] This transmission happens between one living person and another living person:

Tradition is not merely the mechanical transmission of a passive deposit. The very concept implies the delivery of an object from the possession of one person to another, and therefore the transition from one living being to another. It is *incorporated* into a *subject*, a living subject. Living subjects necessarily put something of themselves into what they receive.[21]

THE CHRIST THAT IS TO BE

'When John of the Cross writes, "God has no more to say to us because what he said in the past to the prophets in parts, he has now spoken all at once by giving us the All Who is His Son", he expresses a conviction which we do not dispute, but which needs to be completed. For this "all" is unveiled only through the activity of souls in the unfolding of history [...]. The Gospel is constantly being renewed in previously unseen versions of the unique text. Christians are Christ's future. I love the poem where Tennyson sees the past year being erased and he celebrates the one that is just beginning, still obscurely filled with what will happen. He perceives there the famous Christian reality of "the Christ that is to be". Christ has contained everything, but he has not been everything, nor did he live everything. The gospel branch turns green again constantly in the lives of Christians. This is a perpetual nativity, an incessant return of youth.'

Yves Congar, 'L'Église, antique fontaine d'une eau jaillissante et fraîche', *La Vie Spirituelle* 636 (1980), p. 33

To try to express what is beyond words, Congar resorted to metaphors. But these metaphors themselves could only imperfectly convey what the theologian had set out to communicate. So he was never rigid in using them and employed them only to the extent that they were useful, exercising the freedom to modify them when the reality he was aiming for so required. This was the case when he compared Tradition to a channel or to the phenomenon of the circulation of the blood:

> In its actual role as a channel, since it is not inert but living, it is to a certain extent a source. By nourishing the tissues of the body, the blood is rejuvenated in the arteries that carry it. Tradition is the living artery that receives an increase of the very life it communicates, in its act of transmission.[22]

The subject: A constitutive principle of truth

'Living subjects necessarily put something of themselves into what they receive.' We must not pass too quickly over these words, for they convey an essential aspect of Yves Congar's thought. His conception of Tradition made much room for human experience, for the singularity of every experience, and therefore it is welcoming toward a contemporary disposition and longing. For Congar, the subject is a constitutive principle of truth. Thinking about the subject wards off the spectre of the great machine, of the system that grinds up all singularity.[23] In its place there appears the Christ 'that is to be',[24] and who will never fully be, except through our participation: 'There is the "Christ that is to be" (the words are Tennyson's), and this through a power that comes from his historical incarnation and passion; but also through contributions and a "doing" which are – we hardly dare say it – our part in his mystery.'[25]

To be faithful to Tradition does not mean being uninterested in one's own time, as if Christians had nothing to expect from the specificity of their own day, as if we had to give up a personal way of thinking, as some people fear when they think of the Church. The emphasis on the value of history and the contribution of the person, both of which we find constantly in Congar's writings, helps us understand 'how Tradition is capable of being enriched'.[26] For 'all the generations contribute to its development'.[27] Two texts can be cited here: 'It is not enough to say that there is a living subject; it must be added that this subject lives *in history* and that historicity is one of its inherent features, without, however, implying that its truth is relative or that it is nothing more than the successive and changing thought of men.' In the second text that we are going to read, after recalling that Tradition is the communication between a living being and another living being, Congar explained:

> This communication is made, however, in a history to which it does not remain alien. In other words, this history does not act simply as a setting for it, like a backdrop on a film set, which changes behind the actors without affecting them. It affects the conservation, transmission and even the content of what is kept and passed on in a certain way that does not destroy its identity.[28]

The true novelty: Christ

In giving history such a role, Congar knew that he was in danger of being misunderstood. Was he not underestimating that which has been given once and for all in Jesus Christ? There are many texts that will help avert such a misunderstanding. They do not allow us to think that Congar placed too much emphasis on the act of transmission – with its concern for what is living, for history, and for the demands of time – as compared to the content: 'Tradition implies and even tolerates no alteration in its objective content. It is a communication from one living person to another, but it is the communication of a definite object that retains the identity of its inner nature.'[29] Let us quote another text, one that is less widely known. It comes from one of Congar's innumerable contributions to collective works:

> True, the Church must adapt because it lives in history, where it exercises its mission for human beings. But this adaptation must be an adaptation of the *Church*. So the primary value to

which we must conform is not what is new as such, or what the time calls for (*quod tempus requirit*, as St. Bernard said): 'it is the reality which is communicated to us; we do not constitute it, rather it constitutes us. We can call it "Tradition", and mean by that something other than immobilism or the academicism of "received ideas"'.[30]

In reading this call to conform to the reality that is given to us – that is, the mystery of Christ, and that we do not constitute, but which constitutes us – one is reminded of what Walter Kasper, who learned a great deal from Congar, was writing several decades later about the crisis of transmission: it 'does not consist in an insufficient adaptation to the situation, but rather in an insufficient adaptation to Jesus Christ, because our following Christ is faltering. The ecclesial Tradition does not become meaningful because we keep up with the times, but because it makes Jesus Christ's relevance appear more clearly.'[31]

The art of combining a double fidelity

Kasper, like Congar, was seeking a balance. To quote Henri de Lubac, they believed that 'the work that is called for at the present time is in many respects far more delicate than that required in the Patristic age, in St. Thomas Aquinas' time or even in the "humanist" epoch. It demands a comprehensive combination of opposing qualities, each of them brought to a high degree of excellence, one buttressed so to speak against another, and braced with the greatest tension.'[32] It is a matter of combining a double fidelity: on the one hand, absolute fidelity to the origins, which is the foundation that endures (1 Corinthians 3:11), and on the other hand, the demand that we 'become all things to all' (1 Corinthians 9:22). For Congar wrote: 'As with the Church, one can speak dialectically of Tradition, making contrary statements about it, which are, however, true simultaneously. To say that it is at the center of Catholicism or Christianity means that it shares the same paradoxes and tensions.'[33] Like Congar, Kasper knew that we must be attentive to 'whatever our time calls for', but even more we must direct our attention to the inexhaustible and ever-young newness of Jesus Christ, for it is there, in the fullness of time, that a definitive new beginning was placed by God.[34] Thus, it is by making the unprecedented newness brought by Christ Jesus appear more clearly that we become agents of what Christians call 'Tradition'. Embracing the newness of Christ allows us to understand better how to inhabit our own time; welcoming the questions of our contemporaries can lead us to a fuller discovery of the unexpected possibilities of this same newness.

Congar noted that wanting to preserve what is and has been is frequently the most spontaneous reaction of the Church. This did not surprise him, but he knew that the legitimate concern to conserve is not sufficient, because 'it is also part of its mission to deploy the Gospel as extensively as possible to a humanity that is growing ceaselessly, not only externally and numerically, but also internally'.[35] It is possible to respond to this vocation only if one is like the scribe of the Kingdom of God who knows how to bring from his storeroom both the new and the old (Matthew 13:52).[36] Reflecting on this, Congar quoted von Balthasar:

> In order to remain faithful to itself and its mission, the Church must continually make an effort at creative invention. Paul had to be inventive in order to cope with the problem of the Gentiles who were obliged to enter into a Church that was heir to the Synagogue. The same applies to the Greek Fathers in the face of Hellenistic culture, and also to Saint Thomas in the face of Arabic philosophy and knowledge. We, indeed, for our part, must do the same in the face of the problems of our day.[37]

Discrepancies

It can happen that this capacity for invention and even the perception of its urgency becomes blocked. Congar discerned in history a number of instances when this discrepancy was symptomatic of a capacity for invention that had faltered. One of these moments, which occurred during the Middle Ages, concerned what happens to theology when university teaching is separated from pastoral teaching, that is, from contact with life and its evolution. On the one hand, there is a system that appears to be self-sufficient;

on the other hand, there are 'the almost endless multiplications of human situations in the unfolding of the world's history'. The first to notice the discrepancy are lay people because it is the laity that give 'utterance to the questings and strivings of the world', which can open new paths.[38] Joseph Moingt's explanation helps us to understand Congar's thinking:

> The particular mission of the lay faithful is to experience the life of faith at the heart of the realities of the world and of the historical tasks in which they are more engaged. The Christian people's experience of faith is what the scholastic doctors called *sensus communis fidelium*. They made this into a 'theological locus', that is, a means of elaboration and verification for the understanding of the faith. Of all the factors that influence Tradition, this one is undoubtedly the most powerful, precisely because it is intimately tied in with the evolution of history. At times the Christian people's experience influences Tradition through their resistance to something, and at others, through their push and pressure for something, and there are many instances of this in the history of the Church.[39]

During his life Congar came back repeatedly to this *sensus fidelium**,[40] which he attempted to define with his characteristic precision, for he desired to restore it to its rightful role in doctrinal discernment and theological reflection. He did the same thing with the concept of *sobornost'**,[41] which became important to him as he studied Slavic Orthodoxy. He perceived the essential role of this reality in any truly ecclesial discernment. He was tempted to translate *sobornost'* – a word some commentators said was untranslatable – by the English word 'togetherness', 'the fact of a person being together with others in a whole, the idea that one is oneself together with others, in and through the communion with others'.[42] Elsewhere he proposed to translate it as 'collegiality'*. It seemed to him that this concept of *sobornost'* contained a great core of ecclesiological truth. This need to do things together, this need to participate in the elaboration or maturation of decisions, this was, for Congar, the essence of our Tradition.[43] As for the 'theological locus' that is the life of men and women, to say that Congar was sensitive to it is to say too little, for it was a characteristic of his entire œuvre and theological method.[44]

Another example of a discrepancy can be found in the famous medieval quarrel which set the mendicant orders and the secular clergy against each other. Congar wrote a long article on this subject entitled 'Aspects ecclésiologiques de la querelle entre mendiants et séculiers dans la seconde moitié du XIIIe siècle et le début du XIVe'.[45] The so-called 'article' is 116 pages long! For Congar, 'the mendicants are the men of a world that is changing'.[46] Their existence and their way of being present to a changing world were contested by the secular clergy and aroused their wrath. William of Saint-Amour (1202–72) expressed this anger. In the end they accepted these bothersome religious, for 'one cannot refuse forever to accept what is a fact'.[47] Congar added:

> The opposition to the mendicants, especially in the way it was manifested at the beginning, and particularly in William of Saint-Amour, was clearly an opposition to novelty and to movement, in the name of an established framework that was firm, stable, and fixed once and for all [...] William refused this new form of pastoral care and evangelization in the Church because it represented something different from the ancient forms that were firmly and, he believed, divinely instituted. In the end he took an order of things that was entirely historical to be definitive and unsurpassable, and that was all he accepted. In addition to bishops and curates, there were archpriests, archdeacons, abbots and monks. But he refused to make room for new realities, as if history had stopped.[48]

Being today the Church of always

This fixed vision of history contrasts with Yves Congar's approach. He paid constant attention to the aspirations of his own time, wherever they came from, and with a sustained attention to what is entirely new in history. Like Balthasar, he knew that 'there is never a historical situation that is absolutely similar to any of the ones that preceded it in time. Thus there is no historical situation that can furnish us with its own solutions as a kind of master key capable of resolving all the problems that plague us today. [...] For a new problem there must be a new solution.'[49] Congar put it this way:

The problems of the fifth century and the resources of Augustine
are not those of the third century and Hippolytus; the problems
of the thirteenth century and the resources of Thomas Aquinas
are not those of the fifth century and Augustine. Today we find
ourselves equipped with resources that are new again and faced
with problems and possibilities as yet unknown.[50]

A confident vision of Tradition is at the origin of this attention
and is its fruit: 'To witness to Tradition is to witness to the current
and living faith of the Church. It means expressing this living faith
in its present state of development and conscience in relation to
the problems and errors of the moment.'[51] What is at stake in this
witness is the very identity of the Church: 'the Church of *today* is
the Church of all time. But the Church *of all time* is the Church
of *today* in that she adapts her forms of life and activity to the
requirements of *today*.'[52] In this witness, to be faithful to what is
given cannot mean a simple repetition of the past:

> The old sap, still living, brings life to a new tree. It is not simply
> a repetition of the old, like a new impression of an old record;
> it is an original expression, clothed in new vocabulary; the old,
> belonging to eternity, is indeed repeated, but not in its former
> state; deployed to reply to new problems, it uses new resources
> drawn from a given period, fashioned by human activity.[53]

To shift from an ecclesiology of repetition to an ecclesiology
of actualization was a major task that Yves Congar tackled.[54] It
presupposed living and demanding faithfulness to the mystery of
faith, as well as respect for, and attention to all that is produced
within history:

> Thus, the preservation of identity, because it is faithfulness
> within time – which changes everything – is different from 'the
> repetition of the same thing, which repeats itself becoming
> distorted in the process'. It is the perpetual youthfulness and
> vitality of Jesus Christ, lived out and made actual by new contri-
> butions and by the constant series of questions which demand of
> our fidelity a new response.[55]

The Holy Spirit co-instituting the Church

Congar increasingly understood the role played by the Holy Spirit in this living faithfulness which the Church needs to have:

> The Fourth Gospel attests several times that the disciples under-stood only later, in the light of Easter, the meaning of Christ's gestures or words. It also brings Jesus' promise that the Spirit will lead the disciples to all truth and will reveal to them all that is to come (John 16:13). This does not mean they will be able to predict the future, but it is the promise of assistance, so that their faithfulness to the word of Jesus will be accompanied, in the novelty of history, with new answers. This is the role of living Tradition, of which the Holy Spirit is the transcendent Subject, the guarantor of its fidelity.[56]

Congar increasingly saw the Holy Spirit as co-instituting the Church. Co-instituting, because the Church 'is made by two missions, that of the Son-Word, and that of the Spirit-Breath'.[57] Post-Tridentine ecclesiology had had the tendency to see Christ essentially as a founder. To speak of the Church it stressed the concept of 'society'. It was even called a 'perfect society' to explain that it is complete, furnished with all the means of a society. It could legislate, govern, and constrain via penalties.[58] Consequently, the foundation of the Church by Christ was circumscribed in time; it was a foundation that had happened in the *past*. There were several problems with this vision of the Church, particularly the impression that there was nothing to expect of its current members, as if they had nothing to contribute. For Congar, who was reconnecting here with a more ancient theology, the Church 'was not simply founded in the beginning – God continues without ceasing to build it up'.[59] He does this, according to the metaphor of St. Irenaeus, with his two hands, that is, Christ and the Spirit. In constantly making the work of Christ real in the present, the role of the Spirit 'thrusts the gospel forward into the period of history that has not yet come'.[60] In 'Pneumatology Today', published in 1973, Congar wrote: 'To construct his living Body, Christ has not only assumed in a permanent way and by

mode of institution certain visible and social means which I shall
call the structures of the covenant – the Gospel proclaimed, the
sacraments, the apostolate and its ministers. He calls upon all the
faithful to bring their contribution by placing at the service of his
work the gifts of nature and grace which we call charisms.' And
he added in the same text: 'The Church is not ready-made. It is
always in the process of being built, or rather being built by God.
It is not prefabricated and placed in a frame which has already
been prepared.'[61] Congar applied himself to finding the right
formulations to articulate accurately the work of Christ and the
work of the Spirit. It is with some hesitation and uncertainty that
he felt his way forward. Only in his later years did he find the most
satisfying forms of expression. If the Spirit 'displays something
that is new, in the novelty of history and the variety of cultures,'
Congar wrote, 'it is not something vague and imprecise,' but 'it is
a new thing that comes from the fullness that has been given once
for all by God in Christ.' This leads him to say: 'There is only one
Church, which is at once the Church built on what has been given
and the Church of the future, and it is built up by the "two hands"
of God!'[62]

Entering into the fullness of God

In order to comment on how our awareness of what has been given
in Christ should be deployed in efforts not only to conserve, but
also to develop, Congar made a well-chosen and suggestive use of
a text from Ephesians: 'It is given to us, but also *asked* of us, "to
comprehend with all the saints what is the breadth and length and
height and depth, and to know the love of God which surpasses
knowledge, that [we] may be filled with all the fullness of God"
(Ephesians 3:18–19).'[63] We start with a gift, offered in its totality
to human beings, 'defying perfect comprehension and formulation'.[64] Tradition is then 'the progressive understanding of the
riches possessed objectively from the beginning of Christianity'.[65]
Reflection, circumstances, a new historical situation – all this
can favor the passage from 'what was lived implicitly to what is
explicitly known'. It is in this way, paradoxically, that Tradition is
also connected to the future:

Tenderly inclined towards the past where its treasure is, Tradition proceeds towards the future which is its conquest and light. Even in what it discovers, it humbly feels it is only faithfully reclaiming what belongs to it [...]. Paradoxical though the assertion may seem, it may thus be argued that Tradition anticipates the future by the selfsame effort it makes to remain true to the past.[66]

These words, cited by Congar, were written by Maurice Blondel (1861–1949). Congar was happy to acknowledge his debt to the philosopher from Aix, who was able to reconcile truth and history without falling into relativism. According to Congar, he was the author of 'one of the finest descriptions of Tradition that exist'.[67]

Too fine, some will surely say. This was the view of American theologian John E. Thiel, who was not criticizing Blondel, but those who imagine that the serenity he described might actually correspond to the lived experience of the Church when it has to face something new, especially in the area of doctrine.

The Church's discernment, according to John Thiel

Thiel explains that anything new in the life of the Church seems, at the beginning, to be a threat to Tradition and to continuity with the past. A sense that something is incompatible with what has been taught up to the present can cause enormous resistance. Discernment is almost always arduous and slow. It does not happen without confrontation or debate. Change and novelty – however much care is taken with the language to describe what is happening – appear to be a foreign body and a danger to Tradition. It is only *a posteriori*, sometimes decades later (as was the case for the Council of Nicaea), that what had seemed to be new now seems entirely appropriate within Tradition and the continuity of the Church. In his studies on Tradition,[68] Thiel relied on Congar for a great deal of his historical analysis. Thiel considered Congar's two volumes on Tradition to be a 'magisterial' opus. Thiel also made good use of other works by Congar, and in particular, his important 1972 article on the theme of 'Reception as an Ecclesiological Reality',[69] to which I shall return later. Had Thiel paid greater attention to some of Congar's later works, especially his books on the Holy Spirit, he would have found an even greater ally in the French Dominican.[70]

A good pedagogue, Thiel uncovered four senses of the word 'Tradition'. Though one might disagree with some of the applications of Tradition he suggested, he was more interested in positing the principles for a right conception of Tradition than in imposing his own interpretations. As one reads Thiel's work – and this is one of its merits – one is reminded of what Teilhard wrote long ago about those theologians who imagine that their science can be reduced to understanding well what has *already been said*. As Teilhard wrote to Henri de Lubac, 'Theology is perhaps the most alive of the sciences, the one where there is the most to discover'.[71] Reading Thiel's book, which has been considered the most important work on Tradition since Newman's essay on the development of doctrine,[72] reinforces this conviction.

Two ways of looking

When Thiel studied his second sense of Tradition, what he called 'Development-in-Continuity', he reviewed the main 'models' that have come out of this conception. The contributions of Johann Drey (1777–1853) for the dialectical model, of Möhler for the organic model, and of Newman for the noetic model were presented in turn. Then comes what Thiel called 'the reception model'. He analyzed two ways of considering it, each of which corresponds to a different way of looking at things. He called the first one 'prospective'. The prospective conception belongs to an idealized observer for whom everything is clear: starting from the apostolic age this observer can look towards the future, through the centuries, and see the one same continuity, or at least the possibility of such a continuity in each period. This kind of gaze is far from human experience. It is really the divine gaze, which no human being can claim to possess. Then there is what Thiel called the 'retrospective' way of looking at things. It relinquishes looking for continuity in history from the divine point of view. It does not go from the past to the present, but from the present moment to the

past. It is from the 'present' of ecclesial life, from an act of faith that
gives value to this present, that continuity is discerned in *faith*. This
leads to a new way of looking at the past.[73] For Thiel, Tradition
is the entire ecclesial body's act of faith; it seeks to discern the
presence of the Spirit in history and in the paths it has opened in
history. Continuity is understood to be a reality that appears only
in the act of faith of believers who look at the past and re-interpret
it. 'In other words', Thiel explains, 'traditional continuity is a belief
about the present's relationship to the past, and only indirectly then
about the past's relationship to the present.'[74] One understands,
then, that a developing Tradition opens up a space of creativity for
faith, and this is a discernment of truth in Tradition. Seen in this
way, Tradition necessarily involves openness to novelty. The faith
that allows newness to come forth is a humble reality, both open to
the new and loyal to the old. It is in this sense that Thiel wrote that
'faithfulness is exciting because through it traditions are continu-
ously made'. He can therefore conclude: 'Tradition is a function of
faithfulness.'[75]

These stimulating and fresh views on Tradition are close to what
Congar had to say in his last theological work, *The Word and the
Spirit*: 'The Church is not just an establishment where past forms
are preserved. It is Tradition, and true Tradition is criticism and
creativity as well as the handing-down and preservation of identical
realities.'[76] In their book on Congar, Joseph Famerée and Gilles
Routhier underlined the 'less linear and homogeneous view of
Tradition'[77] that comes through in this later work. Actually, these
dimensions that Thiel is attached to – this openness to novelty,
with a valuing of the present moment and its share of obscurity
and ignorance – were already there in a much earlier writing by
Congar. Congar was writing about catholicity, but the question
he was dealing with there was the same one that any theologian
of Tradition must face. Catholicity and Tradition are, after all,
inseparable.[78] In his *Esquisses du mystère de l'Église*[79] Congar was
commenting on Acts 10, that is, the moment when Peter is taken
to Cornelius and is called to open himself to an action of the Spirit
which he, the apostle, had not expected and which the tradition of
his people had not envisaged. He wrote: 'Can we say that we are
really aware of the catholicity of Church so long as we fail to grasp
it in its concreteness, as it actually absorbs values or realities that
were, at first, or seemed to be, alien to it?' Here is Congar's limpid

response: 'We shall really *know* what it means for the Gospel to be preached to every creature only when *that has been accomplished*.'[80]

Denzingertheologie

To understand Congar's conception of Tradition it can be useful to look at his critique of what he called, following Karl Rahner, *Denzingertheologie*. The *Denzinger* is a compendium of brief doctrinal definitions and statements that was published for the first time in Germany in 1854 by Heinrich Denzinger, and was revised several times afterwards.[81] Neither Congar nor Rahner doubted the utility of this book. Congar even spoke of its 'incontestable usefulness'.[82]

Rahner was responsible for the 18th to the 31st editions of *Denzinger*. What both he and Congar wanted to challenge was the way this book had been used. In a famous article,[83] 'Du bon usage de "Denzinger"' ['On the Proper Use of "Denzinger"'], Congar noted that *Denzinger* 'has been used, especially in the last sixty years, for the formation of the theological mind of the entire Catholic clergy, mainly for the Roman rite. What an honor, and what a historical responsibility!'[84] The critical reflections of Congar on this influential textbook are directed at the notion of Tradition that may be generated by this kind of manual, and more generally he is critical of a certain way of doing theology. Congar was eager to show the limits of *Denzinger*, and even the dangers of a theology based on it.

'Du bon usage de "Denzinger"' recalls the intention of its architect: 'To enable theology students to avoid errors induced by ignorance of the norms given by the Magisterium of the councils and popes, by supplying them with a practical compendium of definitions and condemnations made by this Magisterium.'[85] The manual was thoroughly revised in 1908, and the interpretation of certain themes was skewed by ideological headings that appeared for decades in successive editions. Congar focused his attention on items that were, surprisingly, missing from *Denzinger*. He complained that, in this book, Catholic Tradition was stripped of numerous expressions of its diversity. He noted that despite the fact that the Magisterium has been very diverse, and is so in itself, in *Denzinger* the Magisterium appears to speak with one voice. Congar discerned that an important problem was being posed in theological criteriology and in ecclesiology by the collection's selection of texts. Long before publishing his important 1972 article on 'reception',[86] Congar used this term to explain that the inclusion of certain texts in *Denzinger* and the omission of other texts show that 'reception' really does exist in the Church. This 'reception' must be taken in its historical dimension, for a doctrine that is 'received' at a given time might not be at another time, and vice versa.[87] Certain omissions have a great impact on ecclesiology. For Congar, the most serious of the omissions was that of the letter signed by the German bishops in January and February 1875 and approved by Pope Pius IX in a letter addressed to the German episcopate on March 2 of that same year, and then a few days later in a consistory allocution.[88] Congar was very fond of these texts, which he published himself in the collective work he directed with B.-D. Dupuy, *L'Épiscopat et l'Église Universelle*.[89] They are texts of the utmost importance because they refute Bismarck's argument that 'the bishops [after Vatican I] are only the pope's instruments, his officials without any responsibility of their own'.[90] As O. Rousseau put it, these texts are 'the strongest argument ever produced in the Catholic tradition against any tendency to minimize the rights and value of the episcopate'.[91] Pius IX himself defended in these pages the position of the bishop as pastor of his diocese. One can understand that for Congar, the apostle of collegiality, the omission of these documents was a serious one: 'The inclusion or omission of such texts is decisively important for the orientation of ecclesiology.'[92]

But other dangers could lie in wait for those who would use *Denzinger* in too facile and lazy a fashion. Congar indicated that *Denzinger* 'has excessively favored modern Catholicism's inclination to the juridical approach'.[93] In addition, for Congar who practiced a theology attached to life, rooted in the real, always concerned to take into account the historical and philological contexts within which a thought was elaborated, *Denzinger* was 'the very negation of the historical character of texts'.[94] The *Denzinger Compendium* played an extremely significant role 'in the development of what is a true theological illness, linked with a certain kind of ecclesiology that is all juridical, the one that sees the process that ends in "definitions" as the only one that matters, and sees the major task of theology as the preparation and reaching of such definitions'.[95] Therefore, 'texts which could be truly understood only in their own historical and perhaps philological contexts' are reduced to being textbook categories and to becoming 'juridical statements, detached from the life of faith'.[96]

For Congar, the Magisterium's[97] 'primary function' is not 'to "define", but to transmit the deposit of faith and to give a witness'. In its function of defining – and this is easy to forget – the Magisterium is 'conditioned in great part by the particular point in question, or by the errors that it sets out to exclude. It runs the risk of saying nothing, on the positive side, about very important Christian realities [...].' In other words, if it is limited to the function of defining or reacting against errors, the Magisterium is not operating in all of its fullness; because of the limited task it has taken on, that of defining or rectifying, it no longer proposes 'the totality and the fullness of faith'. To ignore this point and build an entire system of thought based on *Denzinger* can produce deplorable results. This is because 'in intervening against errors, the definition-oriented Magisterium runs the risk of not expressing the most profound aspects of the Catholic faith. In expressing itself at a given time against particular errors, it insists on certain points which, though they may be the most threatened, are not always the most central or the most fundamental'.[98] Congar could then recall that 'the distinctive feature of Tradition, remarkably well-realized in the genius of the Church Fathers and of the liturgy, is precisely that it contains and communicates the *meaning* of things by showing their relation to the whole, to the most radical principles, to the first dogmatic layers, to the Christian mystery at its most intimate'.[99] It is with the Church Fathers that he breathed the spirit of Tradition, its *ethos*, for 'they never lost sight of the totality of the faith, united as it is by its center, that is, the Christian mystery, and converging toward its object, our union with God'.[100] What he most particularly admired about them was this: 'always concentrating on the whole and on its center, the Church Fathers bring the whole to life in each of its parts.'[101]

Tradition and mystery

By focusing on what lies at the center of faith and on its meaning, Congar took Tradition out of the category of apologetics, where it had ended up,[102] and restored it to the place it had at the outset, that is, an expression of mystery. It no longer served extrinsicism*, which was born of the separation between theology and spirituality, where Tradition was reduced to being little more than a coefficient of juridical authority. Thanks to a 'resourcing' that came from a return to the Church Fathers, Tradition is free to be what it truly is: not a system, but 'the action of a living being on another living being, and in the end, the action of the Living God towards a believer in need of new life'.[103]

Congar believed that we enter into an understanding of Tradition only if we are able to view its statements as 'moments in which faith goes forward seeking with difficulty its paths of faithfulness to the mystery'.[104] This is precisely what *Denzinger* does not allow when, as a textbook, it adduces statements that are isolated from their historical context. On the contrary, theologians who wish to become disciples of the Church Fathers do not just repeat what they said. They know they are called to imitate the Fathers' approach: to react to the problems of their time with faith as their primary source. Their understanding of the Word prepares them to welcome what is new: 'The Word of God is always for the present, and it is heard in our time. It is because it is always new that it becomes Tradition. Tradition is not only transmission of the past; it contributes also and at the same time to the opening of a new future.'[105] By drawing again from the sources of Scripture and living Tradition, one can 'find on that basis forms which allow one to evangelize a world that makes itself every day *other* than the one it was yesterday or the day before yesterday'.[106] So, in a changing world, the creative part of transmission cannot be ignored.[107] That this creativity must operate in *faith* and not in clear vision means that nothing is evident from the start. The bold initiative of one or several persons needs time to be recognized as a constitutive part of Tradition. The history of the Church includes abundant examples of this phenomenon.

Twenty years after his article on *Denzinger*, Congar wrote again about this manual that had offered 'in some ways a ready-made theology, one that was independent of the person who was thinking it'. He measured the progress that had occurred in the meantime: 'Theologians today think about issues much more on the basis of sources, and above all, on the basis of the data coming from experience, culture, the various realities themselves.' And he concluded: 'The Church advances in the itinerary of human beings. In that sense, the Church *has to be made* without ceasing. In the Church's confession of faith and in the theology that explains the Church, there are still things that have not been said, that have not been discovered.'[108]

Preserving identity in ways other than repetition

When Congar was writing his books on Tradition, the word 'hermeneutics' in French was not as omnipresent as it is today in exegesis, theology, and other disciplines.[109] It was different in 1972, when he published a lucid text entitled 'Le chrétien, son présent, son avenir et son passé'.[110] In reflecting on the Church's relationship with Scripture, and on the obligation to refer back to a norm, to a canon, Congar was being faithful to the principles that we have already studied. In this new text, where he sought to explain to a general audience the need for a hermeneutic, he used historical examples to illustrate his main points.

First he clearly established the function of hermeneutics: 'Not only to understand the text exegetically, to know what *Paul, Luke, or John* wanted to say, but to reread it personally, to apply it to my life or to the questions that are being posed today.'[111] Then Congar moved on to examples of how the Biblical authors have been solicited in different periods of history to answer questions that they had never imagined during their lifetime: '*John* had not anticipated Arius, and yet he would respond to him through the hermeneutic of Athanasius. *Paul* had not anticipated Pelagius, and yet he would respond to him through the thinking of Augustine. Neither *Paul* nor *John* anticipated Marx, and neither they nor *Luke* anticipated Freud, nor did *Matthew* anticipate the problems of the developing world or of war.' The task that emerges from this wards off all forms of fundamentalism, for the human intelligence must be engaged and is obliged to participate in this adventure: 'It is up to us to bring forth from the authors of the New Testament a word that is both faithful to them, and real in regards to what is unprecedented in history, for by its very nature history is made of such moments.'[112] That is why 'the preservation of the identical is different from "the repetition of the identical"'.[113]

The Alpha and the Omega

In the light of what we have already seen, Tradition's openness to what is new is not at all surprising. This openness can be said to be constitutive of faithfulness. This openness to the future and to the unpredictable can be explained also by the apostolic nature of the Church. 'Apostolic'? Congar knew that this word would convey to many of his readers the notion of a limited call to be faithful to the origins. He was certainly attached to this dimension of faithfulness. The Church claims communion with the apostles in relation to the doctrine and the tradition that it must transmit. Congar said, however, that 'this idea is quite correct, but it needs to be amplified', citing W. Pannenberg almost word for word.[114] In accord with Pannenberg's way of commenting on apostolicity, Congar added that 'apostolic', in the sense of 'in conformity with the origins', 'is in some sense only half the truth'.[115] Christ is not only the *Alpha*; he is also and quite as much the *Omega*. 'In other words', Jean-Georges Boeglin explains, 'the end result of Tradition is as important to understand as its origin.'[116] If there is any notion that brings together and synthesizes faithfulness and novelty, because it is located precisely between the Alpha and the Omega, it is that of *witness*.[117] The apostles are *sent out*, which means they are not only witnesses of events that have occurred (Christ as Alpha), but their words dare to say how the world is transformed by the events they have witnessed. Sent out, the apostles testify to the 'saving value of these events and their present and effective reality for the world'.[118] Pannenberg explained it in this way:

> To be apostolic with regard to the eschatological mission of the apostles is clearly more than merely conserving the heritage of the apostles' doctrine. To be apostolic is to set forth the finality,

that is, the truth, of that which occurred in the person of Jesus and was proclaimed by the apostles. In this context, finality means the future truth of the world, which is not yet brought to completion, that is, has not yet fulfilled its essence. Therefore the apostolic doctrine is not expressed through traditional formulation as such, but only through the proclamation of the finality of the message and work of Jesus, proclamation always related to the present day and always casting light on the present experience, as it sets forth the message and work of Jesus as the truth that brings this unfulfilled world toward fulfilment.[119]

Congar commented: 'Faithfulness to the testimony is therefore not only directed back into the past – it is also oriented towards the future eschatological era and consequently towards the fulfilment of all of history.'[120] He himself used the German word *vorwärtsgerichtet*[121] (meaning 'turned toward what is ahead') to translate this same idea. Indeed the words spoken by those who are sent cannot be limited to a meaning located in the past. They must show how the message they express transforms the world and the life of those who hear them. If the hearers of such words cannot perceive how their future is changed by the message announced to them, if they leave with the impression that what they heard does not concern their own world, but only the world of yesterday, then one can think that they have not been put into contact with the living Tradition. 'The tradition is faithfully passed on only when it is rendered engaging and life-giving.'[122]

Between purity and fullness

Inspired by this understanding of Tradition, and eager to communicate with today's world, Congar wrote: 'Many *representations* of faith cannot be received any more, and thus they cannot be proposed with the terminology, categories, and construction handed down to us by scholasticism, by the apologetics of the eighteenth and nineteenth centuries, and by the school teaching and ordinary preaching of the beginning of this century.'[123]

Thus, the theologian who wants to be faithful to the living Tradition must consent to live in a tension between *purity* and *fullness*:

Tradition, then, comprises two equally vital aspects: one of development and one of conservation. This is why some see Tradition eminently as a safeguard for the purity of the deposit, at the risk of cutting the present off from the future, while others see it eminently as a way of opening the present to the future, in the search for a total synthesis. There is a sort of tension or dialectic between purity and totality, neither of which should be sacrificed.[124]

Congar did not fear the discomfort that might come from this situation, particularly for the theologian:

Instead of starting only from what is given in Revelation and Tradition, as classical theology has generally done, we must start here from a given of facts and questions received from the world and from history. This is much less comfortable. We cannot be content anymore to repeat the old, starting from the ideas and problems of the thirteenth or sixteenth centuries. If not from the ideas, then we must start from the problems of today, as a new 'given' that needs to be clarified, certainly, by what has been 'given' forever in the gospels, but without benefiting from the elaborations already acquired and possessed in the calm of a sure tradition.[125]

Yves Congar dedicated himself, even at an advanced age, to following this path. We see him doing this in a late work intended for the general public, *Église catholique et France moderne*.[126] He was trying to begin a dialogue with those who keep their distance from the Church or even reject it. He accorded a large place to history, and in writing about the institution, about politics, ethics, and certain ways of speaking about God – basically about all the topics that are contentious – he did not hesitate to recognize 'frankly the shortcomings of the past and the deficiencies of the present'.[127] But when the dialogue was about this Church he loved, what he wanted was for people not to be blind to 'the possibilities of its future'. Indeed, for Congar the theologian of Tradition, 'the Church is its future as much as its past'.[128]

3

Reform

Must one choose between tradition and reform? Is it 'either or'?
Yves Congar did not think so. For him, 'reforming prophetism'
and 'fidelity to tradition' are mutually supportive; each of these
attitudes implies the other. Jean-Pierre Jossua rightly recalled how
they are, deep down, in accord.[1] It is in order to be faithful to itself,
to what it truly is, that the Church constantly reforms itself. It does
so not only out of a need for purification or because distortions
are introduced through failures of its members; more fundamentally, it is because it has received the mission to be the witness of
a contemporary God. And because 'the world is being made every
day', Congar affirmed that it cannot be different for the Church.[2]
Before I quote several texts by Congar on this subject, let us listen
to one of his contemporaries, who explains the Church's freedom
to reform itself – a freedom that is not always well understood.

> However rooted in history the Church may be, it is not the slave
> of any epoch or indeed of anything whatsoever the essence of
> which is temporal. The message it is bound to pass on and the
> life it is bound to propagate are never integral parts of either
> 'a political régime, or a social polity or a particular form of
> civilization,' and it must forcefully remind people of the fact,
> in opposition to the illusive evidence to the contrary, which, in
> fact, derives simply from the bonds of habit.[3]

I have quoted this text by Henri de Lubac, for it prepares us to
understand the mentality that Yves Congar clashed with because of

his will to work for Church reform. Let us listen again to de Lubac commenting on resistance to reform:

> There will always be people who identify their cause with that of the Church so totally that they end by equating the Church's cause with their own, and this in all good faith. It does not occur to them that if they are to be truly faithful servants they may have to mortify much in themselves; in their desire to serve the Church, they press the Church into their own service. [...] For them the Church is a certain order of things which is familiar to them and by which they live; a certain state of civilization, a certain number of principles, a certain complex of values which the Church's influence has more or less Christianized but which remain nonetheless largely human. And anything which disturbs this order or threatens this equilibrium, anything which upsets them or merely startles them, seems to them to be a crime against a divine institution.[4]

Unfortunately, examples of situations arising from this kind of blindness are abundant in history. There is something tragic about them, for the resistance to change they manifest has serious consequences.

A courageous book

Specialists on Congar's work agree that *True and False Reform in the Church*[5] is 'his magnum opus and certainly the one that is most characteristic of Congar's genius'.[6] It did not describe a program of reforms, but sought to establish the legitimacy of reform and to clarify the general conditions that would make such reform succeed. The awareness of living in a changing world and culture is a call 'to invent something new'.[7] Congar's great book, which was bold in many ways, was also characterized by great caution; reform had to avoid leading to schism, and it had to be truly *within* the Church, originating from its deepest sources.

Jean-Pierre Jossua's invitation to admire the form and content of *True and False Reform in the Church* rings true especially when one weighs 'the courage needed to publish these pages at the end of the pontificate of Pius XII ... The thought, the tone, and even the writing demonstrate a nobility and a gospel truthfulness to which no one can be insensitive.'[8] We know that Angelo Roncalli, Papal Nuncio in Paris and future Pope John XXIII, 'kept this book, which he had carefully annotated, in his library'.[9] And Monsignor Montini, then Substitute Secretary of State, and later Archbishop of Milan and Pope Paul VI, personally asked Congar to give him a copy of the book, which was already out of print and prohibited from being reprinted.[10]

A traditional theme

The word 'reform', or the 'fact of reform' as Congar called it sometimes, is extremely traditional in the Church. 'Why should we be scared of that? The Church is always reforming itself; it is the way it stays alive, and at any given moment the intensity of its effort to reform is the index of its vitality.'[11] With his vast knowledge of history, Yves Congar had no difficulty offering examples that confirmed this understanding. Other historians agreed with him.[12] The meaning of the word 'reform' can vary. Gerhart B. Ladner has shown that for the Church Fathers, 'reform' meant first of all to reform oneself, to be converted, to become more in God's image. Ladner thought the idea of *Church reform* appeared in the eleventh century.[13] Congar agreed with Ladner, but he thought that the reform of self, that is personal conversion, was insufficient: 'There is in fact a density proper to impersonal and collective structures which has to be reached: otherwise the most generous reformist intentions would exhaust themselves in a never-ending effort that the opposing structures, keeping their place, would condemn to remain only half-effective.'[14]

Congar will go down in history as one of those people who succeeded in bringing about a reform *within* the Church. The fact that he was named a cardinal was seen as an act of gratitude on the part of the Church towards 'one of the artisans of the reform of the Catholic Church as it took shape during the Second Vatican Council'.[15] In expressing himself in 1969 on the theme of reform in the Church during a general audience, Pope Paul VI referred to *True and False Reform in the Church*: 'This is one of the most interesting, grave, and urgent questions of our time. And we ourselves, who desire the just reform of the Church no less than anyone else,[16] we

CONDITIONS FOR A REFORM TO SUCCEED

Congar set out four conditions he considered essential for reform to happen *within* the Church, and without causing a schism:

1 Every effort for reform must give primacy to charity and to pastoral concerns, and not give in to the spirit of the 'system'[17] where the Church is treated like an idea, an intellectual construct. The Church must be accepted as a given of reality. 'This Church, one has both to accept it and not to accept it as it is.' For this is not about making '*another Church*', but 'a *Church* that is *other*'.[18]

2 Secondly, it is necessary to stay within the communion of the whole, for 'the whole truth is grasped only in communion with the whole Church'.[19]

3 A healthy reform will happen through a return to the sources, to the very principles of Tradition. The Church must live in contact with its sources. 'Calling existing forms into question, if that must be done, should proceed not from a weakening but from a strengthening of fidelity.'[20]

4 The last condition consists in showing patience and respecting delays.[21] Congar knew that he was an impatient man in small matters. He acknowledged: 'I do not know how to wait for a bus!'[22] But with the reform of the Church at stake, he was convinced that patience was necessary, and he knew that 'human beings almost always lack this quality'.[23] It is impatience that 'threatens to ruin everything'.[24] It is not a simple matter of reluctantly accepting that the Church moves slowly, but a state of mind. He was thinking about the necessary delays, of course, but beyond that he saw the need for what he called 'a flexibility of spirit'[25], which we could understand as a conscious choice to reject perfectionism. In his writings and in his behaviour, especially during Vatican II, we see how he himself rejected idealism. He denounced the mentality of 'everything or nothing'. One recognizes in him what he himself admired in Lacordaire: 'the sense of what is possible'.[26]

think that the possibility of proceeding with its own reform that is offered to the Church today is a "sign of the times", a grace from the Lord ... We can make our own the program of a continual reform of the Church, understood in its authentic sense, *Ecclesia semper reformanda* [the Church is always to be reformed].'[27]

Why are reforms necessary?

In his introduction to *True and False Reform in the Church*, Congar recalled the questions being asked immediately after World War II. This was a period not only of increasing awareness, but also of great creativity:

> The pastoral activities of the Church no longer had much meaning for the majority of people, especially the more radical and dynamic among them. You might say that this is because people are more easily inclined to be carnal than spiritual; but it was also because people, both priests and lay faithful, received the things of Christ in forms inherited from an honourable but culturally obsolete past, in acts and formulas that were scarcely more than rituals, lacking the power to invite others to life or to express their life.[28]

It is realizing the existence of a gap of this sort that motivates reforms, that opens people's eyes to their necessity. The goal is not to try to update the Church to the latest style or to run after the latest fashion, but the aim is for the Gospel truly to reach men and women as they are, in the reality of their lives. François-Marie Humann, in his recent book on Congar, pinpointed what was new in Congar's way of seeing the need for reform. The novelty was that, instead of explaining the need for reform by referring to sin, he spoke of the 'existential and historical dimension of the Church and of the members who compose it'.[29] Congar wrote:

> Now this humanity [...] does not exist as a kind of timeless and changeless entity, like an inert stone. It lives and grows [...] and becomes diverse, evolving even across time, filling up the changes of time as it fills the space of its progressive developments. The

seed of Adam evolves and develops, expands and becomes
fruitful by pouring out its potential into space and time.[30]

The Church 'has to follow humanity in expanding and evolving
and thus experience a parallel development within itself. If the
Church failed to do this, it would leave between itself and part of
humanity a distance or hiatus, and in this way would fail to carry
out God's plan.'[31] Congar knew that the necessary impetus implied
here is not always easy and that those whose historical sense is not
awakened may not see the need for it: 'If we look around ourselves,
we see that churchmen who are eventually open to reform[32] are
also open to real consideration of historical and social conditions,
whereas churchmen who are *a priori* opposed to any reform
are likewise closed to any consideration of historical and social
conditions.'[33] What is needed is to be plugged into the real, so to
speak, to be attuned to the primacy of facts, to accept the solid
consistency of time.[34]

This is precisely what a system does not do. Congar's strongest
critique of this fact is surely stated in the *Journal d'un théologien:*

I am struck everywhere by the lack of realism in a system which
has its theses and its rituals, and its servants, and which sings
its song without looking at things and problems as they are.
The system is satisfied with its own affirmations and its own
celebrations. This unfolds on a different plane than the one of
real problems, in another universe than that of human beings.[35]

The 'sourcier' [water-diviner] at work

Congar, who loved the Church, suffered from feeling that on the
one hand there was 'a system constantly justified and glorified
[...] and on the other hand, human beings, their questions, their
expectations – with the two never meeting'.[36] What he disliked
about the 'system' was its lack of interest in human beings, its lack
'of consideration for humans, of respect for humans'.[37] He was not
opposed to the Church or to its Tradition, but as the prophet that
he was – like a ancient 'sourcier' [water-diviner] – he was appealing
on the contrary to a deeper tradition and a better fidelity. It was in

the name of the very *ecclesia*[38] that was practically being eliminated 'through fictions, negations of tradition, through the falsifying of history'[39] that he was rebelling. 'It is not outside or against the tradition of the Church' that he wanted 'to find a solution, but in the very depths of the tradition itself'.[40]

If the Church is oblivious to the aspirations of a changing world, lacks openness to it, and refuses the necessary reforms, it deprives itself of the life forces that it needs for the growth of the Body. Congar knew that these life forces were often 'the forces of the periphery, of the frontier, of contact with culture, of assimilation – these are the "missionary" forces of the Church'. To discourage them by rejecting reform would mean accepting 'before history the terrible responsibility of having contributed to depriving the Church of creative forces'.[41]

Structure and life

To give primacy to facts, to accept the solid consistency of time, to pay attention 'to the aspirations of the modern world' – this cannot be done without peril. Congar thought he could avoid the dangers of a flawed theology by means of a distinction between 'structure' and 'life',[42] or between 'structures' in the plural and 'structure' in the singular. In both cases it is necessary to distinguish what is essential for the Church ('the structure') from 'its contingent forms that are relative and subject to time' ('life'). One can recognize here a distinction analogous to the one between Tradition and traditions. *True and False Reform in the Church* is, in great part, built on the distinction Congar posed between 'structure' and 'life'. He was convinced of this: 'Disasters happen whenever one passes inappropriately from the plane of life to that of structure.' Congar has been criticized for this way of presenting things. And he himself, without renouncing it entirely, would evolve toward using other expressions as he came to place a greater emphasis on pneumatology* and when there developed in his thought a better articulation of the connection between Christ and the Spirit. At the same time, we can understand why this distinction was useful for a Catholic theologian who was setting out for the first time to tackle the question of what a reform inside the Church might be. We might add that Congar rarely did theology as a systematician. His approach was more historical and dependent on the reality of the world that surrounded him. He himself wrote of the French theologians of his day, that they 'as a whole have worked very much in contact with the concrete life of the Church and the needs of the faithful; in a less university-focused and scientific way than their German colleagues. Very often it is the circumstances that allow us to understand the meaning of this or that text.'[43]

By fidelity to what is constitutive of the Church, to its 'generative causes', the theologian who wishes to work on reform does not alter 'the deposit of faith, the deposit of the sacraments of faith and the apostolic powers whereby the one and the other are transmitted'.[44] When the object of study is the *life* of the Church, the theologian's space for creativity is much greater, since the focus is forms:

> In order to make the *paradosis* – the transmission – effective and authentic, this or that form in which the transmission occurred in the past, but which would nowadays be an obstacle to its reality, must eventually be revised and renewed. This is why every reform requires not only an analysis of the situation and its demands, but basic resources of a very pure kind in the form of a knowledge of the indefeasible content of the Christian realities which are to be handed on.[45]

Articulating the life of the Church and ecclesiology

According to Congar, the flaw of modernism, what was unacceptable about it, was that it did not give sufficient recognition to the *structure* of the Church; traditionalism [Fr.: *intégrisme*] 'sins against the *life* of the Church by ignoring what the times are asking for', the requests 'for expansion, assimilation, adaptation'.[46] Structure and life: neither of these components should be neglected. 'For if the Church is structured from above, it also lives from below.'[47] According to Congar, life has been studied less than structure in the history of the Church,[48] and it is life to which less space has been devoted. Congar's contribution here is important. It has been

written that he introduced life into ecclesiology,[49] and at the heart
of his method one finds an effort to articulate the life of the Church
and ecclesiology.[50]

Naturally, such an approach implies taking seriously the
experience of the faithful, their questions, their expectations, their
aspirations. It is an approach that rejects the insularity of a closed
system. For Congar, being open to the impact of the real, a real
that is always mobile and changing, and the readiness to put into
practice the reforms that the real calls for, are signs of health, of
vitality. Not being afraid of a dialogue in which the other side
will affect you is indeed a sign of self-confidence. With this in
mind, and as a critique of the opposite attitude in which fear has
the upper hand, Congar quoted the words of Émile Mersch: 'It is
for lack of skeletons that certain animals have to be enclosed in
shells.'[51]

Stones for building the temple

Rooted in Tradition, Congar was one of those Christians who have
refused to enclose Christianity in an outdated culture. At a time of
great cultural and historical change, he wanted the cry once echoed
by Ozanam to be heard again: 'Let us move on to the barbarians!'[52]
Congar knew, as Henri de Lubac recalled, that the Church is not
'the slave of any time' or of any 'particular form of civilization'. No
more than de Lubac could Congar imagine a Church that would
'resign itself to being cut off from those who do not yet know it
simply for the sake of the comfortableness of those who make up
its traditional faithful'.[53] Congar was a man of reform because he
was an apostle,[54] because he was committed to announcing to his
contemporaries an audible Gospel. He knew that 'human history
is like the quarry from which the apostolic ministry must take its
stones to build the temple of God'.[55] He wanted to be attentive to
that which has not yet found its form and aspires to be, knowing
that 'a spiritual organism is more likely to *grow* out of the elements
searching and striving for expression'.[56] He found a confirmation
of this fact in history.

WHAT IS A REFORM?

' A Reform is not a revolution, for it respects continuity, but it is something else besides a restoration, for it does not seek simply to reestablish what was there *before*. If I saw conformity to the present situation as the only possibility, there would never be any reform. If I imagined something entirely other, that would not be the reform of the *Church*. We must keep Catholic fidelity, but not a flat fidelity, given only to the actual form of things. Building on the foundations that were laid at the beginning, my faithfulness has to take on the future. In short it has to come to terms with and accept the solid consistency of time.'

Yves Congar, *Au milieu des orages* (Paris: Cerf, 1969), p.14

A major characteristic of the modern world: the discovery of the subject

It was because he was equipped with this apostolic sense that Congar wanted to welcome a characteristic of modernity whose importance he discerned very early in his career as a theologian: *the discovery of the subject*. As others have noted, for a man not particularly aware of contemporary philosophy, Congar was still 'remarkably attuned to the thought of his time'.[57] Congar tried to define the discovery of the subject, one of the great themes of the modern world, in *True and False Reform in the Church*, hinting that he would devote other works to this theme in the future.[58] As we saw above,[59] his article on Kierkegaard already showed an early interest in this theme. Congar now wished not simply to understand his contemporaries' interest in a philosopher, but also to make room in ecclesiology for the human beings who wish and need to be the *subjects* of their actions. Congar realized that he was not entirely alone on this path:

A number of level-headed minds within Catholicism have thought that there was a certain truth in the subject's point of view, and particularly in the idea that knowledge and assent are conditioned by the dispositions of the subject. It is remarkable that the same people who made room for this point of view applied the idea of development to Christianity, giving legitimacy within Catholicism to the psychological and the historical. Such is the great interest of Möhler and Newman, who for this reason were considered by some – quite wrongly in my view – as ancestors of modernism.[60]

Congar reflected a great deal on modernism. He saw what was unacceptable about it, and at the same time he wanted to honour its potential truth or at least its valid aspirations. In the winter of 1932, long conversations with Marie-Dominique Chenu helped him to see more clearly: 'we agreed also on this point, that one of our generation's tasks would be to address successfully the valid concerns of modernism.'[61] Insofar as it was a phenomenon internal to Catholicism, modernism was a heresy condemned by Pius X in his 1907 encyclical *Pascendi*. As is often the case, this heresy represented an inadequate answer to real questions. 'That is what is frightening', Étienne Gilson wrote, 'orthodoxy in the hands of her destroyers. The tragedy of modernism was that the rotten theology promulgated by its opponents was in large part responsible for its errors.'[62]

According to Congar, modernism was seeking to answer two new questions: 'Both of these questions have been distorted and spoiled by it, but both of them also concern real problems.' First, 'there is the attempt to apply to Christian reality, which presents itself as a historical reality, a critical methodology'. The historian Émile Poulat, a specialist in modernism, agrees with this analysis and sees in the modernist crisis the result 'of the harsh collision of traditional ecclesiastical teaching with the new religious studies which were forged far from the control of orthodox ways of thinking and often against them'.[63] For the first time methodologies emerging from these new approaches were being applied to an area previously considered beyond their competence. On this first point, Congar explained his position clearly. He held to the principle that the faith of the Church 'has not forgone the possibility of a dialogue with the historian, but the Church asks the historian to accept it for what it is, something irreducible to the narrow limits admitted by historicism as its proper domain'.[64] We cannot develop this further here, but suffice it to say that, on this point, Congar owed a great deal to the theology of faith of Ambroise Gardeil; the Saulchoir School, under the direction of Chenu, had made this one of its foundations. In *La théologie au Saulchoir*, M.-D. Chenu wrote with serenity:

> It was the conjunction of modernist historicism with a false theology of faith that provoked around 1900 such a malaise in the study of the sources of revelation and in the development of theological methodology. Modernist historicism considered history to be an absolute; but only faith is absolute.[65]

The other reality Congar discerned in modernism was 'a religious philosophy that included an entire interpretation of the act of faith, the insertion of the believer in the Church .... Of this philosophy, I have found that there is a valid underlying concern. It is what I call "the point of view of the subject".'[66] Congar believed that Christianity is able to honour this concern which comes from modernity; he considered it to be valid and legitimate. This concern consisted of the will to be the subject of one's actions, to be responsible and free. In old age, when he was commenting on people's massive desertion from the churches, he could still say: 'That is one of the reasons for the present crisis in any case: people do not feel that they are being sufficiently treated as subjects ...'[67]

Congar sought to honour this concern as an ecclesiologist. The reform of ecclesiology brought by Vatican II, especially in the recognition, 'remarkably granted by the Council, of the role of charisms in the building of the Church'[68] crowned his efforts. Christianity for Congar is 'at heart an affirmation of the person, of the human's freedom to choose, of the free initiative of God's grace in the person, and of the freedom which this grace brings'. This is why Congar did not fear the personal principle which 'has taken in our day a new character. With the modern age we have passed from an objective world, fixed and hierarchical, where the person was situated in a total order encompassing all of creation to a world where subjects affirm their own subjectivity and their own personal free choice.'[69] Inspired by Möhler, but ultimately simply to be faithful to the great Tradition, Congar proposed a *Gemeinschaft* theology, that is, a Church which is a *community* of persons, where each one brings his or her own riches. Indeed, 'the Church is not ready-made. It is always in process of being built, or rather, of being built by God. It is not prefabricated and placed in a frame which has already been prepared. It is a living organism to whose functioning people contribute their help and their creativity.'[70] As a result, Congar was critical vis-à-vis the Church's response to modernism: 'In the necessary reaction against modernism, what was valid was swept out along with what was corrupt. What triumphed was a set of petty points of view coming from a theology (?) that was both non-critical and ready-made, emptied of the sap of sources and of the content of the contemplation of faith.'[71] Clearly, the question mark he attached to 'theology' in the text that I have just quoted marks not only his disagreement with the answer that was given, but also a doubt as to its theological quality. For Congar, this question was not resolved by the condemnation of modernism. Along with others, he considered the ever-increasing importance given to the formal principle of authority to be a danger for the future of the Church in a society built more and more around freedom. He also questioned whether this tendency was in keeping with the Tradition of the Church.

The subjective turn of culture

The sixty years that have passed since the publication of *True and False Reform in the Church* have, to a large extent, confirmed what Congar had perceived before many others, and this despite all the vicissitudes the understanding of the subject has undergone and the new insights that have been brought to its study by the social sciences and philosophy. Recent books by a contemporary philosopher, Charles Taylor, who learned a great deal from Congar,[72] allow us to measure the importance of this subjective turn of culture. Taylor is the author of a recent and monumental work on secularization entitled *A Secular Age*. In this book and in earlier works, Taylor characterizes our age as 'The Age of Authenticity'.[73] As a particularly attentive and rigorous observer of modernity, Taylor manifests rootedness and openness, balanced judgements, and a rejection of dualism – all of which remind us of Congar's own approach. Like many others, Taylor believes that North-Atlantic civilization is undergoing a cultural revolution, and he considers the 1960s to be the moment of transition. This was in part an 'individuating revolution'. Taylor recognizes that such a statement can seem surprising for, to a great extent, individualism has characterized the modern world for a long time. However, he sees a new axis that does not supplant the others. In addition to moral, spiritual, and instrumental individualisms, there is a widespread 'expressivist' individualism as well.[74] Here too Charles Taylor recognizes that this is not a new phenomenon, since the 'expressivism' that appeared at the end of the eighteenth century emerged from Romanticism. Intellectual and artistic elites have forever looked for the most authentic ways of expressing themselves. What is new here is the fact that this is now a mass phenomenon. What Taylor calls 'the culture of authenticity' consists of:

> the understanding of life which emerges with the Romantic expressivism of the late-eighteenth century, that each one of us has his/her own way of realizing our humanity, and that it is important to find and live one's own, as against surrendering to conformity with a model imposed from outside, by society, or the previous generation, or religions or political authority.[75]

This kind of situation is frequently assessed in a rather pessimistic way by religious authorities. If everyone sets out to find 'his or her own' truth, are we not on our way to relativism and problematic spiritualities, a terrain in which New Age thinking will prosper? We can be grateful to Taylor for his resistance to this kind of pessimism and for his nuanced appreciation of the potentials of our time, which he sees as far more open than a number of other authors do. Taylor indeed denounces a tendency to confuse 'the main phenomena of the Age of Authenticity with their most simple and flattened forms' which in the end produce 'a simplified and distorted view of what is happening in our civilization'.[76] He agrees here with Wade Clark Roof,[77] who argues that 'the spiritual ferment we observe today may be far deeper and of greater significance than many commentators, who point simply to its faddish qualities, would have us believe'.[78]

The subjective turn of culture conditions our contemporaries' approach to spiritual questions. The culture of authenticity now shapes what used to pertain to a world ruled by authority and objectivity. However, is it really so worrisome that, when faced with a religious tradition, our contemporaries ask, 'Does this have a meaning for me?' Or that they ask, 'To what extent can this faith help me to live and to grow?' Where the mistake lies is in the belief that this kind of quest is fated to be limited to an experience centered on the self in a totally immanent way. Taylor and Roof argue, on the contrary, that there will always be people who will want to go beyond egocentrism. For some authors, critiqued by Taylor, 'finding out about oneself, expressing oneself, discovering one's own way of becoming all that one can [...] be' is opposed to 'denying or sacrificing oneself for the sake of a super-self order of things, or even [...] living by reference to such an order'. Taylor criticizes these authors for underestimating the evolution and maturing that can happen: the personal quest, the desire to find one's own path without there being any authority imposing its dogmas. None of these characteristics of the culture of authenticity exclude the eventual discovery that there is more than the self, something more important than the self, a reality that merits the gift of self. Rather than accepting the false dichotomy – personal quest versus religion based on authority – it is important to see that the legitimately personal quest can lead to the discovery of community and its demands.[79] Nothing guarantees such a conclusion, but then nothing certifies its opposite either.[80]

The fruitfulness of Congar

Paying attention to the question of the subject and how it resonates in the thought of a philosopher such as Charles Taylor can help us better understand the importance and fruitfulness of Congar's thought. With the increasing importance of the subject, Congar could see the danger of falling into subjectivism. But such a danger, though real, was not all he could see. He knew that the questions posed by our age are 'the world's way of knocking to get the Gospel to open at the page that concerns it; they are so many wounds piercing the side of the Church, so that through the Church the water and salutary blood might flow.'[81] As a theologian of Church reform, Congar knew that the Church is taught by its time and that 'changes which affect the people of today have their impact on the Church and on theology'.[82]

In her book on Congar,[83] Elizabeth Teresa Groppe has also shown to what great extent his theology is able to enter into dialogue with the various currents of contemporary thought. Other theologians have been involved in this dialogue in a much more systematic way. We have already discussed Rahner's attempt to set out a theological anthropology. Congar's contribution, as Groppe emphasizes, is that he reminds us that Christian anthropology cannot be separated from an ecclesiological framework and context.[84]

In dialoguing and allowing himself to be challenged by his contemporaries' sensibility, Congar developed a more elaborate pneumatological ecclesiology, an ecclesiology of communion and community. The questions posed by his contemporaries and their aspiration to be subjects of their actions contributed to a better understanding of Christian Tradition. As Joseph Famerée and Gilles Routhier put it in their book on Yves Congar, there are

> realities or truths that truly belong to the Christian Tradition but remain latent, veiled, or potential, not actualized, and that become effective only in particular historical circumstances. It is then that the Church takes full possession, in its life, of what it carried before that had not yet been fully discovered.[85]

I must dwell a moment longer on the question of the subject to point out what appears in some of Congar's later works. I am thinking of 'Le monothéisme politique et le Dieu Trinité',[86] 'La Tri-unité de Dieu et de l'Église',[87] 'Pneumatologie Dogmatique',[88] *Diversity and Communion*[89] and, of course, the three volumes of *I Believe in the Holy Spirit*.[90] Congar became more aware of the consequences in the Church's life of what he called 'a pretrinitarian monotheism'. Among these consequences, Congar underlined 'legalism, uniformity, a purely pyramidal logic that is therefore clerical and paternalistic'. The contrast with the other vision, the one proposed by Congar, is sharp:

> A Church with a Trinitarian and pneumatological reference point accords to persons and to particular communities the quality of being *subjects*: they are subjects of their activity, with a role in determining the rules of their lives; they are subjects of their own history, as they put into practice their own gifts

and charisms. This means a great deal in the lived ecclesial experience.[91]

In certain periods of history, a political context or cultural setting may have favoured in the Church 'a patriarchalism, even a paternalism, with a monotheistic backdrop that was a-trinitarian, or insufficiently Trinitarian'.[92] Congar explained what he meant by 'paternalism', and his explanation reveals an obvious connection with our theme: 'There is paternalism when one treats subordinates as if they were children whom one must care for, for their own good, without their having to decide for themselves or take in hand their own destiny.'[93]

The awareness of a need for reform, born of this confrontation with a new sensibility, the one where the subject comes forward with unexpected new requests, must lead the Church to examine more fully the treasure of faith and Tradition, and to discover untapped potential. Thus the questions that arise do not lead the Church to dilute the mystery to suit the style of the day, but rather serve as a starting point for the Church to probe the mystery more fully, and with eventual reforms, to express it more authentically with renewed faithfulness.

The mystery that is probed by the theologian can reveal that human expectation still needs to be broadened and enriched. Thus, though Congar considered that it is legitimate to welcome 'the point of view of the subject', and though he did not fear 'the personal principle', he would stress that 'it is not true that persons are reducible to individuality. There is not in us only an individual without human reference or roots and therefore without dependency.'[94] The person is fulfilled in the meeting, in the exchange. Thus, he wrote:

> The knowledge of the Trinity of God, of the mystery of the Persons and of their procession, allows us to honour at a new depth a truth which contemporary philosophy is happy to explore: the person is fulfilled not by isolating himself/herself but through a relationship of knowledge and love with another.[95]

Although he took heed of the subjective turn of culture, Congar never promoted a disincarnate individualism, or a superficial vision of autonomy that confuses autonomy with an autarchy that does not owe anything to anyone.

A Church of persons

When he spoke of the Church or wrote about it, Congar was always careful to show that it is a communion of persons: 'The Church is not only the enclosure or "sheepfold" (aulē), but also the "flock" of individual sheep (poimnē), each of which the shepherd calls by its own name (John 10:1–3, 16).'[96] Thus, 'lay people are not only *objects* in the Church, objects though they are of its goodness and care; they are also religious *subjects*, and therefore active persons. They are not only *made* by the Church, in as much as it is a hierarchical institution; they *make* the Church ...'[97] And again, in 'Pneumatology Today', this passage is worth quoting again: 'The Church is not ready-made. It is always in process of being built, or rather, of being built by God. It is not prefabricated and placed in a frame which has already been prepared. It is a living organism to whose functioning people contribute their help and their creativity.'[98] In the same sense, Congar also wrote: 'The Body of Christ is not a hive, but a city of free human beings, willingly harmonizing with one another in love.'[99]

Joseph Famerée and Gilles Routhier have convincingly described Congar's contribution to ecclesiology: 'The originality of Congar's methodology in ecclesiology is that, in his writings about the Church, "human beings are taken as a starting point and his is a Church *for* human beings". The Church is not thought of as a reality that can exist apart from human beings, for itself, as an apparatus.'[100]

How to honour this desire of our contemporaries to be the subjects of their actions? What reforms would need to be undertaken in the life of the Church to reach that end? Congar did not make a list, and creating such an inventory was not the aim of *True and False Reform in the Church*. But he did hint at what he had in mind in this great book and in his subsequent writings. These indications come from his work as a theologian, but the theologian that he was did more than seek knowledge in learned libraries. A book published in 1960 by Georges Michonneau, a parish priest in a working-class setting, entitled *Pas de vie chrétienne sans commu-nauté*,[101] includes a remarkable preface by Congar. He mentioned some of the ecclesiological ideas and pastoral accomplishments of his time. In commenting on their meaning, he discerned 'a reinvention of the Church as an assembly or community made of human beings'.[102] He recalled what the word 'Church' means for many: 'the authority, the system defined by this authority of which it is the guardian'. He added that 'the word [Church] evokes less the idea of an assembly made up of human beings than that of a prestigious framework, ready-made, that issues the dictates to which they will have to submit'. When this conception of Church prevails, 'one is attached most of all to the frameworks, one is likely to see human beings as uninteresting or, in sum, interchangeable; hardly any attention is paid to the original contributions that each person might make; one might even be suspicious of such contributions'.[103]

'Interchangeable persons', suspicion of the 'original contri-butions': these are strong expressions with which to describe a Church where the subject has not yet found a place. But already Congar could glimpse the emergence of a Church where things would be different, and he imagined the implementation of reforms that would steer it in a more promising direction:

Such a Church demands that, in pastoral care, one find beyond the collective frameworks, moments or proceedings that would allow human beings to truly express themselves, when they can bring the problems or the values of their humanity – a humanity that is not reducible to the generalizations that are found in our literature textbooks, in the chapter on the great French classics [...]. It is necessary for the specific experiences of real human beings to be welcomed and heard.[104]

For Congar, time had come to modify a certain way of operating and certain practices of the Church. In 1963, he wrote:

We proceed too much as if we believed that what is important is simply to go through the motions. We liken the Church to a business that has to be successful, while in fact, what is important, is that we be instrumental in bringing about *spiritual actions*, that we help others meet God, that we bring others to the Gospel to be converted [...] Often we put into practice a pastoral plan of *things*, a pre-determined framework which human beings do their best to fit into, as if their role were to keep a system going and if possible, make it flourish.[105]

In describing the Church, Congar asserted: 'It is not a kind of great machine where an undifferentiated mass of believers would receive from the clerics some form of religion.'[106] The Church of Yves Congar was ready to live in a culture in which the place of the subject is great, because he knew that 'the Church does not build itself only from on high but also from below'.[107] Elizabeth Teresa Groppe captures this well when she writes:

Congar believed that the Church is built up by the graced initiatives of all who are members of the Church universal, for the Church does not exist as an unchanging institutional form that absorbs new members who are homogenized to a common mold. Rather, the Church is a living communion that grows dynamically as each person and each local community contribute its gifts to the service of others.[108]

In 1973, the magnitude of the cultural changes that followed the Council was for Congar a call for more radical reforms than those he had intuited in 1950 when he published *True and False Reform in the Church*. He wrote: 'Our epoch of rapid change and cultural transformation (philosophical ferments and sociological conditions different from those which the Church has accustomed itself to until now) calls for a revision of "traditional" forms which goes beyond the level of adaptation or *aggiornamento*, and which would be instead a new creation. It is no longer sufficient to maintain, by adapting it, what has already been; it is necessary to reconstruct it.'[109]

Undoubtedly this statement is not easy for all to hear. It is good to recall that its author was profoundly attached to continuity.[110] But fidelity to continuity is precisely what demands reform, for Congar knew that 'the only way to say the same thing in a changed context is to say it differently'.[111]

Congar saw the need for reform in many domains, practically all those areas that Vatican II undertook to address: ecclesiology, ecumenism, liturgy, religious liberty, the way of conceiving and practicing the various ministries, the theology of the laity, the presence of the Church in the world. His belief that the liturgy was in need of profound change can be underlined, and it is not difficult to see the connection between the changes he hoped to see occur in liturgy and the importance Congar gave to the person and the subject.

A compelling call for meaningful gestures

At the time when he was publishing his great book on reform in the Church, a dozen years before the Council, Congar did not hide the fact that he was unhappy with a liturgy that was followed in a passive way and that to many people seemed like ritualism:

> In our beautiful and holy Catholic liturgy, as it is too often celebrated, there are many things that have lost their original meaning and have become a mere ritual vestige of an action that, at its origin, did express a genuine initiative of some person or some community.[112]

'The compelling call for truly meaningful gestures' was, for Congar, one of the fruits of what he called 'the great thing of the modern world: the discovery of the subject'.[113] He wanted to take seriously the fact that

> our age certainly goes further than others in demanding truth in actions and attitudes. Clearly, previous generations did not have difficulty in adopting the habits and customs that tradition had laid down before their time and without their assent, although our contemporaries do feel that reluctance.[114]

Congar, who was sensitive to liturgical prayer his entire life and was very aware of what was at stake, wrote in his introduction to *True and False Reform in the Church*:

> Today there is a compelling call for true gestures carried out in such a way as to really be the gestures of living persons and to

really express what they are meant to express. (We need to direct
and guide this tendency, but who, in the name of the Lord,
would dare to suppress it?)[115]

Once again we admire Congar's lucidity, and we can understand
that he joyfully embraced the liturgical reform of Vatican II.[116] 'The
whole meaning of the liturgical renovation of the twentieth century,'
he wrote in 1967, 'is to keep liturgical celebrations from being
self-contained "ceremonies" but rather the worship of *someone*.
The whole current movement aims to (re-)integrate the subject
into the dogmatic, sacramental, and disciplinary objectivism.'[117]
According to Congar, the movements of renewal which, at least
partially, succeeded at the Council and thanks to the Council, came
in response to two great aspirations that he had noticed among his
contemporaries. He himself had formulated them in *True and False
Reform in the Church*: to restore the authenticity of gestures, and
to find the appropriate forms enabling the Gospel to be proclaimed
effectively in our time. According to Congar, 'these two demands
corresponded to the two great temptations to which the Church is
liable: first, the temptation of Pharisaism, which triumphs when
formalism prevents structures from really serving their end and
fulfilling their meaning'. Then, there is also another temptation,
which is 'refusing to hear the appeals of the times and carry out
the adaptations or renewals required by the times'. Solid references
had been furnished by Congar to justify his way of thinking, most
notably St. Augustine, who did not cease to affirm 'the going
beyond all forms, and the primacy of the meaning of things in the
service of the spiritual man'.[118]

We should note that, in the wake of the reforms promulgated
by the Second Vatican Council, Congar did not deny the existence
of certain deviations, but he considered it unfair that the attention
was focused so often on the negative when the positive side, in his
view, should have prevailed.[119] 'The crisis' after Vatican II had been
real, but in 1979 Congar expressed this belief:

Many of the realities that preoccupy us today were already
present in the 1950s, and even in the 1930s. The Council did
not give rise to them. On the other hand, the current crisis is
clearly due to a considerable extent to causes that have revealed
their strength since the Council. Indeed it warned against them,

warding them off instead of bringing them about. Vatican II has been followed by socio-cultural change more extensive, radical and rapid and more cosmic in its proportion than any other period in history.[120]

Coming from the pen of a significant historian, these words should not be taken lightly.

* * *

We opened this chapter with the words of Henri de Lubac who, like Congar, devoted a great deal of thought to the reforms needed in the Church.[121] Like Congar, he suffered and he spared no effort in working towards their implementation. I would like to conclude this reflection with a page from the great Jesuit on the dangers of immobilism. De Lubac's terminology may be somewhat dated, but the call he enjoins us to hear could not be more timely. His remarks highlight Yves Congar's clearsightedness. Henri de Lubac recalled the situation described in the Acts of the Apostles, about certain people he calls 'carnal men [...] who, turning the Church into their own private property, practically stopped the Apostles from announcing the Gospel to the Gentiles'.[122] De Lubac then exhorted: 'Let us take care not to be like them, for if we do that, we lay ourselves open to something yet more calamitous – collaboration with militant irreligion, by way of making it easier for it to carry out its self-assigned task of relegating the Church and its doctrine to the class of the defunct.' In this vibrant page, de Lubac was aiming at Renan (1823–92), and all those who understand nothing about 'the actuality of the eternal'. Their message is: 'Let the Church remain what it is.' Henri de Lubac knew what sort of 'petrification such a wish implies,' and the seeming respect that is displayed is 'that always accorded to historic relics'. When reading these pages, it is difficult not to think of twenty-first-century Renans. We easily recognize what was termed 'irreligion' in his day and that today would be called militant atheism. Characteriscally, it 'mixes up at will cases of the most widely differing kinds, confusing with dogma opinions or attitudes inherited from situations which have ceased to be'. The efforts made by Christians to actualize their faith are considered with contempt, as 'concessions' dominated by deceitfulness. This militant atheism has 'made up its mind once and for all that there can be nothing reasonable in Christian beliefs.' And this is the logic de Lubac saw at work in these ways of thinking: 'The Church can never cut loose from its past [...]. Religion is a whole [that] must not be touched [...]. As soon as you reason about it, you are an atheist.' 'The principle is "all or nothing".' And de Lubac added: 'provided that the "all" is understood in the terms dictated – which are not those of the Church.' He cited Renan as an example, 'making the Catholic faith involved forever with the historicity of the Book of Daniel and other things of the same kind', as if everything had the same value, as if one could put on the same level the resurrection of Christ and the veneration of St. Christopher. In conclusion, in a poignant manner, evoking the sympathy within the Church itself for the ideology that holds the Church to be something that is dead, de Lubac wrote: 'And it is a day of rejoicing [for that ideology] when voices are raised within the very heart of "this poor and aged Church" which sound like approval. A false intransigence can certainly cause an enormous amount of harm in this way – quite in opposition to its own intentions.'

With de Lubac and Congar, the question must be asked: Do those who systematically oppose all reform always realize with whom they have become allied?

4

A sense of wholeness

The concept of catholicity governs all of Congar's work. Due to his keen understanding of catholicity, which stands out even in his earliest writings,[1] Congar was immune to the spirit of the system. The Christianity he expounded was never ideological.[2] As a result, he was never a reductionist when he engaged with human beings, encountered new realities, and examined philosophies. The concern to live and think 'according to the whole' – this is the meaning of the word 'catholic'[3] – 'was the foundation for that never-completed search for the truth' which he eagerly desired to see 'recognized wherever it is found'.[4] Any reader prizing truth and respect for the real will be sympathetic to Congar's work.[5] It is Congar's fervent sense of catholicity that made him appreciate the words of Ivan Kireevski: 'For the whole of truth, we need the whole of being.'[6]

A deficit of catholicity

When he was still a young theologian,[7] Congar became aware of 'a deficit of catholicity' in the Church and assessed the harmful consequences of such a deficit, particularly in the way the faith was perceived by his contemporaries. When reading Congar, it becomes clear why the themes of *tradition, reform,* and *catholicity* are not only closely connected, but also contained one within the other.

What is a 'deficit of catholicity'? This happens when the Church no longer lives or thinks in relation to the whole or with a sense of wholeness. If the church leaves out part of reality, particularly

if it ignores emerging realities because they are new and do not
fit into 'what is already known', then the church is not faithful to
its vocation. This is a permanent risk, for the world continues to
change, it is new every day.[8] It can be tempting to keep to the status
quo, to reject what is new or to give in to fear of the unknown.[9]
Yves Congar was born in a time when the Catholic Church had
developed an extreme distrust of the modern world. As a young
man, Congar had sought to understand the origin and the consequences of this distrust. In 1935, Congar was asked to write the
conclusion to an inquiry on modern unbelief. He set out to expose
the reasons for this distrust with 'absolute sincerity'.[10] He described
how faith 'now appears as a particular thing, a thing apart and
cut off from life'. The Church then seems to be nothing more than
'a *particular* group, [...] a *fenced off part*, like a closed, peculiar,
anti-progressive party'.[11] 'Under the triple attack of secularism, the
Reformation and rationalism', the Church contracted, 'retreated to
its positions, barricaded itself, took on an attitude of self-defense',
and lived 'in a real state of siege'.[12] Opposite this Church, a humanistic spiritual world was emerging, marked by Christ's absence.
This absence is what saddened and worried the young Congar
above all. That humanistic world is 'abandoned to its own inner
light, that of reason; freed from all the historical and dogmatic
complex whole of Catholicism, and making of this autonomy, of
this liberty, the very substance of its spiritual heaven'.[13] To such a
world, the Christian universe appears to be an apparatus, 'with all
its regime of dogmatism, authority, submission, conservatism'.[14]
This is a tragic situation, for what is being shown of the Church,
and what people take to be its real face and essence, is nothing
more than a grimace and a distortion. They believe that the Church
is intrinsically anti-progressive and hopelessly mired in an outdated
way of thinking and behaving. 'Do we really appear as if we lived
in a fullness of life? Do we not all too often display a meager and
insipid kind of Catholicism, not in the least attractive, so that in
us the resplendent catholicity of the Church becomes small and
repellent?'[15]
    The consequences of this are serious:

Thus, an enormous slice of human activity, an entire expanse
of humanity, of human flesh and blood – modern life with its
science, its wretchedness, its greatness – has not had within it

the incarnation of the Word; the Church has not given her soul to this body which has developed and which should, like every human value, receive the communication of the Spirit of Christ in order to become in this way his Body and to give glory to God.[16]

For this theologian filled with a sense of catholicity, the remedy is evident:

To all growth of humanity, to all 'progress', to all extensions of the human in any one of the domains of creation – in knowledge just as much as in action – there must correspond a growth of the Church, an incorporation of faith, an incarnation of grace, a humanization of God [...]. This is the Church, this is catholicity.[17]

These lines are reminiscent of the writings of Jules Monchanin, who said: 'Until all that is human has been embraced and welcomed into the Church, the Church will remain an adolescent: the Church must grow.'[18]

Reform and catholicity

Although Congar's theology was turned toward the totality of the real and was open to history and its developments, he was nonetheless quite nuanced in his reactions to what is new, for he was aware that errors of various kinds can inhibit the life of the Church. It is not only that the Church is vulnerable to being out of step with the rest of the world in a way that is damaging for its catholicity. There is another danger: the possibility of being misled by what is only a temporary fashion – the superficial expression of a sub-culture – and taking it for true cultural change.

Congar realized how much was at stake here, for he knew this concerns the very being of the Church. Therefore, he recommended a certain caution,[19] even regarding authentic aspirations, and he emphasized the need for patience. He understood that authority can hesitate and even postpone action, and he saw that there are benefits to the delays that the Church allows itself. However, some

brutally honest passages of *Journal d'un théologien*[20] deplore that
prudence has become an absolute. The prophetic dimension of
the Church is lost when 'the category of "true" is replaced by
the category of "sure" and "prudent"'.[21] Congar also feared that
an insufficient openness to people's authentic aspirations might
discourage them, that they might 'be driven to despair of ever
getting a hearing for what they believe to be true'.[22]

There was concern for balance here, but his deep understanding
of fidelity was anything but static. Congar devoted an Appendix[23]
to this theme in *True and False Reform in the Church*, and he
himself indicated that a certain type of fidelity is at the heart of
his book:

> Fidelity to Christian reality can be a fidelity to the present state
> of things, to forms presently expressing this reality, that is, a
> fidelity to what is at present achieved. It can also be a fidelity
> to its future development or a fidelity to its principle. The two
> expressions come to the same thing [...]. A profound, not
> shallow, fidelity to this dimension of Christianity is at once a
> fidelity to principle, to the tradition, and to the future, that is,
> to what Christianity can and ought to become in order to arrive
> at the truth given at the beginning, in substance, in its principle.
> Catholic (= embracing the whole) fidelity will have to embrace
> the two aspects.[24]

Congar knew that 'there is a tension' between these two aspects
of faithfulness, but also that 'there can and there must exist a
communication, even a continuity, and thus a harmony between
them'.[25]

It is faithfulness to the future that incites reforms. For if there is
a duality between the essence and the form in which this essence
is expressed, the essence of a thing is stronger than this form, and
'thus the form has the tendency to move beyond itself to become
commensurate with the essence and to conquer thereby its full
truth'. For Congar, then, reform and truth went hand in hand.
Reforms are needed in order to grow in catholicity, for 'the church
is its future as much as it is its past'.[26]

ANACHRONISM

'The drama of the modern world comes in large part from the fact that while the process of restoring autonomy to the profane structures which began in the thirteenth century continued inexorably into the following centuries and until today, Christian spirituality did not follow the path suggested by St. Thomas but returned to an outdated Augustinianism in the sixteenth and seventeenth centuries. This inexcusable anachronism forged for modern society a type of Christian person who met the needs of medieval society, but did not correpond to the needs of current society, and thus was ineffective. As a result, it was outside of Christianity that modern society would forge the type of human being that it needed.'

M.-J. Le Guillou, *Le visage du Ressuscité* (Paris: Éditions Ouvrières, 1968), pp. 231–2

A radically new approach to ecumenism

After rereading *Divided Christendom*,[27] Yves Congar's first great book, Ghislain Lafont wrote in 1964:

It is hard not to be moved in reading again, after a quarter century, this truly prophetic book. This is less because of its ecclesiological orientations than because of the ecumenical principles which were developed in chapters VII and VIII; indeed, these principles are today the common heritage of the Catholic church, and it is in large part due to this book that they have penetrated so deeply into our ordinary religious consciousness.[28]

Fifty years later, the contemporary reader can still marvel at Congar's prophetic vision.

In the Table of Contents of *Divided Christendom* there are brief summaries of the content of each chapter. Congar explains one of the objectives of Chapter VII and how it relates to the search for unity: 'It is not a question of having one system triumph, but making it possible for the Christian life to reach the fullness for which it was made'.[29] Even though many perspectives articulated in this book are now dated and do not represent the beliefs that Congar was later to have as a mature ecumenical theologian (in a context that allowed it!), it is still with pleasure that we can read passages on catholicity such as this one:

> To this end, the Catholic Church must make full use of its powers of assimilating all the problems, needs, aspirations, and values which are currently exiled from it and which must once more find their place in unity. How can there ever be reunion if, instead of appearing to them as fullness, our Church looks to those Christians outside it like one particular denomination, one system among others, an 'ism' as limited and exclusive as any other 'ism'?[30]

It has been said, rightly, that Congar made catholicity 'the principal category of his ecclesiology'.[31] We must note that catholicity is first of all at the heart of his ecumenism, and that his ecumenical vocation is the best explanation for his vocation as an ecclesiologist. 'It is the ecumenist who became an ecclesiologist', wrote Hervé Legrand, a colleague of Congar.[32] To support this statement, Legrand recalled how Congar himself recounted the origin of his vocation, and most notably his ordination retreat in 1930 when he recognized 'a definite call to work so that all who believe in Jesus Christ would be one [...]'. It was Congar himself who wrote: 'I then *recognized* an ecumenical vocation which was, at the same time, an ecclesiological vocation.'[33] According to Hervé Legrand, this is an exceptionally useful key that allows us to understand Congar's vocation.[34] Indeed, Congar always refused to see ecumenism as a 'specialty'. It is in order to be more fully itself, to live its catholicity fully, that the church must be one. And it is in trying to bring to fulfilment its grace of catholicity that the church accomplishes its true ecumenical work.[35]

In relating the ecumenical question to the theme of catholicity, Congar profoundly renewed ecumenism. Largely because of his insights, the Catholic Church went from an ecumenism of return, which was practically the only sort of ecumenism advocated at the time, to an ecumenism based on the consciousness of needing the gifts of others in order to express its full catholicity. One admires here the clarity of his thought:

> [...] the Church is deprived of a Slavic expression, a Norse expression, of the one and many-splendoured grace of Christ. In these temperaments and others besides there is an innate manner of human living which ought to be, in the unity of the Church, an innate manner of living in Christ, and of glorifying God in Him; there is an expression of values which have as such no equivalent in Latin or Anglo-Saxon races, because in these values humanity has felt and lived a real growth of human experience. To the extent to which such growth is not integrated into the Church it is clear that something is wanting to its actual and effective Catholicity.[36]

ECUMENISM IS NOT A SPECIALTY

'I felt very strongly that the great transformation required by the ecumenical movement was consistent with the entire ecclesiological, pastoral, biblical, and liturgical movement. Early on, I perceived that ecumenism is not a specialty, that it presupposes a movement of conversion and reform which is coextensive with the life of all the Communions.'

Yves Congar, *Une passion: l'unité* (Paris: Foi Vivante, 1974), p. 41

By linking ecumenism to catholicity, Congar contributed in a powerful way to the development of a new understanding of Martin Luther[37] and Protestantism. He considered Luther to be 'one of the great religious geniuses in all of history'.[38] Post-Tridentine Catholicism*[39] tended to push the controversialists systematically to oppose the Reformation, and thus impoverished Catholicism by introducing an imbalance in its expressions and its doctrine. The controversialists of the time wanted 'to reaffirm, against the challenges of the Reformation, the continuity of the Church, its faithfulness to all that it had been before. But such a reaffirming was directed *against* others, and by that very fact colored the development of doctrine.'[40] Citing de Lubac, Congar wrote: 'It is a great misfortune to have been taught a catechism [that was written] against someone.'[41] *Divided Christendom* contains excellent passages on this phenomenon that are still relevant:

> ... in general our theology has [...] too often grown one-sided, and developed systematically those aspects that are least congenial to even the legitimate aspirations of non-Catholics, dissidents or unbelievers.[42]

Congar, who had thought a great deal about what characterizes the various heresies, knew that they are often unilateral distortions of the truth, and particular and partial points of view that have been built up into systems. The portion of truth they contain is distorted because it is set up as an absolute and excludes other truths. How does the Catholic church react to heresy? In some of its reactions Congar discerned an imbalance stemming from the obligation felt by the leaders to accentuate what had been denied in the heterodox position. Hence there is a danger of finding in what is being affirmed 'a truth that is hardened and incomplete because its formulation, partial and unilateral, was determined by a particular set of circumstances'. Congar concluded:

> For orthodox theology heresy is, therefore, at once an opportunity for progress and a danger of one-sided progress. Whenever an erroneous emphasis or statement is made, the organism of the Church stiffens, and forces are polarized to resist the evil. In regards to the false affirmation, which is, as we shall soon see, a truth that is disconnected from its centre, the true affirmation is refined and stated. In most cases, the dogma in its fullness is not summoned, and one is content to give greater relief and precision to the truth that is mistakenly stated or denied by the error. As a result, since error is always partial, the dogmatic truth that it opposes runs the risk also of being partial.[43]

These reflections inspire Congar to write: 'Thus the Reformation brought in its wake the Counter-Reformation. But in so far as something is done merely or predominantly *counter*, or *anti*, even though it be directed against error, it is not fully *catholic*.'[44]

To the reader of Congar, the history of the division among Christians appears in a different light. We see more clearly the extent to which certain differences were artificially exaggerated:

> Insofar as we are content merely to affirm what the other denies or distorts, instead of integrating partial truths into the wholeness of truth and transcending the plane of mutual opposition and contradiction, to that extent we ourselves help to impoverish the full realization of the Church's innate Catholicity and its full expression within the Life of the Church.[45]

Consenting to fullness

Entire portions of ecclesial Tradition were indeed marginalized, considered suspect, or simply forgotten.[46] Other aspects were hardened or inflated.[47] Congar denounced what denomination-alism for centuries had considered compulsory: taking the exact opposite position to that of another denomination. His approach was entirely different:

> I have bet my whole life on the conviction that a truth cannot be the opposite of another truth. We must therefore recognize every truth, wherever it comes from, and try to give it its place in an enveloping organism, many elements of which will probably elude us.[48]

'What does our ecumenism seek?', he asked. His answer is crystal clear: 'the *fullness* of the gifts of Christ.'[49] What matters is to be 'children of fullness'.[50] Or again, as he wrote in a section he intended to add to a revised edition of *Divided Christendom*, the basis of an authentic catholicity is 'a kind of consent to fullness'.[51]

Likewise, *True and False Reform* quotes a German author, W. Foerster: 'For a great number of zealous Catholics today, it is enough that something be Protestant in order for it no longer to be considered Catholic. For them Catholicism is expressed in the formula: *Christianity with Protestantism subtracted* [...].'[52] In the same spirit, Congar wrote in 1976 about the liturgical reforms of Vatican II: 'That the Church has delighted Protestants by giving a greater prominence to the Word of God in its celebrations can scandalize only those who think that Catholicism and anti-Protestantism are the same thing, in the same way that there once existed in Protestant circles those – though there are happily few of them left now – who identify anti-Catholicism with true Christianity.'[53]

Congar quoted another passage from Foerster to demonstrate how the attitude I have described above has impoverished the faith:

> All these repercussions of the Reformation ended up creating in modern Catholicism a kind of exaggerated mistrust of the personal element in religion. Instead of assimilating and socializing new liberating tendencies, the Church confronted them and ended up rejecting spiritual elements that were formerly part of its concern.[54]

We can see here how far Congar stood from a denominational identity based on the opposition to another denomination. On the contrary, Congar valued the truth inherent in other denominations, in order to integrate it into the life of the entire Church. Such an approach was practised at Vatican II. Congar, one of the Council's main artisans, wrote about it: 'One of the most decisive aspects of Vatican II was that, in moving beyond a certain part of the Middle Ages, the Counter-Reformation, and the anti-modern restoration of the nineteenth century, it reconnected with the inspirations of the undivided Church.'[55] When the Council voted to reject the schema containing the two-source theory of Revelation, Congar shared the opinion of Father Rouquette that this 'marked the end of the Counter-Reformation'.[56]

Already in his first book, *Divided Christendom*, Congar proposed a way out of those sterile and systematic oppositions that had not only sustained divisions, but had also, as we have seen, impoverished the Christian heritage. The attitude he sought to describe consisted 'in returning to the sources and a profound life':

> The source and the living principle of such an attitude as we have here outlined is an interior life which has grown beyond all partisan outlook and the clash of forms and systems, and found the deep springs which nourish the life of the spirit. The person

who lives on the surface, heeding the letter rather than the spirit, can find no mean between an indifferentism which will come to terms with anything and a rigidity which sets up one formula again another. A superficial life has no capacity to comprehend and unify, but the deeper the life the more it develops such powers of assimilation and response. Only the most profound life of all, that of our Lord Himself, has the universal capacity to comprehend and satisfy.[57]

Let us add a last quotation from *Divided Christendom*. It underscores the negative effects of a rigid attitude [Fr.: '*l'esprit de système*'], and, conversely, the benefits of a true sense of catholicity:

Moreover, since action brings about reaction, in the end everyone gets the hearing he or she deserves. Whoever approaches souls in a rigid attitude of mind [Fr.: '*dans un esprit de système*'] finds people with their backs up and a corresponding rigidity [Fr.: '*système*'] ready for defence against attack. But if we were to try to get back together to questions above all institutional paraphernalia, to the common sources of life in all that truly lives, should we not find, far more often than we could have believed, that we had been meeting with a brother?[58]

We need our brothers and sisters to ensure that the treasure given by Christ to the Church might shine in all its splendor: for Congar, to become aware of this was what it meant to be awakened to the ecumenical vocation. In writing a 'magisterial'[59] introduction to the anti-Donatist treatises* of St. Augustine – where precisely the catholicity of the church is at stake, against a sectarian attitude – Congar quoted in the last pages of *Divided Christendom* this magnificent text by the bishop of Hippo:

When on one occasion He [Jesus] was preaching to the people and a man demanded of Him, 'Lord, speak to my brother, that he divide the inheritance with me', the Lord would not assent to division, for He had come to create unity – the unity of which He spoke when He said, 'Other sheep I have which are not of this fold. Them also I must bring, and there shall be one fold and one shepherd.' He therefore who loved unity and hated division would not confirm this division, but said, 'Who has set me to divide your inheritance?' And I say, not what this man said, but 'Lord, speak to my brother that he may safeguard the inheritance with me'.[60]

The mystery of catholicity

Congar had a profound view of catholicity that he never ceased to enrich as he read and reflected.[61] In another remarkable preface, this one for the book written by the great exegete André Feuillet, *Le Christ, Sagesse de Dieu*, Congar wrote with much humility: 'Our theology of catholicity (mine, in any case) is certainly too timid, not cosmic enough.'[62] Congar saw that 'we have overly separated (not overly distinguished) the church from the world. Both seek the same thing, but with different resources and on different planes: both want to bring creation to its fulfillment, to make humans successfully achieve their end.'[63]

Actually, in his earliest writings Yves Congar was already elaborating a profound vision of catholicity, breathing new life into it for many of his contemporaries. With Congar, catholicity was no longer considered in a polemic or apologetic manner. It recovered the richness of its theological flavour, of which a purely denominational understanding had deprived it.[64]

'The Catholicity of the Church has long been interpreted in an exclusively geographical or, at any rate, quantitative sense, as the temporal and especially the local extension of the Church among all men and throughout the whole world.'[65] This quantitative rather than qualitative understanding is not mistaken; we find it in the writings of the Church Fathers. 'But in the Fathers, except perhaps St. Augustine, and in the early theologians, this quantitative aspect is never affirmed in isolation.' Congar goes on to recall other aspects of the Church's universality: the universality of truth; the universality of redemption and healing for humanity; the universality of gifts, virtues, and spiritual endowment; and finally, universality in time.[66]

Congar led his readers from the quantitative to the qualitative without opposing the one to the other: 'In thinking this over [...] one is very quickly led to see that there cannot be quantitative Catholicity without the qualitative, with the latter being the necessary cause of the former.' He could then propose the following definition of the Church's catholicity: 'The Catholicity of the Church, regarded as a property of its being, is the dynamic universality of its unity, the capacity of its principles of unity to assimilate, fulfil and raise to God in oneness with Him all human beings and every human being and every human value.'[67] We should take note that this catholicity does not belong to any human organization or system. This is a catholicity entirely received from Christ,[68] 'in whom dwells the fullness of the divine energy capable of reconciling, purifying, unifying and transfiguring the world'.[69]

The two sources of catholicity

For Congar, 'the catholicity of the church has two sources that must enter into relationship with one another: there is the fullness of Christ's grace, but there is also the virtual undefinedness of humanity's creations and developments'.[70] We note that in his early writings Congar emphasized unity with Christ as the source of the Church's catholicity, and he viewed catholicity essentially as a principle of unity. In an article published in 1948 in the journal *Dieu vivant*, the eastern Orthodox theologian Vladimir Lossky had critiqued this limited way of approaching the question, even though he did not deny the 'Christological condition which is at the basis of catholicity'.[71] Lossky thought that 'the Christological condition alone – the unity of human nature recapitulated in Christ – was insufficient'. He took issue with Congar for not having sufficiently taken into account this other condition for catholicity: Pentecost.[72] Lossky wrote: 'We should not underestimate the pneumatological condition of the Church, but rather give it full recognition, on a par with the Christological condition, if we want to find the true foundation of the Church's catholicity.'[73] Congar accepted this critique[74] and modified his theology accordingly. We know that his work made more and more room for the Holy Spirit, and he himself admitted[75] that he had become much more sensitive to diversity and pluralism. A Polish author who has studied the theme of catholicity in Congar's thought puts it this way: 'In his first writings his reflection on catholicity was based on the concept of unity, while in his late writings diversity or plurality dominated his thinking. The model of unity's deployment within plurality was replaced by that of the tension of the diversities toward unity.'[76] Actually, it is not necessary to wait for this later period to find Congar's attentiveness to the role of the Spirit and to the Spirit's specific way of establishing unity. In 1950, Congar was already writing: 'What is specific to the Holy Spirit, indeed, is that when the Spirit enters the intimacy of consciousness, the Spirit establishes a communion among diverse things, bringing them to unity without doing any violence to them.'[77] And in 1960, incorporating Lossky's remarks, Congar proposed an enriched conception of catholicity and unity by being more attentive to the role of the Holy Spirit who 'on the one hand internalizes and personalizes that which is common, and on the other hand makes common that which is personal'.[78] This conception had nothing to do with 'a military or mechanical style of obedience in which the contributions of the personal subject are not considered relevant'.[79] Congar wrote: 'If a multitude without unity is anarchy, a unity which does not depend on the multitude is tyranny.'[80] The role he gave to the Spirit in his understanding of catholicity stands out again in this passage written in 1970: 'It is through the Holy Spirit that the source of catholicity from below meets and is united with its source from above.'[81] However, it is true that it was in his later writings that Congar made most explicit the consequences of an insufficiently Trinitarian theology, or as he called it, an 'a-Trinitarian' one, especially on this topic of catholicity. In 1981, when he published his article entitled 'Le monothéisme politique et le Dieu Trinité',[82] he was ready to draw the conclusions from his long reflection on these questions. He knew that a 'pneumatology is not simply a theology of the third Person', but that 'its impact on the conception of the Church and on ecclesial practice'[83] is a real one. The absence of a true pneumatology can be seen in an inclination towards uniformity and exclusion. A monotheism that is at the source of a catholicity that honours particularity calls for a Trinitarian pneumatology and theology.[84] Since in the Church there is no vague and abstract unity, just as in God there is no nature outside of the three Persons,[85] this kind of Trinitarian theology leads to an appreciation of difference and pluralism. But this is to say too little. Catholic unity, as Congar conceived of it, does not abolish 'diversities, but to the contrary is *constituted* on the basis of these diversities'.[86] This conviction appeared forcefully in one of his last works, *Diversity and Communion*, where catholicity is a principle not only of unity, but also of the legitimate and fruitful diversity of traditions in the Church.[87] He wrote: 'The firmest tradition is that, given the unity of faith, a diversity of customs and opinions is quite legitimate.'[88]

We begin to perceive how deep an authentic reflection on catholicity can go. If it is cosmic, encompassing every thing and every time, it is also eminently personal:

> The answer which apostolic faith offers to human beings is the one that brings a satisfactory response to the *ultimate* questions they have, those which concern them and their all ('This concerns us and our all': Pascal), connect with their greatest depth, in their *total* depth, and consequently, make a unity out of all that is in them.[89]

The Spirit's unpredictability

If there is one text by Congar by which the reader is easily persuaded that he is facing a non-ideological thought,[90] the opposite of a system in which everything is predictable, a theology that is open to the boldness of the Spirit, to the unknown, to the newness of history, it is certainly Congar's text on the Acts of the Apostles, and particularly the passages where he comments on how the first Christians discovered their calling to catholicity.

We know that one of Luke's intentions in writing Chapters 10 to 15 of Acts was to show that the Church had become aware progressively of its universal vocation. This awareness had arisen not because it corresponded to a human project or established strategy. If the church moved in this direction, it is because it had been led by the Spirit, despite much human reticence. Here, actions precede conscious reflection. In Acts 10, Peter visits Cornelius, baptizes him, and witnesses how the gift of the Spirit is given to him. The intention of St. Luke, which is very clear, is to help us understand that what happened exceeded what the apostle had expected (Acts 11:17). Peter's actions do not correspond to the existing religious schemes. The reader is brought to realize that it is not humans who control what is unfolding, even if Luke does want his readers to understand as well – and this is in large part the objective of Acts 15 – that God wants collaborators who freely enter into his designs.

As Congar meditated on these texts, he had this to say about them: '[...] it was in the course of actually becoming universal that the Church became aware of its universality.' He then posed this legitimate question: 'Can we say that we are really aware of the catholicity of the Church so long as we fail to grasp it in its concreteness, as it actually absorbs values or realities that were, at first, or seemed to be, alien to it?' We should note the answer that Congar placed in his conclusion: 'We shall really know what it means for the Gospel to be preached to every creature only when that has been accomplished.'[91]

5

Authority the Christian way

Yves Congar was far too conscious of the complexity of the issues to attribute contemporary unbelief to a single cause. He knew that several factors have led to the rejection of God. More than once, he quoted the words God spoke to the prophet Samuel: 'It is not you they reject, it is me.'[1] As his thought on modern unbelief developed over the years, he never laid responsibility for it on the Church alone, or on its past. He became increasingly aware that a certain way of speaking about God, faith, and revelation had become incomprehensible. In 1935, however, what was foremost in his mind was the ecclesiological obstacle. And so, when looking back on his own evolution, he wrote: 'Insofar, however, as we have a responsibility for unbelief, it seemed to me that this unbelief was generated by the face the Church was showing to humanity, a face that belied more than it expressed the Church's true nature, in conformity with the Gospel and its own deepest tradition.'[2]

The young Congar had already seen and described this problematic face of the Church. On 17 September 1930, while he was in Düsseldorf, he wrote about it in the form of a prayer or 'elevation': 'My God, why has your Church, which is holy and one […], why has it so often such an austere and forbidding face when in reality it is full of youth and life?'[3]

In the same text, he asked: 'My God, why does your Church always condemn? True, it must above all guard the "deposit of faith"; but is there no other means than condemnation, especially condemning so quickly?' Such words do not come from the pen of an impassive intellectual who is content to explore abstract ideas and toy with concepts. Congar wrote as an apostle, eager for the Church to be understood for what it truly is and a Church understanding of all human beings:

> My God, my God! you who wished your Church, even in its cradle, to speak all tongues; not in the sense that it would vary the expression of the truth, still less the truth itself, but in the sense that the truth which the Church alone professes should be intelligible to every human ear. My God, enlarge our hearts! Grant that human beings may understand us and we may understand human beings, all human beings![4]

Congar's decision in 1935 to launch a series aimed at the renewal of ecclesiology was born of this desire to enable the true face of the Church to shine out. Several volumes of this series, *Unam Sanctam*, deal in one form or another with the question of authority at the centre of this final chapter.

All who are keen to announce the Gospel to their contemporaries, for whom freedom is so all-important, realize that they must address this thorny question. It is a major stumbling block and, at the same time, the point where numerous and varied problems are crystallized.[5] We can recall here the remark made by Congar (without restricting it to reactions directed towards the Catholic Church) when commenting on the Legend of the Grand Inquisitor in *The Brothers Karamazov:* 'The more I study opposition to Catholicism, whether it stems from Eastern Christians or from Northern European Protestants, the more I see that what they have in common is expressed in this text of Dostoyevsky; they accuse it of stifling human freedom and the creative value of the religious subject.'[6]

Modernity and the rejection of authority

In many ways, modernity is the product of reactions against authority[7] that extend to all areas of culture. Over time, the phenomenon has grown, sparing nothing: family, education, society, politics, science, religious beliefs. Some authors have spoken of an 'end of authority' to characterize our times. Congar showed how clear-sighted he was on this question. He knew that 'our contemporary is mistrustful of everything that is given from outside and from above: norms, laws, authorities, institutions'.[8] Ahead of many others, he gauged the great crisis of ideas and of culture that began with the Renaissance[9] and that came to a head with the Reformation:

> The Reformation was roughly contemporary with the rise of the great forces that created the modern world (the sciences of observation, the primacy of individual personality, the passion for invention and continual progress, historical and philosophical criticism, perhaps even the beginnings of rationalism).

And so authority is challenged 'not only in its historical forms, but as a principle'.[10] In a world 'turned towards the future, a Church whose role is to communicate a Revelation, sacraments, apostolic ministry that have been given once and for all in the past, seems obsolete'.[11] Furthermore, for modern people, 'truth lies in what is to come, it is more practical than speculative, inseparable from experience and from what can be verified'.[12]

The crisis progressed from 1680[13] onwards and escalated with the Enlightenment. Congar summarized the decisive developments in this way: 'An entire society went from rules and explanations coming from above, by what is superior to the human being, and instead it looked for explanations from within human beings, their nature, and their reason, leading to a knowledge of things themselves based on experience.'[14]

The besieged fortress

The Catholic hierarchy reacted energetically to these developments, issuing a host of condemnations. Congar's youth unfolded in such an atmosphere. Granted, the hierarchy's intention was not to reject the 'modern' on principle. It declared that its 'condemnation was limited to the errors, deviations and dangers of modern civilization'.[15] However, in what was called a 'struggle for God', an all-too-human element was mixed in, that of a Church 'holding on to the thought forms and structures of a stable, rural world, quite foreign to the new current of ideas'.[16] When expressing the uneasiness this reaction inspired in him, Congar was specific: 'This struggle for God, for which Christendom remained the model, not only became an expression of opposition to rationalism but also, under the guise of the fight against liberalism, ran counter to the achievements that are constitutive of modern society, such as freedom of the press, tolerance of other forms of worship, realities that do not threaten morality or public order.'[17] Such a posture reinforced in many minds the notion of a Church that is intrinsically conservative and reactionary. This was *yesterday's* Church trying to exist in *today's* world, a Church that was subordinate to an obsolete form of civilization, unable to welcome a new world and opposed to it.[18] It is useful to recall with Joseph Moingt that 'the crisis of Christianity and principally of Western Catholicism goes back to the origins of modernity. Such a crisis was the result of the emancipation of the subject not from the Gospel, but from the Church, in the name of freedom of thought, that is the freedom to think and to express oneself publicly.'[19] The scandal barring the path to faith was not the crucified God, but the superfluous scandal of a Church that was colluding with the conservative forces in society, those that were opposed to progress. Congar, like other authors, used the image of the besieged fortress to describe this situation, which reached its climax at the beginning of the twentieth century.[20] The Church was defending itself not just from attacks, 'but against any infiltration of the ideas of a corrupt century'. It multiplied 'rules, controls and condemnations', 'in order to protect the faithful, more particularly young people and seminarians, from the contagion of subversive ideas'.[21]

It would be unfair to see only a backward-looking feature in this defensive position. A number of attacks were directed against the very soul of the Church and not simply against its powers and privileges. Conflict seemed inevitable. Unable to respond to new questions, those raised notably by the introduction of historical analysis into practically all religious questions, the Church considered it was better not to ask these questions. For the Church to put off answering questions when it felt unable to answer them well, was perhaps not lacking in wisdom, but in Congar's opinion the necessary reaction was 'excessive, too purely negative, and the consequences of this excessively negative reaction can be felt to this day'. He wrote: 'The crisis was repressed. The problems remained.'[22]

In order to repress the crisis, authority was reinforced. A famous study by Congar was entitled appropriately: 'Ecclesiology: From the French Revolution to the Vatican Council under the Banner of Authority'.[23] Congar was deeply interested in nineteenth-century ecclesiology[24] because he was convinced that understanding that century's tendency increasingly to appeal to authority in texts (not only those emanating from the hierarchy) and practice (in spite of other more promising trends) was a key to understanding the problems and the failings of our time. An historical approach can often shed light on an issue, and this is especially true regarding the question of authority.

Let us begin with two quotations that in the crudest light will reveal to what extent the notion of authority had been distorted. We will then understand more fully Congar's need to go back to the sources. Comte Joseph de Maistre (1753–1821) wrote in 1819: 'What need is there for an ecumenical council when a pillory would have the same effect?'[25] Our second quotation comes from a conversation Congar had with 'a prominent theologian of preconciliar mentality'. Congar writes: '[He] congratulated me on my Latin and then said: "You speak of the Holy Spirit, but that is for Protestants. We have the Magisterium".'[26]

How did we get to this point? We will follow in this chapter a lecture given by Congar in 1961 at the Monastery of Notre-Dame du Bec[27] on the notion and exercise of authority in the history of the Catholic Church. We will let Congar take us by the hand and be our guide in this chapter through twenty centuries of history that he has divided into five periods. It is stunning to witness the ease with which he covers two millennia of history, marking out the dominant characteristics of each period. We will journey through these with him, and we will supplement what he said in his 1961 lecture with other writings. We will discover that there is a specifically Christian way of understanding, living and exercising authority. This comes across powerfully in the first period studied by Congar.[28]

Historical overview in five steps*

I. The New Testament and the Apostles

Congar's study of the vocabulary of the New Testament allowed him to remark that it 'avoids or rarely uses the words which signify authority or power in classical Greek'. He writes that the word 'hierarchy' 'does not appear at all' (HDA, 120).

Archè, in the sense of 'power', is used a dozen times, but it never refers to Church authorities; *taxis*, which is translated by 'order', is used ten times, however, it does not refer to the Church either; *timè* is only used in the sense of the "dignity" of Christ and the priesthood of Aaron'. *Exousia* (authority, power) occurs ninety-five times in the New Testament: only seven cases are relevant to our topic. After studying these words, Congar concluded: 'St. Paul declares that he has received *exousia* in order to build and not to destroy. His power is strictly related to the aim which the Lord pursues and towards which he orders the play of events' (HDA, 120).

After these general remarks on vocabulary, Congar proceeds to study the nouns by which the various functions or specific ministries are designated in the New Testament. He provides the following list: apostles, doctors, prophets, evangelists, teachers, pastors, bishops (= supervisors or overseers), presbyters (= elders, ancients), ministers, leaders or superintendents, presidents, stewards or administrators (HDA, 120). Congar observes that all of these terms refer to a task or an activity that is viewed as a service to be performed in the community. He then draws our attention to the fact that when speaking of these ministries or functions the early Christians used a vocabulary borrowed from everyday life and that the words they used eventually developed a religious connotation only because they were lived in Christ and for Christ within the context of Christian life. In no way does

---

*I will frequently be referring to the lecture given by Congar in the monastery of Bec Hellouin: 'The Historical Development of Authority in the Church. Points for Christian Reflection' in *Problems of Authority*, ed. John M. Todd (Baltimore: The Helicon Press, and London: DLT, 1962). References to this book will be included in the text with the initials HDA followed by the page number.

this reduce their power; on the contrary, it points to a specifically Christian characteristic that Congar goes on to define: 'All of these offices are included in the *diaconia*, even that of the apostle. All of them are forms of *service*' (HDA, 120–1). We have now reached the heart of the distinctive nature of Christian authority. Authority belongs not to the category of honour, but to the category of *service*: 'All of them are forms of *service*; or better, "service" or the "diaconia" transcend and involve these offices. It is a universal value coextensive and identical with the Christian life itself' (HDA, 120–1). Congar listens to St. Paul, and what he hears is not a man wrangling about his *rights*, but someone speaking of his *duties*. Paul, in keeping with other apostles, 'continues the teaching of the Gospel that combines priority of rank and the greatest degree of humble loving service' (HDA, 121; tr. modified).

'The secret of the New Testament concept of authority', writes Congar, 'consists in the fact that authority does not take priority.' (HDA, 121; tr. modified). What comes first is Christian existence that is essentially a service. It is *within* this existence that authority, instituted by Christ or by the apostles, must be situated. Any type of 'domineering' attitude in the Church would be in contradiction with Christian identity. Conversely, the spirit of exchange suffuses all things, for God, the sole giver of divine gifts, when giving, is thinking of the good of all. 'Hence the Law of the Christian life is that we should consider ourselves as stewards of God's gifts, which are for the good of all' (HDA, 122). Congar quotes from 1 Peter 4:10 to ground his argument. But even more frequently he likes to quote from Ephesians:

> He who descended is the same one who ascended far above all the heavens, so that he might fill all things. The gifts he gave were that some would be apostles, some prophets, some evangelists, some pastors and teachers, to equip the saints for the work of ministry, for building up the body of Christ, until all of us come to the unity of the faith and of the knowledge of the Son of God, to maturity, to the measure of the full stature of Christ. We must no longer be children, tossed to and fro and blown about by every wind of doctrine, by people's trickery, by their craftiness in deceitful scheming. But speaking the truth in love, we must grow up in every way into him who is the head, into Christ, from whom the whole body, joined and knitted together

by every ligament with which it is equipped, as each part is working properly, promotes the body's growth in building itself up in love. (Ephesians 4:10–16, NRSV)

These texts reveal that all Christians, those whom the New Testament calls 'the saints', are called to service and have been endowed with gifts to that effect. In an article entitled 'Authority, Initiative and Co-responsibility', after having quoted from this passage in Ephesians, Congar comments: 'This is a work of service which consists in building the body of Christ: it is incumbent on all Christians. The role of functions or ministries is to organize Christians so they can do this work.'[29] The Church of the New Testament is not a society in which God would take pleasure in allocating places at different prices according to rank, as though there could be different classes of Christians. Hierarchy there is, but it is a 'functional'[30] hierarchy, one of service, which is in place to facilitate the community life, to allow each person to play his or her role, so one person's gift may be placed at the service of others. 'So each becomes a means of life and growth for all the rest.'[31] Congar laid great stress on this point: 'Hence the hierarchy must not only *live* its life *in the spirit* of service, it *is* service intrinsically because it is established within a life which *is* service' (HDA, 123). Congar liked the way Father Laberthonnière had put it: 'The exercise of authority in general is only one of the forms of what we each have to do through others and for others to further our common destiny.'[32]

To speak of destiny is to speak of the future, of a people on a journey, one that has therefore not yet reached the fullness of its vocation. St. Paul speaks of 'the progress of the Gospel' (Philippians 1:12). Ministries and all forms of service are given for the growth of the body. So it is right to say that ministry and authority are spoken of properly only in the context of growth. 'Within the body and for its growth', Congar writes, 'Christ bestows ministries and services.'[33] Gustave Martelet, who often expressed how much he was indebted to Congar, offered perhaps the clearest comment on this reality: 'Authority in the Church is only a service of the head to bring about an authentic growth of the body. The etymology of the word is significant. "Authority" comes from the Latin verb *augere,* which means *to grow, to increase.* "Authority" thus refers to "a work's dependency on the one who brought it into existence and leads it to its full maturity".'[34]

By failing to maintain this perspective of growth and the means that are ordained to it, theology has at times been led astray, mixing in ontological notions with the question of ministry, and more particularly with the question of hierarchy. When the concept of hierarchy is moulded on the structures of the world, then the 'originality of the mystery of Christ is lost'.[35] When describing the people of God in its deepest identity (its ontology*), the New Testament knows of no other ontology than that of service.

II. The Church of the martyrs and monasticism

The second period scrutinized by Congar is the Church of the martyrs and of monasticism. The Church of the martyrs extends, according to Congar, from the apostles to the peace of Constantine. As for monasticism, the period defined by Congar in his lecture at the Abbey of Bec Hellouin extends from Constantine to the eleventh century. When we consider the third period, from Constantine to Gregory VII, we will therefore not be in an entirely new era. Congar warns us that these great moments must not be viewed as distinct from one another. A number of traits characterizing one period can be found in another; his intention is above all to present us with the dominant characteristics of each period.

Three features are underlined in the notion of authority in the Church of the martyrs: a strong insistence on authority; a very close link to the community of Christians; and a marked charismatic or spiritual character. These three features will be examined successively.

A strong insistence on authority

This is clear in the writings of Ignatius of Antioch (†110), and the same can be said for Cyprian (200–58), St. Irenaeus (bishop around the year 180) and St. Hippolytus (170–235). In this insistence on authority 'the religious or mystical value of salvation or of grace coincides completely with the juridical status of the authority presiding over a society and regulating its life' (HDA, 124). This may sound surprising, but it will become clearer when we look at the second feature of this period's way of understanding and exercising authority.

Link to the community

It is in fact impossible to understand the exercise of authority in the early Church without first realizing that for ancient Christianity the *ecclesia** refers to the entire Christian community, the assembly or unity of Christians. Two texts by Cyprian are quoted by Congar: 'The Church is the people united to its pontiff, and the flock abiding with its shepherd. This will make you see that the bishop is in the Church and the Church in the bishop' (HDA, 125n. 1). And this second text shows how Cyprian exercised his ministry as bishop: 'I have made it a rule, ever since the beginning of my episcopate, to make no decision merely on the strength of my own personal opinion without consulting you (the priests and the deacons) and without the approbation of the people' (HDA, 126; tr. modified). Both of these texts correspond to a discovery made by Congar when doing his research on the laity in early Christianity: 'there is no antagonism, but a union between the hierarchical structure and the communal exercise of all Church activities' (HDA, 125; tr. modified). What is involved is the living and organic reality of the whole Church.[36] A fascinating page from *Lay People in the Church* allows the reader to watch the theologian at work:

> Our theology, which is insufficiently inductive and too often ignores what can be learned from facts, has almost completely failed to see how the actual Church, whose structure is life-bearing, follows a law of existence that can be formulated thus: the meeting and harmonizing between a hierarchical communication from above and a community's consent. The Church is actualized in a living relationship between two poles, which can be called the hierarchical and the 'communitarian' poles. Once one has seen that, a host of texts and facts are clarified, the history of ecclesiology takes shape.[37]

He goes on to write that the texts of early Christianity 'are all at the same time both resolutely hierarchical and unquestionably communitarian'.[38] Unlike some other authors, Congar does not speak of a 'duality of authority', 'but the duality of the hierarchy pole and the community pole: of a hierarchy by which the Church is constructed, and of a community in which alone she finds her plenitude and fulfills her life; one single Church made from above and from below'.[39] For Congar the affirmation of one pole is not at the expense of the other: 'no Church without an apostolically instituted bishop; nothing in the Church without the bishop'. However, Congar also observes that 'the texts – often exactly the same ones – also say: nothing without the consent of the community, all living by the Spirit of God; each one can give his opinion; each gives thanks according to his rank'.[40] He then adds: 'That is why in the writings of the Apostolic Fathers one passes so often and so easily from very strong hierarchical statements to communal statements, and vice versa. [...] They reflect a state of things in which the two principles harmonize.'[41]

A few examples taken from the liturgy illustrate this: 'The ancient liturgy has no "I" distinct from the "we" of the whole assembly. The celebrant, that is, the president of the assembly and the head of the community, speaks in the name of all for he is one with all its members' (HDA, 125). Congar takes this insight further in a study entitled 'The *Ecclesia* or Christian Community as a Whole Celebrates the Liturgy'.[42] The study appeared shortly after the publication of the Second Vatican Council's constitution on the sacred liturgy. Referring to this constitution and to *Lumen Gentium* no. 11, Congar is pleased to note that, in keeping with the early Church, the Council teaches 'that the *ecclesia*, or this organically structured body that is the Church, is the subject of liturgical acts'.[43] Is this not obvious, asks Congar, 'since liturgical acts are precisely public acts of Christian worship?'[44] To prove this point, we can supplement the examples given in his study with other examples, more numerous in other writings than in his lecture on authority at the Abbey of Bec Helloin. Let us take an example from the post-Constantinian period, from Augustine, the doctor of the Church who was most attached to understanding the *ecclesia* as the unity of Christians. Congar illustrates the way Augustine sees forgiveness when speaking of the 'power of the keys': 'It is the *ecclesia*, or rather the corporate unity of the *ecclesia*, that has received the keys and that exercises them.'[45] For those who might be frightened by such a statement, Congar adds immediately: 'Augustine does not misunderstand the role of the ministries or the efficacy that follows upon their actions when Christ acts through them, but he refuses to isolate ministry from the community of believers.' Congar connected this theme and the theme of spiritual motherhood, which interested him a great deal. Can we legitimately speak of 'spiritual motherhood' with regard to the faithful? Are they not themselves the Church's children? According to Congar, St. Ambrose and St. Augustine have already answered this question: 'The faithful, taken separately or individually, are sons and daughters of the Church; but if taken together, incorporated in its unity, they form the *Ecclesia-Mater*, and as such they give birth to souls. The reason is always the same: the Holy Spirit is bestowed and operates within the unity of the Church.'[46] How should this be applied to the forgiveness of sins? Congar answers:

> There is a simplistic habit, alas far too widespread, of linking forgiveness exclusively to sacramental absolution. This leaves out a number of the main teachings of the Catholic Tradition. According to this Tradition, receiving the Eucharist, granting forgiveness to those who have sinned against us, and finally the entire life of charity, the whole *vita in Christo*, all the good we do, all of these things constitute a permanent communication of forgiveness. The healing of sinful nature is accomplished by the Christian life in its entirety, and other people are constantly involved in it: just as all of a person's life and health takes part in the healing of a wound [...].[47]

With this elaborate existential consistency, we are at the heart of Augustine's great ecclesiology, far from the individualism and the legalism of subsequent centuries. Drawing on his careful study of Augustine's anti-Donatist writings, Congar points out: 'St. Augustine particularly developed this doctrine that is at once ecclesiological and pneumatological. It is the heart of his ecclesiology.'[48] We understand that 'the Holy Spirit is actually the principle of our communion with Christ and, in Christ, of communion among ourselves. The Holy Spirit is the principle by which the faithful form themselves into an *ecclesia*, and thus become the organic unity of the body of Christ, the subject of liturgical actions.'[49]

Let us now turn to a few other examples that illustrate the link between authority and community in the early Church. 'Several letters dating from the sub-apostolic period are written by the community and by its head, and the two are inseparably linked' (HDA, 125). Clement of Rome's letter to the Church of Corinth can be quoted as an example, as well as Denys of Corinth's letter mentioned by Eusebius in his *Ecclesiastical History*: 'it is addressed by him and by the Church he governed to Xystus and the Church of Rome' (HDA, 125n. 4). In other writings of this same period, Congar underlines, 'there is a constant alternation of assertions of the hierarchical principle and assertions of the community principle' (HDA, 125 and n. 5).[50]

Finally, Congar recalls the active role that was played by the laity in all of Church life, including the election of bishops and the designation of ministers. He explains: 'Their intervention as occasion arose was accepted all the more willingly since the early Church, whilst possessing a firm canonical structure, wanted to be ready for any movement inspired by the Holy Spirit. And God is pleased to make his will known through the humblest and the least esteemed of his children' (HDA, 126).

The charismatic or spiritual nature of authority

This is the third feature in the life of the early Church studied by Congar. As he has stressed already elsewhere, there is no opposition between the spiritual and the institutional, or between charisms and hierarchy. 'The bishops were the men who possessed the principal charismatic gifts of the community.' […] 'In the early Church, in fact, the mystical and the juridical elements were closely interwoven and the idea of grades of spirituality was linked with that of grades of dignity' (HDA, 126–7). The bishop is considered both a leader and a spiritual man, that is, someone filled with the Spirit and the Spirit's gifts. He was chosen for this very reason, because the one leading God's people must himself be someone who listens to the Spirit. This is the only way the people can be led by God. In this period, the bishop's 'actions, and in a more general way, all the decisive factors in the life of the Church, whether due to decisions emanating from the authority of the bishop or of synods, or from some other sources, were attributed to God's intervention' (HDA, 127). 'It is GOD who controls the life of the Church' (HDA, 127n. 1). Congar summarizes in the following way the spirit that characterizes this period in Church history:

In the early Church, authority was that of men who were like princes in a community which was wholly sanctified, *plebs sancta*, and overshadowed by the Spirit of God. The Church leaders were all the more conscious of their authority in that they saw it as the vehicle of the mystery of that salvation which God wishes to accomplish in his Church. They wanted to be, and knew that they were, moved by the Spirit, but they also knew that the Spirit inhabits the Christian community and in the exercise of their authority they remained closely linked to this community (HDA, 127).

III. From Constantine to Gregory VII

Congar deals with this period with the greatest respect. Anybody looking for stereotyped images of the early Middle Ages will be disappointed with Congar's analysis. He concedes that remaining faithful to a Christian understanding of authority was a challenge and that the danger of succumbing to another conception of authority was real. In the years that followed the peace of Constantine, 'the clergy were given important privileges, the bishops became *illustri*, and for all practical purposes, ranked with the senators. They were invested with public authority within the framework of the empire, even in the sphere of the secular life of the cities' (HDA, 128). Should we not expect a betrayal of the early Church's conception of authority and a shift towards something different? The question is legitimate, and Congar becomes more explicit about what is at stake:

> Under these conditions, we ought perhaps to expect that authority would change its character and that it would acquire a much more secular, much more juridical meaning, based simply on the relation of superior to subordinate. It would cease to be open onto the higher sphere of a marked charismatic action on God's part and onto the lower sphere of the influence of the action of the community, and so close in on itself and become authority for its own sake, authority pure and simple (HDA, 128).

The risk was real, and our theologian does not deny it. He compares it to the dangers faced by Christian thought when it entered into symbiosis with the philosophy of pagan culture. For this very reason he admires all the more this period's fidelity to the mystery of the Church. 'The juridical form of thought had not yet taken over ecclesiology.'[51] Congar goes on to explain, and we can appreciate more fully the contrast that he emphasizes when we compare this period of history with others: 'People are not content with the formal validity of institutions or functions as if what they are in reality were not important or as if you could be oblivious of the way in which they act. Unceasingly the content passes judgment on the form, and determines its authenticity and validity.'[52] The authority of Peter can be given as an example: 'The pope has the authority of Peter, insofar as he has the faith, the righteousness, the mores of Peter. His decisions are received when the people recognize in them the faith and the voice of Peter.'[53] In short, content is important. And this content determines whether authority is acknowledged or not.

At the request of the German publisher, Herder, Congar undertook a careful study of this period of history, when the word *ecclesia* 'indicated Christian society and included the empire or the various kingdoms as well as the Church as such' (HDA, 136; tr. modified). His book on the ecclesiology of the early Middle Ages[54] was hailed by some of the greatest historians as a work of singular erudition.[55] Unquestionably, the conception and exercise of authority in the early Middle Ages owed a great deal to monasticism. Congar thinks 'it would be a mistake to see any conflict between this type of authority and that exercised by the bishops during the period from the peace of Constantine to the Gregorian reform' (HDA, 130). Many of the bishops of that time had themselves been monks, or at least they were trained in monasteries. They often pursued some kind of religious life and were nostalgic for the life they had left behind.

The type of authority that existed in monasticism was spiritual and charismatic (HDA, 128). It was the authority of a man of God. The patriarchs of monasticism wanted to be 'transparent' to God, unceasingly listening to the Spirit. Their authority was entirely dependent on this listening.

In Western Europe, along with other examples that he does not dwell upon, Congar mentions Celtic Christianity which preserved a structure of its own down to the twelfth century:

There was no diocesan pattern, that is, there were no specific territories under the authority of bishops, but a whole complex of spheres of spiritual influence. A 'saint' had his own sphere of influence in which he was in a sense a permanent spiritual lord of a given place. A territory was affiliated to a holy man, and eventually, there was a grouping with a monastery at its centre and the jurisdiction belonged to the Abbot who was often, but not necessarily, in bishop's orders. Sometimes even, as in Kildare, jurisdiction was in the hands of an abbess. Authority was attributed to the man of God, and not to a particular grade in the priestly hierarchy (HDA, 129–30).

In the period under discussion, 'the bishop, whether or not a monk, is a spiritual man, a man of God'. Congar, whose survey goes beyond theological treatises and extends to liturgy, underlines that when a bishop is mentioned 'the oldest sections in the Latin ritual of ordination state his duties rather that his powers' (HDA, 130). St. Gregory (540 to circa 604), Congar reminds us, referred to the study of scripture as one of the necessary qualifications for one to be elected bishop (HDA, 130–1n. 1). The bishop must pray, fast, practise hospitality, be a man who listens to others. He must edify his people by his words and by the celebration of the liturgy. He is to defend the poor and the weak. In short, 'he must be aware that he is exercising not a *dominium* or a *potestas*, but a *ministerium* [a service] in keeping with the vocabulary St. Augustine has passed on to the Western Church' [HDA, 131; tr. modified]. At the time, '*Servus servorum Dei*' was not a mere official phrase (HDA, 132), Congar says. Bishops such as Gregory the Great 'took a genuine interest in the welfare of those under their command' (HDA, 132; tr. modified). This concern for the welfare of others shapes this period's conception of authority. In his study 'Quelques expressions traditionnelles du service chrétien', which he published in the wake of his text on 'The Hierarchy as Service',[56] Congar examines some of the traditional expressions that are used to describe the legitimate exercise of authority, such as *prodesse-praesse* [to serve-to rule over] that appear in various forms. For example, *The Rule of St. Benedict* reminds the abbot 'that his duty is rather to profit his brethren than to preside over them'.[57] The same is true of *The Pastoral Rule* of St. Gregory the Great and down to St. Bernard who in many regards had more in common with the spirit of the period we are studying than the next.[58] Bernard wrote to Pope Eugenius III that he should '*non ministrari sed ministrare*', which means 'serve rather than be served'.[59] Bernard also advised him to 'lead in order to serve, not in order to rule' [*praesis ut prosis ne ut imperes*]. Repeatedly Bernard used this expression, which was one of St. Augustine's favorites.[60]

Congar's closing remarks on this period of history are noteworthy. Before the West adopted Roman Law, that is, before the twelfth century, there was a different conception of authority, one in which the strong influence of Christianity can be discerned:

> The early medieval period was biblical, patristic, liturgical, and monastic. Roman law seems to have been alien to it, as there are hardly any signs of it between the sixth and the eleventh centuries. In those situations where the influence of Roman law can be discerned, one notes a tendency to replace the Christian, spontaneous, and traditional view of power as ordered to a good and subordinate to this good, with the notion of an absolute power that justifies itself.[61]

At the very end of his study, Congar is more specific as he summarizes:

> When it exercises its own proper influence on the conception of social life and power, Christianity acts in a communitarian, non-statist direction. The priority is not power or authority as such, but the well-being of persons, which is maintained to the highest degree in the community that they form.[62]

We can add to these closing remarks a brief unsigned text that can be found at the end of *Problems of Authority*. It is presented as a summary of the discussion that took place at the Abbey of Bec Hellouin, following Jacques Leclercq's lecture on authority. Congar's style and concerns are easily recognizable and not surprisingly so since the book appeared in French in the series *Unam Sanctam* that Congar founded and directed:

> Historically, whenever the Church has been free to create its own institutions it has always created authority in the context of community rather than in an autocratic sense. Whenever

autocracy appears, it comes from outside the Church, not from its own inspiration – from Roman Law, from barbarian tradition, or some other origin independent of the Church itself. (HDA, 259; tr. modified)

Let us now return to authority as it was exercised by Gregory the Great in his community. It elicits the following commentary from Congar: 'he [Gregory] took a genuine interest in the welfare of the men under his command. He loved and respected their progress in virtue as resulting from their own free will. He took care to explain to them the reasons for any of his decisions in the light of some good or some truth which their souls instinctively sought' (HDA, 132). And Congar concludes: 'In a word, he exercised his authority like a kind of supreme and universal Father Abbot, combining the tender care of a mother with the authority of a father. The Church for him was not a vast organization or a system but a community of human beings moving towards the perfection of charity' (HDA, 132; tr. modified).

In the passage I just quoted, Congar underlined the words 'explain the reasons'. If he is keen to stress this, it is because he remembers a Church dignitary saying to him: 'Authority's proper characteristic is that it has not to give any reasons' (HDA, 132n. 4). The exact opposite is what Congar observes in the early Church. For example, in his letter to Theoctista, the emperor's sister, 'Gregory notes that the Apostle Peter himself explained to the Church the reasons for his baptism of Cornelius' (HDA, 132n. 4).

Congar reinforces his claim that it is normal for the people to be consulted and that their views play a role in decision making by quoting formulas elaborated by various popes in the fourth and fifth centuries and taken up by a number of councils. For example, Congar cites St. Leo: 'Qui praefuturus est omnibus ab omnibus eligatur' [Let him who will stand before all be elected by all!]. He also cites Pope Celestine: 'Nullus invitis detur episcopus' [That a bishop must not be imposed on people against their will].[63] Let us now turn to an example that Congar takes from the life of St. Augustine. At Hippo, around the year 424, a member of the clergy named Januarius had misbehaved. In order to live a life of prayer together with Augustine and others, he claimed that he had given away all his possessions. However, when he died, a

will was discovered revealing that he had actually concealed his
wealth, leaving instructions for it to be given to the Church after
his death. If Augustine had accepted this inheritance, he would
have deprived Januarius' son, still a minor. This was a delicate
matter. It could have been taken care of discreetly. In a sermon,

RECEPTION

A legal mind[64] might have a hard time understanding this
notion of 'reception' which Congar studied carefully and
considered to be of major importance for 'a wholly traditional
Catholic ecclesiology'.[65] Reception 'derives from a theology of
communion, it is no more than the extension or prolongation
of the conciliar process: it is associated with the same essential
"conciliarity" of the Church'. It rests on the belief that the whole
body of the Church is enlivened by the Holy Spirit.[66] Consensus
is seen as an effect of the Holy Spirit and the sign of his presence.
Subscribing to this view is not to reject authority, 'for the Christian
faith does not conceive of authority as a form of domination'. It
is a matter of acknowledging that the faithful are not merely
passive, but are 'true subjects of activity and free initiative'. When
it comes to determining the form their lives will take, they have
a true capacity for discernment and cooperation. Reception is
seen by Congar as 'the process by means of which the *ecclesia*
takes over as its own a decision that it did not originate in regard
to itself'.[67] Obedience certainly has a place in the Church, 'but
not everything is laid down in the tradition of the Church'. The
assent which faith requires 'does not call merely upon volition, but
upon intelligence'. In this way, faith is just as much 'consensus
as it is obedience'. The notion of reception, very present in the
first millennium of the Church, was practically eliminated when a
pyramidal conception was substituted for the older conception of
the Church as the Body of Christ, the people of God. Obedience
is insisted upon when the Church is conceived of as a society
subject to a monarchical authority (this was the case from the
eleventh century to Vatican II); reception and consent are important
when the universal Church is seen as a communion of churches.

however, Augustine openly spoke about it to his people, giving his reasons for not accepting the inheritance. Congar comments: 'Augustine gave his people an account of his line of conduct and of the principles on which he wished to base the cooperation of his clergy in his work as their bishop.' And Congar went on to ask: 'Who would do anything of the sort today?' (HDA, 134). The concluding remarks of Congar's lecture at the Abbey of Bec Hellouin, which are cited almost word for word in *Lay People in the Church*, bring together the essential components of his view of authority: 'When St. Augustine explained to his flock on what terms he expected his clergy to live with him, he made the whole life of the Church perfectly clear and ensured the wholehearted assent of the faithful to a government for which he did not cease to be wholly responsible.'[68]

Before addressing the issue of how priestly authority was conceived and practised in the Middle Ages, Congar's Bec Hellouin lecture discusses features of Church practice in Late Antiquity that prepared and hinted at the change that was coming. For instance, he pointed out the gap between the clergy and the faithful was widening. 'Clerics were to observe a special rule of life modelled more or less on that of the monks and inspired by the Levitical regulations of the Old Testament' (HDA, 135). Most people today would be surprised to read Pope Celestine's letter sent in 428 to Honorat, the abbot of Lerins, who had become bishop of Arles. The Pope upbraided him for *innovating* when he introduced specific ecclesiastic clothing for the clergy.[69] According to Congar, the clergy began wearing special clothing in the first third of the fifth century. 'Hitherto, priests' dress had been exactly the same as that of other men. Even in the celebration of the Liturgy they merely wore *clean* clothes' (HDA, 134n. 4; tr. modified).

These examples reveal a shift that will grow in the subsequent periods. The tension that had existed earlier in the Church of the Martyrs was between the *ecclesia* and the world. 'Henceforth within a society entirely Christian, tension grew inside the Church or within Christian society between monks or priests on the one hand, and laymen on the other' (HDA, 135).

The most positive aspects of this period are summarized by Congar when he explains that 'the great bishops of the centuries we have understandably called those of monastic Catholicism were very careful to relate authority to its transcendent spiritual principle' (HDA, 132). We must add to this that 'at this period in fact the primal and decisive reality in ecclesiology was still the *ecclesia* itself, that is, the totality, the community, the unity of the faithful' (HDA, 132–3). The consequences of this emphasis on the *ecclesia* were extremely significant and determined how authority was understood. 'The whole concept of authority in the treatise *De Ecclesia* and the whole balance of the treatise itself depend upon it' (HDA, 133). 'For the Fathers and the Early Christians, the *ecclesia* comes first. Then, in the *ecclesia*, come the *praepositi ecclesiae*, the presidents or heads of the Christian community' (HDA, 133). And so we are able to understand why, in the early Church, the bishop introduced himself first of all as a Christian. 'St. Augustine constantly tells his flock: "I am a bishop for your sake, I am a Christian together with you"[70], "a sinner together with you", "a disciple and hearer of the Gospel together with you", "Vobis sum episcopus, vobiscum christianus"' (HDA, 133).

Other important themes in the thought of Yves Congar appear in his final remarks on this early period: 'The foundation of all this and of patristic ecclesiology, which continued to be that of the early Middle Ages, is doubtless the fact that the Church is composed of human beings and that all that is done within the Church is aimed formally and immediately at the formation of spiritual human beings. Ecclesiology and anthropology are not in separate compartments, and the former is a continuation of soteriology, which is itself but one chapter of Christology' (HDA, 133; tr. modified). We may add with Congar:

> What is involved is not a system or a juridical set-up but a body of people praying, fasting, doing penance, asking for grace, engaging in a spiritual combat and struggling for the triumph in themselves of the spirit of Jesus Christ. This is why authority is *moral* and requires human beings who are themselves spiritually alive. (HDA, 133–4)

IV. Priestly authority in the Middle Ages

As we might expect, it is now time for Congar to focus on the Gregorian Reform. Knowing Congar's standpoint on this period, we are not surprised to read: 'We are convinced that the reform begun by St. Leo IX (1049–54) and continued with such vigor by St. Gregory VII (1073–81) represents a decisive turning-point from the point of view of ecclesiological doctrines in general and of the notion of authority in particular' (HDA, 136). As I have already pointed out, Congar had no doubts with regard to the positive intention of the Gregorian Reform, which was to purify the Church. Furthermore, we would be mistaken if we thought that his analysis of the Gregorian Reform was limited to its shortcomings. He was convinced that it was essential that the Church 'rid itself of its identification with political society, an identification indicated by the word *ecclesia* itself which meant both the mystical Body and the Empire with no distinction made between them' (HDA, 136). Pursuing his objective of clarification, 'Pope Gregory VII claimed for the Church the completely autonomous and sovereign system of rights proper to a spiritual society' (HDA, 136).

The papacy takes on an unprecedented importance in the new ecclesial configuration. Papal power 'enters into the dogmatic definition of the Church, not simply to take up a place, but to take up the key place and crucial role: the place of a constitutive principle'.[71] It becomes 'the foundation of the ecclesiastical construction', and the authority attached to it 'comes directly from a positive divine institution'.[72] Claiming 'the sovereign rights of this authority not only over the Church, but also over kings and their kingdoms', Pope Gregory VII had 'asked churchmen to discover the maximum number of juridical texts in favor of this view'. And Congar, who throughout his theological writings often showed interest in legal history, adds: 'In point of fact, a whole series of canonical collections owes its existence to this request. For all these reasons, the eleventh-century reform set in motion a powerful wave of canonical studies' (HDA, 136–7). Canon law became an academic discipline in this period, and Christendom's most famous law school was in Bologna.

Authority proceeded to state and to claim its rights in unprecedented ways. It is legitimate 'to speak of a new chapter in the history of the notion of authority itself' (HDA, 137). It would be a mistake to believe that this new tendency was limited to a juridical or academic expression. Alongside the strong personality of its promoters, the movement was carried by 'a vast and profound "mystique"'. Congar attached great importance to the specific power that derives from a 'mystique'. 'The strength of a movement', he writes, 'always lies in its "mystique"' (HDA, 138).[73] The mystique in question here is distinctive. It is expressed and invested in legal arguments that result in 'a genuine political theology'. Moreover, a number of texts that had been hitherto considered to be in the realm of spiritual anthropology (HDA, 138) were now interpreted legalistically. What had been understood as applying to spiritual life is now translated 'into terms of law (and of rights!) together with a specific application to the Pope and to the Pope alone' (HDA, 138). We may use the words addressed to the prophet Jeremiah as an example: 'Lo, I have set thee this day over the nations and over kingdoms, to root up, and to pull down, and to waste, and to destroy, and to build, and to plant' (Jeremiah 1:10). In the new mystique of papal authority this 'becomes an assertion of the supreme authority of the Pope and of his right to depose kings'.[74] Pope Pius V (Pope from 1566 to 1572) used these words of Jeremiah in his bull *Regnans in excelsis* to depose Queen Elizabeth I (HDA, 138).

Congar made a careful study of the expression *Vicarius Christi*. He felt that an understanding of how the meaning of this expression had been transformed would lead to a better understanding of the evolution of the notion of authority. Congar's analysis is helpful if we want to understand how the modern mystique of authority came into being:

> Its older sense in Catholic *theology* was that of a visible represen-tation of a transcendent or heavenly power *which was actually active* in its earthly representative. The context and atmosphere surrounding this idea were those of the actuality of the action of God, Christ and the saints, working in their representative. This is a very sacramental, iconological concept, linked to the idea of constant 'presences' of God and the celestial powers in our earthly sphere. (HDA, 138–9)

It is important to understand what Congar means here when he speaks of an 'actually active' power – elsewhere he sometimes used the uncommon French term *actualisme* to convey this idea. He explained this in an article entitled 'Remarks on the Council as an Assembly and on the Church's Fundamentally Conciliar Nature'.[75] The objective of his article was not to study the expression *Vicarius Christi*, but, as its lengthy title indicates, to look at what happens

when the Church is gathered in a council and to study the ways in
which such a gathering can help us understand the nature of the
Church. What Congar affirms on 'actualisme' in this article will be
helpful for understanding his views on the true meaning of *Vicarius
Christi.* When in the early Church the Fathers speak of councils,
they 'say that they are assembled together in a certain place
"with the Holy Spirit" or even "by the Holy Spirit"'. A council is
gathered. 'It is so by and in the Holy Spirit, who is, invisibly, the
most authoritative Person of this gathering.' The role attributed to
the Spirit is an interior action of 'suggestion' or 'inspiration'. The
presidency is attributed to Christ – 'a mystical presidency often
given visible expression by placing a representation of Christ in
the middle of the basilica or, more regularly, the book of Gospels
open on a throne'. The Fathers are keen to show that 'Christ and
the Holy Spirit are not present inactively: of their sovereign power
they operate the council'. Congar is attentive to 'the consciousness
which the councils had of being "inspired", that is, of having been
visited by the Holy Spirit'. This led the early Christians to believe
that 'it is Christ and the Holy Spirit who act in councils and are
the real authors of their decrees so that the final judgment, the sole
act which is properly the conciliar act, is the common act of the
assembled college *and* of the Holy Spirit'. Congar refers also to
St. Cyprian, who spoke of the Spirit intervening in a perceptible
manner. Thus 'the decisions of the council come from God, set
forth by his authority'. And this is where Congar explains more
precisely how he thinks such a statement should be understood:
'The Fathers understood this not so much as a juridical assertion of
the authority of the bishops or the council representing or pledging
Christ's authority, communicated by him to them, but as a *reality*:
it is God, Christ, the Holy Spirit, who *act* in the lawful and holy
assembly.'

We are now able to understand the evolution that Congar
discerned in the use of the expression *Vicarius Christi.* The idea
that it is Christ at work through the one representing him has not
disappeared; however, it is 'overlaid by another quality that also is
not entirely new – what is new is its marked predominance over the
former one – namely, the idea of a "power" given at the beginning
by someone, by Christ, to his "Vicar", that is, to a representative
who takes his place and who hands on to those who come after him,
in a historical sequence of transmission and succession, the power

thus received' (HDA, 138). This represents a major shift because the predominant feature is now 'not a vertical movement, an actual presence, an iconological representation, but the "horizontal" transmission of a power vested in the earthly jurisdiction and which, although received from on high, is yet genuinely possessed by this jurisdiction which uses it in the same way as any authority may use the power attached to it' (HDA, 139). Congar thought that the modern mystique of authority prevalent in the period we are now studying, all the way to Vatican II, was due to the change that has just been described. It would be a mistake to think that the mystical element has ceased to exist; rather, it 'has combined the actuality of the power possessed with the vision of the "vertical" descent of the divine power upon the actual historic authority' (HDA, 139). This is where Congar put his finger on what was truly new: the emergence of legalism. How does such a legalism manifest itself? Where is it seen? Congar's answer to these questions contrasts with his description of the early Middle Ages.[76] He depicts the period extending from the Gregorian Reform to Vatican II with characteristics that are the exact opposite of the early periods. 'We see this legalism at work', writes Congar, 'in the importance attached to the formal validity of authority, to its possession of a title in law. There is no insistence on the need of an actual intervention of God's grace, nor therefore on the need for human beings "to pray for this intervention", to be open to this intervention' (HDA, 140). In the time preceding the emergence of this legalism, those exercising authority or a council gathered to deliberate on a question knew that openness to God is possible only through the 'mortification of the flesh'.[77] A word of explanation is required about this expression Congar uses and that contemporary readers are likely to misunderstand. Mortification of the flesh consists in resisting the urge to impose one's own point of view, to forego the tendency to seek one's own interest. It is to refuse to be authoritarian and renounce the need to have the last word at all costs. Various spiritual disciplines including fasting, prayer, chastity, and liturgical celebrations are there to facilitate the openness to a reality greater than oneself. We can grasp in this light how the exercise of authority, one that is faithful to the Spirit, is in this way *openness to the unknown*, the opposite of a self-centred system.

If the period under study is a far cry from the positive realities that we have been describing, we should nevertheless recall the distinction Congar made between ecclesiological *theory* and Christian life. The holiness of Christians active in real life, their way of living, was far superior to the misguided theory. It should be noted, however, that this period is characterized by many movements demanding more simplicity and less pomp in the Church. Pomp there certainly was. From the eleventh century on, wrote Cardinal Congar, 'the supreme authority of the Pope borrowed many of the features of vocabulary, insignia, ceremonial, style and ideology of the imperial court. These factors sometimes go back to pagan days and even by way of the Hellenistic monarchy of Alexander, to the Persian paganism of the fourth century B.C.' (HDA, 142). St. Bernard wrote to Pope Eugenius III: 'All this goes back to Constantine, not to Peter' (HDA, 142).

When the conception and exercise of authority are no longer modelled on the Gospel, when

> instead of being seen as a relationship of superior to subordinate *within* the vast system of mutual love and service between Christians who are Christians as the result of a grace for which each is accountable to all, does not *authority* run the risk of being posited *first and foremost* for its own sake, and so of being looked upon in a purely juridical and sociological way, and not from a spiritual and a Christian standpoint? (HDA, 141)

Congar believed that up to the death of Thomas and Bonaventure, the two great doctors of the thirteenth century, theology was able to balance the various elements of ancient ecclesiology and thus avoided ascribing purely juridical and formal value to authority. As for the fourteenth and fifteenth centuries, they represent the most assertive expression of ecclesiastical power up to 'the thunderclap of October 31, 1517'. Congar is of course referring to the Reformation, which 'refused the right to any human authority whatsoever to enter into the field of the human person's religious relationship with God. This relationship was to be conditioned by the authority of God alone, and this authority was simply and solely that of his Word as contained in Scripture' (HDA, 143–4; tr. modified).

V. From the Council of Trent to Vatican II

In order to understand the importance of the period we are about to examine, we should remember what Jean Delumeau said about the Council of Trent: 'It forms a watershed in the religious history of the West that separates two eras; the second era only came to an end with the Second Vatican Council.'[78] The Reformation had challenged the very principle of authority, and not only the forms it had taken in history. A vigorous reaction from Rome soon followed.[79] From the Council of Trent onwards, authority was reasserted and became more centralized.

With regard to the reassertion of authority, aspects of the hierarchy were emphasized to such a degree that the term 'Church' came to stand for 'nothing more than a society in which some commanded and the rest obeyed'. The Church came to be considered 'from the viewpoint of its rights and the powers that made it a social structure; in a word, as a juridical subject of authority and rights'.[80] This tendency, characterized by a reassertion of authority, can be noticed in practically every area. Let us begin with a few examples taken from the nineteenth century. Congar mentions the way in which Vatican I* speaks of Revelation, Pope Leo's manner of speaking of the state in his encyclicals, the creation of the feast of Christ the King, as well as the reassertion of parental authority. Congar concluded: 'Ecclesiology, as far as the instruction of clerics and of the faithful is concerned, became fixed in a set pattern in which the question of authority is so predominant that the whole treatise is more like a hierarchiology or a treatise on public law.'[81] Congar is not alone in making such a diagnosis. Other experts on the nineteenth century have observed that even for a writer as subtle as Tocqueville, the Catholic Church is 'identified purely and simply with authority and law'.[82]

In his lecture at the Abbey of Bec Hellouin, Congar drew his examples from the nineteenth and twentieth centuries. We must turn to some of his other writings for an analysis of Tridentinism,[83] whose main features were listed in the introduction to this book. I would like to quote here a remark that sheds light on the widening gap between Church and society: 'At a time when the modern world was attempting to build its life on the principle of the individual personality, even to the point of disregarding or denying the objective rights of God and of his law, from the sixteenth century onwards the Catholic Church put into practice a genuine "mystique" of authority' (HDA, 145; tr. modified).

Not surprisingly, in this reassertion of authority, the papacy receives the lion's share. 'The idea of authority, the exercise of

authority in contemporary Catholicism, are first and foremost
the idea and the exercise of papal authority' (HDA, 144). Congar
offers abundant examples of this fact by enumerating instances
when Rome intervened: encyclicals, liturgy, rules concerning
fasting, marriage preparation, content for courses in seminaries
and faculties of theology ... The saints are those canonized by
Rome; 'the religious congregations ask Rome for the authori-
zation of their rule and it is from Rome that the secular Institutes
have received theirs. Rome intervenes directly in the question
of adapting apostolic methods to the needs of the time (worker
priests, *Mission de France*). It keeps a sharp eye on publications
[...].' Congar summarizes: 'In short, the exercise of authority in the
modern Catholic Church is largely that of its central and supreme
seat in Rome' (HDA, 145; tr. modified).[84]

In all of this, Congar lamented an imbalance that history[85]
can partially explain. If he pleaded for more collegiality in the
Church, we must note that the primacy of the bishop of Rome
and his ministry of unity remain essential to Congar.[86] Even in
the darkest time in his life, when the hardship he experienced
originated precisely in Rome, and when some of his friends were
urging him to leave his order and the Church, Congar wrote
in his diary: 'There is truly something apostolic in Rome.'[87] He
believed in conciliarity*, as it 'pertains to the deepest nature of
the Church',[88] but we fail to detect in his thought any sympathy
for conciliarism*.[89] He was delighted by Pope John XXIII's plans
for the Council that was in preparation in 1959. Those plans
were aimed indeed at a readjustment, i.e. to complete the received
teaching and to favour both in theological reflection and in practice
a revitalization of the role of bishops. The episcopal function was
to have the same vitality as the papal function, and one was to
complement the other.[90] In his report on the third session of the
Council, Congar rejoiced that the fifteenth-century misconception
that placed the Pope and the Council in opposition had been cast
aside. And he added: 'What is distinctive with Vatican II with
regards to the councils of Constance and Basel and even Vatican I
is the peaceful restoration of the organic unity between the Council
and the Pope, between episcopal collegiality and the authority of
Peter's successor.' In the same text he stresses that this 'restoration
was lived out even before it was expressed theoretically'.[91] In his
article on the papacy in the French *Encyclopædia Universalis*,

Congar remarked: 'With Pope John XXIII and Vatican II, the Catholic Church has reconnected with a number of ecclesiological values of the first millennium and breathed new life into many realities inspired by the Gospel: collegiality, the communion of local churches, horizontal catholicity, a Church less centered on the papacy and affording a greater place to the episcopacy, less focused on hierarchical ministry and thus able to give a greater place to the communion of the faithful.'[92] The term 'reconnected' was deliberately and carefully chosen. It indicates that what has begun can still grow. Consequently, Congar explained to Jean Puyo that the Council 'had begun a work that remains unfinished. Whether it be with regards to collegiality, the role of the laity, mission work, or ecumenism, it would be absurd to think that matters should remain where they were left at the end of the Council, on 8 December, 1965.' And again to Puyo, he said: 'All of the Council's work is half-finished [...]. The Council gave the initial push, but life must now determine what will come next.' [93]

A year before the Council started, near the conclusion of his long and insightful lecture at the monastery of Bec Hellouin, Congar acknowledged the progress that had been made in the exercise of authority, remarking that there is now 'a predominance of pastoral care over prelacy' and an awareness 'of tasks and responsibilities over the claiming of privileges'. Congar felt nevertheless impelled to add: 'And yet an ecclesiology that is still too juridical, too remote from spiritual anthropology, continues to give a somewhat external character to the aims of authority, a character that is sometimes inclined to be sociological rather than interior and spiritual' (HDA, 148).

Vatican II

'I could not have asked for anything more.'[94] Father Congar used such words when he looked back on the work accomplished at the Second Vatican Council.[95] So many of the themes that were dear to him were heartily embraced by the Council, and among them the question of authority and the related question of ministry.

The Council marked the beginning of a new era, but it was also, as Cardinal Suenens wrote, 'the heir and beneficiary of those great movements of renewal which were and are stirring in the heart of the modern Church; we mean the biblical, liturgical, patristic, theological and pastoral renewals'.[96] Since Congar had taken an active role in the drafting of the texts produced by the Council, he was frequently called upon later to write commentaries on them. In one such commentary, he gave an account that is related to the topic we are examining. On 21 November 1964, the Fathers of the Council voted on the dogmatic constitution *Lumen Gentium*. Yves Congar wrote about an event that had occurred a few months earlier, one that he considered particularly important.[97] During the plenary session of the theological commission that was held 2–5 March of that same year, Cardinal Garrone indicated the six reasons that led the Commission to insert Chapter 2 on the people of God in the new constitution. Reasons 2 and 3 will be quoted here. Reason 2: 'To set forth, prior to any distinction regarding states of life or ministries, what pertains to the entire Church'. Reason 3: 'In this way, the hierarchy as a form of service inserted within the community would appear more clearly'.[98]

As is well known, this is the path that was taken by the Council. The people of God are mentioned first (Ch. 2 of *Lumen Gentium*), before any mention is made of the hierarchy (Ch. 3). The order of the chapters is of utmost significance. Congar commented on this more than once, praising the positive consequences that ensued for the notion of authority:

> [...] the sequence adopted was: Mystery of the Church, People of God, Hierarchy. Thus the highest value was given to the quality of disciple, the dignity attached to Christian existence as such or the reality of an ontology of grace, and then, to the interior of this reality, a hierarchical structure of social organization. [...] Is this not, also, what we find when we study the theme of service and of the hierarchy as service in the New Testament? It is within a whole people characterized by service as by its own proper form of existence that certain members are placed in a position of command which is, in the last analysis, a post of responsibility for service.[99]

In a similar text published in his *Le Concile au jour le jour, Troisième session*, Congar explained how the Council had avoided giving to the hierarchy an absolute value, but instead emphasized how it only finds its proper place in relation to another reality that has priority:

The entire Church is presented as composed of *disciples*, it is the 'we' of Christians […]. By that very fact, the first value put forward is not the hierarchical structure (that is obviously not negated or played down!) but what could be called the ontology of grace, Christian existence, the Christian human being. The rest of the schema is consistent with this option: when speaking of the episcopacy, for example, it focuses on its sacramental nature. With regard to this priority given to Christian existence, the value of 'hierarchy' comes in *second* place: I do not say that it is *secondary*, i.e. unimportant, but that it takes second place. Hierarchy is not laid out as an absolute value that would exist independently, without reference to others. It appears above all as a *service* rendered to Christian existence and to the community of disciples.[100]

When reading the text quoted above we can grasp the distance covered thanks to *Lumen Gentium*. The Council recovered the reality of the *ecclesia** as the fundamental reality. As a result, ministries, hierarchy and authority could be considered in a manner consistent with the mystery of which they are a part.

Congar liked to stress the importance of finding the proper door to enter on a question. 'In general terms it may be said that the door whereby one enters on a question decides the chances of a happy or less happy solution.'[101] Entering through the door of the 'people of God' allows one to affirm that all the baptized are equal, 'an unfettered equality', 'the absolute rejection of any kind of discrimination', 'since the love of God is poured out on all and on everyone without the slightest distinction'.[102] At the same time, one can speak legitimately of 'hierarchy', because it can now be perceived as a service; it is functional,[103] a service provided within a people that is itself at the service of humanity. This is clearly expressed by Congar: 'The notion of people of God as it can be drawn from Holy Scripture allows us to affirm both the equality of all the baptized in the dignity of their Christian existence – which is described as priestly, royal and prophetic – and the diversity of services or offices, which involves an inequality from a functional perspective.'[104]

A healthy conception of authority emerges from the texts I have just quoted. They also show how Congar evolved towards a vision of the Church that was less clerical. In no way does this mean that Congar failed to recognize the irreplaceable role of ordained ministry or that he played down its importance. To think that clericalism reinforces the sense of ordained ministry is a mistake, because in fact the negative reactions aroused by clericalism[105] in the end jeopardize the very reality it is intended to promote.

Congar himself gave an account of how his thought evolved on this question. A remark made by another expert at Vatican II seems to have been decisive: '[...] Fr. Daniélou, who had very keen insights and fell on sensitive points like a hawk on a field mouse, noted in *Dieu vivant* that I had defined the laity in terms of the clergy.'[106] In a remarkable text published in 1971 entitled 'My Path-Findings in the Theology of Laity and Ministries', a text which has rightly been compared to St. Augustine's 'Retractations', Congar wrote:

> In *Jalons* [*Lay People in the Church*] I put a reasoned construction on the data by distinguishing two titles of participation or two fashions of participating in the priesthood, kingship and prophetic office of Christ: one title referring to the dignity or quality of existence common to all Christians, the other to the authority, and thus superiority, that characterizes instituted ministers. I now wonder whether this is a happy mode of procedure.[107]

As we have just seen, he henceforth preferred 'the door' of community and the people of God. As a result, 'the decisive coupling is not "priesthood/laity", as I used it in *Jalons*, but rather "ministries/modes of service to the community"'.[108]

Authority and freedom

Affected by the upheavals of 1968 and striving to understand them, Congar reflected once more on the question of authority in the Church. The two texts that he published at the time, 'Autorité, initiative, coresponsabilité'[109] and 'Autorité et liberté dans l'Église',[110] were for him an opportunity to re-evaluate and take stock. It would be impossible for me to bring this chapter on authority to a close without mentioning a few of the helpful insights that can be found in these two texts. 'Autorité et liberté dans l'Église' has preserved the tone and style of the talk that it originally was. His article 'Authority, Initiative, and Co-responsibility', which first appeared in *La Maison-Dieu*, is more structured. Although we can easily recognize the same beliefs that Congar put forward in his lecture at Bec Hellouin Abbey, we can also perceive in both these texts that the theologian was expressing himself in a world that had undergone radical change. Realities that were taken for granted yesterday are now rejected. 'The roots of the difficulties which we run into today are philosophical,'[111] wrote Congar. According to Congar, many of the things questioned by our times represent the legacy of the Middle Ages, an era that he loved, but 'that is after all', he reminds us, 'nothing more (in spite of all its greatness), than one historical achievement, and one moment in the life of the Church'. His comments on the historical legacies that have weighed upon the conception and practice of authority were not limited to the Middle Ages; his article published in *La Maison-Dieu* refers also to the sixteenth through to the nineteenth centuries. He joined Emmanuel Mounier in a plea for the Church to free itself from a 'certain sociological burden and from certain forms inherited from the past that have become questionable'. Yves Congar was open to the questions of his contemporaries; this questioning was for him legitimate, but he could only regret that the questions and discussions were sometimes rushed, with no time to get to the bottom of things.

Congar, a remarkably open-minded man, was not naive. He knew that the talk about being open to modern society could be a pretext to ignore a call to conversion. The meaning of the term *reform* in the early Church, he reiterated, is to be reconfigured to Christ. Openness must not be an excuse for self-indulgence or the rejection of authority. Congar was aware of the danger of substituting one sociological conformism for another. The conformism of the late 1960s – characterized by a systematic rejection of authority – is not better than the nineteenth century's infatuation with authority. The true challenge for the Church is to recover what is specifically Christian.

In a world that had drastically changed, the theologian observed that 'young people, consciously or not, participate in a philosophical current for which the point of departure is not a given that is objective and external to the self. It is a question of interpreting oneself to oneself in contact with the world, with others, and even with the Gospel and the Church or the different institutions that exist in the latter.'[112] In this new context, 'tradition and obedience appear as a domination of the object, of the cut and dried, and therefore as a bullying, an alienation harmful to the free realization of the subject'.[113] Congar used a non-scholarly yet effective expression to summarize an aspiration he had noticed among the young: 'one just wishes to be oneself and freely sing one's own song.'[114] Congar warned of the danger of seeing the law and the institution exclusively as agents or factors of alienation. He reminded his readers that St. Thomas 'presents the law as being (from without) with grace (from within) an auxiliary of true self-realization, through the coincidence of our will with the good'.[115] In another text, written approximately a year earlier, he had already recalled the 'traditional and revolutionary formulations of St. Thomas Aquinas' that keep us from false dichotomy: for Thomas, 'the evangelical law – the Christian religion – consists principally in the grace of the Holy Spirit, and secondly in what is necessary or useful to dispose people for this grace or for the use of what pertains to it'. This led him to conclude with wonder: 'What interiority! What personalism! The institution is referred entirely to the event of the Holy Spirit and to the interior edification of persons.'[116] Congar was not unaware that in a legalistic climate, the objectivism of the institution can alienate and trample under foot. But of this same objectivism, he could also write: 'It can, on the other hand, if it presents itself as a group of models which require that one personally assume and live them, promote spiritual liberty and the creative movement whose subject, under the influence of the Holy Spirit, is the person.'[117]

Initiative and authority

Respectful of the positive aspects of modern culture, particularly its attachment to initiative, Yves Congar summarized in the following way a thirst he detected: 'In the Church, there is a desire to think through, in an authentically and fully Christian manner, the relationship between personal initiative and authority, the latter having obviously to take responsibility for the harmonizing of the whole and for unity, for the preservation of unity, or rather the promotion of unity.'[118] This understanding of authority involves a specific conception of unity. Now it is important to see that the conception one has of unity will determine one's way of exercising authority. If unity is considered as a given already in place, then authority will be exercised in a negative way. It will consist in 'keeping people from straying out of the existing framework' or 'in bringing back those who have wandered off'. It is a unity into which one 'must enter or remain without raising questions'.[119] Congar did not hesitate to support another conception of unity: 'Today, we see unity as something that must be *achieved* every day, in a world that ceaselessly asks new questions and is equipped with new resources.'

Was Congar simply yielding here to a modern trend of thought? A closer look at what motivated him leads us to think quite the opposite. New insights can be gained from the article he wrote in 1974 entitled 'La Tri-Unité de Dieu et l'Église'. For Congar, a specifically Christian way of exercising authority, one that is in conformity with faith, must be bound up with a truly Trinitarian faith. 'A Trinitarian view of God, a pneumatology', writes Congar, modifies 'in a notable manner the way one practices initiative and freedom'.[120] It is worth listening to him once more on this important question that we have already come across when we examined the themes of catholicity and reform. What he says has particularly important repercussions on the theme of this chapter: 'A pre-Trinitarian understanding of monotheism is easily reflected in a paternalistic conception of authority. There is no denying that this has existed in history. Paternalism is stamped with kindness and care, but it fails to recognize in a lower rank a capacity for intelligence and initiative.'[121] Let us recall Congar's definition of paternalism: 'Paternalism exists when subordinates are treated as children that have to be looked after, for their own good, depriving them of control over their own lives.'[122] Congar's wish to leave behind a paternalistic conception of authority was in no way a rejection of the role of authority in the Church. Congar always tried to defuse potential misunderstandings on this question.[123] He attempted to do this in his article 'Authority, Initiative, and Co-responsibility'. At a time when almost everything was being called into question, he dared to write: 'Authority is the right that a person has to determine something in the life of other persons.'[124] This relationship to authority must be personalist in nature, that is, it must be respectful of persons and can be so only by acknowledging the inviolable rights of their intelligence. Congar considered personalism to be a legitimately Christian value;[125] it is only when it is diverted and corrupted that it degenerates into subjectivism and individualism. He valued respect and envisioned it as an important component of the dialogue between superior and subordinate. Together they are called to seek as much light as possible in order to respond to their respective missions. The relationship that unites superior and subordinate 'should not be conceived only in two terms', for when it comes to the exercise of authority within Christianity, 'the authority does not by itself place itself in a position of superiority; constituted in this position, it seeks and serves the same good, the same truth as the one who is subordinated.' Mission, then, is the third term that situates the other two in their proper place. And so Congar concluded: 'Thus, without denying its obligations, obedience assumes an aspect of cooperation, of co-responsibility and, therefore, to some degree, of dialogue.' Congar, however, always aware of possible misunderstandings, felt the need to clarify: 'That does not mean that the superior is only a brother with whom one discusses and decides *ex aequo*. Rather, this means that he is actually a brother and that each adapts jointly to the good that both the one and the other seek.'[126]

What would happen if Christians were more Trinitarian in the faith they profess?[127] Authority would be exercised differently. 'A Church that is Trinitarian and pneumatological sees in persons and in particular communities the quality of subjects: subjects of their activity, having their say in determining the rules by which they live; subjects of their personal history, putting to use their gifts and charisms. This has far-reaching consequences in ecclesial life.'[128]

Congar hailed such a theology in a document produced by the *Groupe des Dombes* which he quoted and then commented on: 'The relationships that establish themselves between the ministry and the community in the unity of the Church reflect those between the persons of the Trinity in the divine unity: ministry and community find their source of authority in the person of the Father, of their service in the person of the Son, and of their freedom and communion in the person of the Holy Spirit.'[129] In his comment, wishing to clear up possible misunderstandings that might arise, Congar explained:

> It would be inadequate to associate the image of God the Father with the instituted ministries that occupy the apex of the hierarchy, or the image of the incarnate Son with those who, on an intermediary level, carry out duties of supervision in a spirit of service, or lastly the Holy Spirit with the community of the faithful. The entire people of God, as it is structured, but also as a living body, reflects, each one at his/her place, the qualities belonging to the Three persons. All authority comes from the Father, its source and fundamental origin (cf. Ephesians 3:14). All authority is service; in Christianity, every function should be ascribed to an ontology of service; from one end of the Body to the other, from top to bottom, in width and in depth, all of the living members receive life from the Holy Spirit and communicate through that same Spirit, who is *koinônia*, communication and communion.[130]

Such beliefs led Yves Congar to speak of 'co-responsibility'[131] in the Church. In his lecture 'Autorité et liberté dans l'Église', he called the term 'co-responsibility' 'admirable', and then he added: 'the longing to do things "together", the longing to participate in the decision-making process, is a Christian aspiration that should not surprise us; it belongs to our tradition.'[132] The same Yves Congar who once said, 'My life has been all about rediscoveries',[133] could add: 'What is asked of us is not to give in to some fad or to adopt the taste of the times. No, we must simply rediscover our own deepest tradition.'[134]

* * *

One last point can be added. Congar ascribed to authority a different purpose than that of keeping people in check or bringing back those who have strayed from the fold. Authority, he saw, should walk alongside those who are seeking without merely 'going with the flow'. In this respect, 'authority must learn to become more forward-looking than backward-looking, studying a future to which it rouses us and guides us, accepting the lack of a comfortable viewpoint, because what is being considered is so bound up with the unknown [...]'.[135] In his book, *The Mystery of the Church*, as in other writings, Congar was fond of quoting what Father A.-D. Sertillanges had written on authority: 'Authority teaches itself by its own decision, as an intelligent grain of wheat might learn by watching itself grow, only dimly aware of what it bears within itself.'[136]

CONCLUSION

Yves Congar was fond of Lacordaire (1802–61), someone he often preached on and who comes up frequently in his writings.[1] He admired 'the sense of the possible'[2] that characterized the great French Dominican who restored the Dominican Order in France. He admired his rejection of the 'all or nothing' that kept him from extremes and shielded him from a sterile idealism; he admired his trust. Lacordaire believed that it was possible 'to save the Church *through the Church*'.[3] Cardinal Yves Congar shared the same trust, as his entire life exemplified and as is manifested in his outstanding contribution to Vatican II.

But something else is common to both Dominicans. Congar described Lacordaire as a man who was 'consubstantial with his age'. He had learned to understand the deepest aspirations of his time, and he had loved its ideal of freedom. He believed that 'in the human heart, in the intellectual climate, in the development of human opinion, in laws, in events and historical periods, there exists a fulcrum, a point of support[4] that God can use'. But of course, one must be able to identify this point of support and make use of its potentialities. And Lacordaire considered that ability to be a great art.[5]

It is easy to recognize several features of Congar in Lacordaire. Congar, like Lacordaire, exercised discernment and tried to find points of support for God in the culture of his day. Accordingly, Congar was able to envision an ecclesiology that could embrace the contribution of the subject and allow a Church comprised of persons to emerge. It is in this way that he became aware that 'today perhaps more than ever the Holy Spirit moves the world towards an ideal of fullness'.[6] Congar was an apostle, driven by his faith. He felt the call to resist the atmosphere of pessimism that surrounded him. Congar sought to love the world because ours is the world God loves. He understood that the art of discernment requires the ability to be open to new questions, to the aspirations of the day, to what is entirely new in history, to what can possibly surprise and astonish. He believed that, in discernment, 'there must be a link between what has already been given and the unexpected, between what has been acquired once for all time and what is always new. This link is forged by the Holy Spirit, the Spirit of Jesus, Jesus as Spirit, who is also both "Spirit of truth" and "freedom".'[7] We have seen how his vast knowledge of history kept him from absolutizing what is relative, and he was thus able to help the Church of his day to understand that 'the forms that exist, as true and respectable as they may be, are not the last word about the realities they attempt to translate: dogmas are perfectible, the Church is, in its structures, an open system'.[8] Not only did Congar help the Church to understand these truths, but also he was instrumental in setting up the reforms they require.

The young man who, in the 1920s, for the sake of his love for life, was strong enough to resist l'abbé Lallement; who refused to turn his back on history, possessed as he was by a fundamental realism; who knew intuitively that 'there is novelty; there is something truly real happening in history'[9]: this man became the author of a bold theological corpus.

In his old age, his respect for history remained vigorous, as can be seen when he quoted the words of his friend Marie-Dominique Chenu: '[...] our time is a dimension of the eternity of God.' And he added in the same text: 'by the Incarnation, God has become the subject of a human history. A human history has entered into the eternity of God.'[10]

Cardinal Walter Kasper once said of Congar: 'He foresaw the problems and challenges that we are now facing in the twenty-first century'; and he added this comment about Congar's later works: 'We are still far from having explored all the perspectives he has opened for us.'[11]

And yet, Yves Congar was a humble man who never played the prophet. 'Nothing is more miserable than a false prophet', he once wrote.[12] He simply wanted to be faithful to the God of Jesus Christ, to the Living God, to the mystery of God's unpredictable Breath. For the man of the system, everything is predictable. There can be no surprise. There is no question that does not already have its ready-made answer: 'it is simply a question of taking out from shelf or drawer the appropriate article.'[13] As for Congar, he knew that 'sometimes true spiritual depth is to be found in a mind that does not know the truth but seeks it, whereas superficiality, a lack of any serious spiritual commitment, is apparent in one who goes forward armed with a ready-made orthodoxy whereby all errors are known and refuted. The whole truth is known and formulated [...].'[14] However, Congar cautioned, 'this little game soon proves unplayable when one enters into a dialogue with a real person'.[15]

Congar was a privileged witness of the breaking through of the unpredictable in the life of the Church. He said of Vatican II: 'What I imagined would take thirty years to come about took place in three months.' 'For example, I saw the bishops gathered for the Council come round to the idea of ecumenism in an almost unanimous fashion, in a handful of minutes. That makes me think that the Spirit was at work.'[16]

Congar was disappointed that a number of his contemporaries had failed to understand that the *aggiornamento* (updating) that took place at the Council was not about making the Church fashionable. For him, the Council was about the Spirit's faithfulness that beckons our own. As a result, we would become a people who 'are ready, if necessary, to go beyond what exists at present, who are open to possible developments'. Congar wanted us to 'know how to criticize our assumptions in view of a better fidelity to the tradition, so that we will not only be people with solutions, but also be people who can face up to problems and not turn away from challenges'.[17] For Congar this should come about 'not because of lack of fidelity, but because we have learned to exercise a more difficult and deeper fidelity'.[18]

We have seen how, within each of our themes – Tradition, reform, catholicity, authority – the unexpected could arise at every moment and lead the Church to where it had not planned on going. A system leaves very little room for the unpredictable. That is why the Church is not a system: when the Church lets itself be guided by the Spirit, the Spirit who blows where it chooses, it becomes the home of freedom.

* * *

It is a well-known fact that Congar spent an entire year in the Holy Land. That is where I have chosen to take leave of him. It is not hard to imagine him pacing up and down the seafront at Jaffa, which is the place where for the first time the apostle Peter (Acts 9–10) was made aware of a call to universality. Congar wrote that it was not by accident that Peter had his vision of catholicity at that particular location, because 'the sea attracts and conjures up the notion of immensity'.[19] That is where, for the first time perhaps, a Christian experienced the intimation of a call to be faithful to the future.

NOTES

Notes to the Preface

1   He suffered, according to E. Fouilloux, from medullary angiomatosis. See E. Fouilloux, 'Un théologien dans l'Église du XXe siècle', *Bulletin de Littérature ecclésiastique* CVI/1 (2005), p. 35. Congar explained to Jean Puyo that his illness was not 'multiple sclerosis, but an ailment that was fairly close to it' (*Jean Puyo interroge le Père Congar: Une vie pour la vérité* [Paris: Centurion, 1975], p. 154).

2   Y. C., *Dialogue Between Christians*, trans. Philip Loretz, S.J. (Westminster: The Newman Press, 1966), pp. 32–3.

3   There are many references to meals with Taizé brothers in Y. C., *My Journal of the Council*, trans. Sr. Mary John Ronayne, O.P. and Mary Cecily Boulding, O.P. (Collegeville, MN: Liturgical Press, 2012).

4   Y. C., *Power and Poverty in the Church*, trans. Jennifer Nicholson (Baltimore: Helicon, 1964), pp. 111–12; tr. modified.

5   Y. C., *My Journal of the Council*, p. 613.

6   J. Famerée and G. Routhier, *Yves Congar* (Paris: Cerf, 2008). Before that, J.-P. Jossua, *Yves Congar, Theology in Service of God's People*, trans. Sister Mary Jocelyn, O.P. (Chicago: Priory Press, 1968) is particularly remarkable, as is the unforgettable set of dialogues published in *Jean Puyo interroge le Père Congar. Une vie pour la vérité* (Paris: Centurion, 1975).

7   Y. C., *True and False Reform in the Church*, trans. Paul Philibert, O.P. (Collegeville, MN: Liturgical Press, 2011).

8   I use the word here in its etymological sense: 'according to the whole'. For other explanations of this term, see the Glossary.

9   The word 'authority' comes from the Latin verb *augere*, which means 'to increase', 'to make grow'.

10   Y. C., *La Tradition et la vie de l'Église* (Paris: Cerf, 1984), p. 5. I
     quote here from the 1984 edition, which includes a new preface
     by Congar that is not included in the latest English translation:
     The Meaning of Tradition, trans. A. N. Woodrow (San Francisco:
     Ignatius Press, 2004).

Notes to the Introduction

1   Congar knew that Saint Irenaeus and John Henry Newman had
     used the word 'system' in a positive manner, as had the theological
     'systematicians' who knew that the word of revelation must be
     connected with the questions that concern our entire existence and
     that aim to show the articulations and overall coherence of the
     mystery of faith. These authors did not endorse the approach that
     Congar was criticizing. The 'system' that Congar denounced covers
     another reality that is close to the pejorative meaning which the
     Petit Robert dictionary gives for the word 'system': 'The tendency
     to value internal coherence and the integration into a system over
     the right appreciation of the real.'

2   *Fifty Years of Catholic Theology, Conversations with Yves Congar*,
     edited and introduced by Bernard Lauret, trans. John Bowden
     (Philadelphia: Fortress Press, 1988), p. 70; tr. modified. He also
     said: 'The scholastic way of conceptualizing things that I was
     steeped in is not always helpful when one is trying to understand
     realities like the Church' (quoted in M. Vidal, *Cette Église que je
     cherche à comprendre* [Paris: Éditions de l'Atelier, 2009], p. 39).

3   'I do not regret my formation at the school of St. Thomas and his
     modern disciples. It is a school that privileges an ordered mind.
     But today I realize what this tradition, so focused on definitions
     and analysis, may be missing in regards to the full traditional sense
     of the Church as community.' See Y. C., *Ministères et communion
     ecclésiale* (Paris: Cerf, 1971), p. 15.

4   Y. C. *True and False Reform in the Church*, trans. Paul Philibert
     (Collegeville, MN: Liturgical Press, 2011), p. 318; tr. modified.

5   Y. C., 'Moving Towards a Pilgrim Church', in *Vatican II By Those
     Who Were There*, ed. A. Stacpoole (London: Geoffrey Chapman,
     1986), p. 144. In this article Congar gives a striking example of
     a religion divorced from the world. Citing a study sponsored by
     the Union catholique des scientifiques français, he made a list of
     article topics that were missing from the *Dictionnaire de Théologie*

Catholique (fifteen enormous volumes published between 1903 and 1950). To name a few: Profession, Work, Family, Paternity, Maternity, Economy, Politics. There is a similar formula in Congar's *Le Concile au jour le jour, Troisième session* (Paris: Cerf, 1965), p. 147: 'To a religion without a historical and cosmic vision there corresponds a cosmos without God.'

6   See Y. C., *Lay People in the Church: A Study for a Theology of the Laity*, trans. Donald Attwater (Westminster, MD: Newman Press, 1965), p. 282: 'To put these different aspects into opposition with one another, even separate them [...] is to misunderstand the living organic reality of the total Church.' Only a cursory and superficial reading of Congar could lead one to doubt this point. At Vatican II, he wanted to avoid a council of theologians; for him, this was above all the council of the bishops. See G. Alberigo, 'Réforme et unité de l'Église', in *Cardinal Yves Congar (1904–1995)*, ed. A. Vauchez (Paris: Cerf, 1999), p. 22. Congar did not minimize the role of the hierarchy, but he did not speak *only* of the hierarchy: 'By means of history he wishes to bring back to ecclesial consciousness the buried layers of its treasure' (J.-P. Jossua, *Yves Congar, Theology in the Service of God's People*, trans. Sister Mary Jocelyn, O.P. [Chicago: The Priory Press, 1968], p. 89).

7   See Congar's prefatory letter to G. Michonneau, *Pas de vie chrétienne sans communauté* (Paris: Cerf, 1960), p. 11: 'Father Michonneau, you do not have a system. You are taking into consideration the data that are appropriate to each situation.'

8   Y. C., *Tradition and Traditions: An Historical and a Theological Essay*, trans. Michael Naseby, Part I, and Thomas Rainborough, Part II (New York: The Macmillan Company, 1967), pp. 505–6: 'My studies in the history of ecclesiology have led me to think that perhaps the most important turning point in that history came between the end of the eleventh and the end of the thirteenth centuries. In the way they used a whole number of themes and texts, theologians passed gradually from the level of the spiritual man to that of an assertion of hierarchical privileges, both guaranteed and understood in a juridical way.'

9   Y. C., *L'Église de Saint Augustin à l'époque moderne* (Paris: Cerf, 1970), p. 103. Not available in English translation.

10   Y. C., *L'Église de Saint Augustin à l'époque moderne*, p. 90.

11   Y. C., *L'Église de Saint Augustin à l'époque moderne*, p. 112.

12   Y. C., *L'Église de Saint Augustin à l'époque moderne*, p. 101.

13   Y. C., *L'Église de Saint Augustin à l'époque moderne*, p. 102.

14 Y. C., 'The Historical Development of Authority in the Church. Points for Christian Reflection', in *Problems of Authority*, ed. John M. Todd (Baltimore: The Helicon Press, and London: DLT, 1962), p. 137.

15 Y. C., *L'Église de Saint Augustin à l'époque moderne*, p. 103. On legalism, see also Y. C., *Dialogue Between Christians*, trans. Philip Loretz, S. J. (Westminster, MD: Newman Press, 1966), pp. 233–4 for a good summary of the differences between East and West. For the eastern Christians: 'Our statements seem to them to lack ontological consistency. It is this impression which is so often expressed in the accusation of "juridicism" levelled against us, a juridicism defining *external* situations and relationships. They maintain that this attitude is revealed in our way of speaking of nature and grace, reason and faith, of cosmic and temporal realities and of the Church. Similarly, they feel that our concept of the relation between the faithful and the hierarchy within the Church is juridical in as much as we think of the latter as having *"power over"* the former. Even within the Church the West appears to think in terms of relations between individuals whereas the East thinks of a certain social or community intimacy and inwardness.'

16 Congar is referring to pre-Vatican II ecclesiology.

17 Y. C., 'The Council as an Assembly and the Church as Essentially Conciliar', in Y. C., *Report from Rome II, On the Second Session of the Vatican Council*, trans. Lancelot Sheppard (London: Geoffrey Chapman, Christian Living Series, 1964), p. 185. This text first appeared in German in *Gott in Welt (Festgabe Karl Rahner)* (Fribourg: Herder, 1963), pp. 865–95; tr. modified.

18 Y. C., *L'Église de Saint Augustin à l'époque moderne*, p. 364.

19 Y. C., *L'Église de Saint Augustin à l'époque moderne*, p. 367. See also Y. C., *Essais œcuméniques* (Paris: Centurion, 1984), p. 10: 'We must distinguish between Tridentinism and the Council of Trent.'

20 Y. C., *Église et papauté* (Paris: Cerf, 2002), pp. 59–60. Congar attributed this phrase to the Italian historian G. Alberigo. He came back to this at length at the end of his life in his *Fifty Years of Catholic Theology, Conversations with Yves Congar*, pp. 3–4.

21 Y. C., *Essais œcuméniques*, p. 10.

22 Y. C., *L'Église de Saint Augustin à l'époque moderne*, p. 368. One should underline here the word 'theoretical', for Congar knew that in the actual life of the Church there was more than this 'juridicism'.

23 Y. C., *L'Église de Saint Augustin à l'époque moderne*, p. 381.

24 Y. C., *L'Église de Saint Augustin à l'époque moderne*, p. 382.

25 'He was undoubtedly the greatest ecclesiologist not only of the twentieth century but of the entire history of the Church as well' (Richard McBrien, 'I Believe in the Holy Spirit. The Role of Pneumatology in Yves Congar's Theology', in *Yves Congar, Theologian of the Church*, ed. Gabriel Flynn [Louvain: Peeters, 2005], p. 305).

26 Y. C., *L'Église de Saint Augustin à l'époque moderne*, pp. 382–3.

27 Y. C., *L'Église de Saint Augustin à l'époque moderne*, p. 383.

28 Y. C., 'The Historical Development of Authority in the Church', p. 140.

29 Y. C., 'The Historical Development of Authority in the Church', p. 140.

30 For this notion and its evolution, see Y. C., *L'Église de Saint Augustin à l'époque moderne*, p. 383 and n. 42, as well as Y. C., 'Moving Toward a Pilgrim Church', in *Vatican II by Those Who Were There*, ed. Alberic Stacpoole (London: Geoffrey Chapman, 1986), pp. 132–4.

31 Y. C., *L'Église de Saint Augustin à l'époque moderne*, p. 383.

32 He described this conception of the Church as 'Catholics living together and forming a cultural world of their own, [...] quite self-sufficient' (Y. C., 'Moving Toward a Pilgrim Church', p. 138).

33 Y. C. 'Two Aspects of Apostolic Work: The Priest as Head of his People and as Apostle', in Y. C., *Priest and Layman*, trans. P. J. Hepburne-Scott (London: DLT, 1967), p. 198.

34 Y. C., 'L'Ecclésiologie de Saint Bernard,' in *Église et Papauté*, pp. 167–8.

35 Y. C., 'The Historical Development of Authority in the Church', p. 133; tr. modified. See also Congar's Introduction to the *Traités anti-donatistes de Saint Augustin* (*Œuvres de Saint Augustin* 28, Quatrième série, Vol.1 [Paris: Desclée de Brouwer, 1963], pp. 9–133).

36 See John Paul II's telegram to Cardinal Lustiger and to Fr. Timothy Radcliffe in *Documentation catholique* 92 (1995), p. 690. Also Y. C., *My Journal of the Council*, trans. Sr. Mary John Ronayne, O.P., and Mary Cecily Boulding, O.P. (Collegeville, MN: Liturgical Press, 2012), p. 871. Congar himself lists there the conciliar texts that he authored. *My Journal of the Council* contains a wealth of information about the spirit and atmosphere in which the Council worked.

37 H. Legrand, 'Yves Congar (1904–1995): Une passion pour l'unité', in *Nouvelle Revue Théologique* 126/4 (2004), p. 547. See there the quotation by Monica Wolff on p. 529: 'Yves Congar is one of those theologians whose work was so well-integrated into the theology of Vatican II that it is almost impossible to measure its initial impact and originality.' In the year of Congar's death, Peter Steinfels wrote of Congar in the *New York Times* that he was 'one of a handful of scholars who utterly changed Roman Catholicism' (quoted in E. T. Groppe, *Yves Congar's Theology of the Holy Spirit* (New York: Oxford University Press, 2004), p. 12.

38 Y. C., Congar, 'A Last Look at the Council', in *Vatican II By Those Who Were There*, ed. Alberic Stacpoole (London: Geoffrey Chapman, 1986), p. 338. The passage by Pope John XXIII was part of a speech he gave to the diocesan leaders of *L'Azione Cattolica*, on 9 August 1959.

39 J. P. Jossua, *Yves Congar, Theology in the Service of God's People*, p. 40.

40 Y. C., *The Meaning of Tradition*, trans. A. N. Woodrow (San Francisco: Ignatius Press, 2004), p. 59; tr. modified.

41 Y. C., *The Meaning of Tradition*, p. 163; tr. modified. See also Y. C., *Tradition and Traditions, An Historical and a Theological Essay*, trans. Michael Naseby and Thomas Rainborough (London: Burns and Oates, 1966), pp. 395–96: 'This Church exists principally in spiritual people, or, in the Pauline and Augustinian sense of the word, in the saints. […]. The use of such a title serves to indicate the preference given to the realities of spiritual anthropology over juridical categories.' And p. 394: 'The Fathers and the medievals understand by "Church" not only, as we have seen, the whole Christian community, but a fundamentally spiritual reality. It is true that beginning with the Gregorian Reform (last third of the eleventh century) a juridical mode of thought slowly infiltrated into ecclesiological ideas and ended by an invasion of the modern treatises *De Ecclesia*.' And p. 395: 'They understand it [the Church] as the totality of human beings who are converted to Jesus Christ, and in whom the Spirit is at work' (tr. modified).

42 Y. C., 'L'ecclésiologie de Saint Bernard', in *Église et papauté*, pp. 162–3; and see p. 163n. 203, for the references to St. Bernard. Congar also writes, p. 173: 'Bernard sees the Church less as the total set of the means of grace – the Church is that for him also, obviously –, but as the total set of the people seeking God who live the drama and struggles of sanctity.'

43 Y. C., *The Meaning of Tradition*, p. 59.

44 Y. C., *Journal d'un théologien* (Paris: Cerf, 2001). Not available in English translation.

45 See Jossua, *Yves Congar, Theology in the Service of God's People*, p. 52 and p. 60 on truth; and *Jean Puyo interroge le Père Congar. Une vie pour la vérité* (Paris: Centurion, 1975), p. 38: 'I had a real cult of Truth.' And Congar recalled this quotation by Madame Swetchine: 'I loved truth with the love one has for a person.'

46 Y. C., *Journal d'un théologien*, p. 185.

47 *Jean Puyo interroge le Père Congar. Une vie pour la vérité* (Paris: Centurion, 1975). Not available in English translation.

48 *Jean Puyo interroge le Père Congar*, p. 102.

Notes to Chapter 1

1 Y. C., *Journal d'un théologien* (Paris: Cerf, 2001), p. 46.

2 J.-P. Jossua, *Yves Congar, Theology in the Service of God's People*, trans. Sister Mary Jocelyn, O.P. (Chicago: The Priory Press, 1968), p. 41.

3 Y. C., *Journal d'un théologien*, p. 46.

4 Y. C., *Dialogue Between Christians*, trans. Philip Loretz, S.J. (Westminster, MD: The Newman Press, 1966), p. 4; tr. modified.

5 Y. C., *Journal d'un théologien*, p. 48.

6 Under the title *Journal de la Guerre, 1914–1918*, the Éditions du Cerf published in 1997 the five school notebooks written by Yves Congar as a child during World War I. This book's annotations and commentary are by S. Audoin-Rouzeau and D. Congar.

7 Y. C., *Dialogue Between Christians*, p. 4; tr. modified.

8 After three years at the Carmelite seminary, Congar changed direction and entered the Dominican order in 1925. From 1926 to 1931 he was at the provincial *studium* of Le Saulchoir, which was moved to Kaïn-la-Tombe, near Tournai in Belgium, following the 1903 expulsion from France of religious communities. Congar studied philosophy there for a year, and did four years of theology. See E. Fouilloux, 'Un théologien dans l'Église du XXe siècle', *Bulletin de Littérature ecclésiastique* CVI/1 (2005), pp. 21–38 (24–5). The Dominicans kept the 'Saulchoir' name (it means 'place planted with willow trees') when they returned to France and settled in Étiolles, near Évry, in 1939. They stayed there until 1971,

at which point Le Saulchoir moved to the 13th *arrondissement* in Paris.

9   Y. C., *Journal d'un théologien*, p. 26.

10   'In a more general way it gave me the presentiment of the benefit which the mind of a Frenchman could derive from contact with Germany [...]. I owe a great deal to German genius and science and to my numerous German friends' (Y. C., *Dialogue Between Christians*, p. 6; tr. modified). See also M. Vidal, *Cette Église que je cherche à comprendre* (Paris: Éditions de l'Atelier, 2009), p. 31: 'Yves-Marie Congar wrote a history of ecclesiology. He is one of the great masters on the history of ecclesiology, and he is recognized as such even by the Germans: that is saying a lot, for a Frenchman!'

11   D. de Rougemont reported these facts at the Colloque de Dourdan in 1982. See G. Lurol, *Mounier I, Genèse de la personne*, Philosophie européenne, Éditions universitaires, 1990, p. 147, and n. 625. See also Y. C., *Une passion: l'unité* (Paris: coll. Foi Vivante, 1974), pp. 18–19. According to J. Famerée, Congar's reading of the Orthodox theologians influenced him more than his writings might seem to indicate. See his article 'Orthodox Influence on the Roman Catholic Theologian Yves Congar, O.P.: A Sketch', in *St. Vladimir's Theological Quarterly* 39 (1995), pp. 409–16. In addition to the names cited here, one might add Khomiakov, Soloviev and Florovsky. We know that Congar learned Russian. Father Gratieux, a specialist on Khomiakov and the Slavophile movement, was his first Russian teacher. See *Une passion: l'unité*, p. 19.

12   Y. C., *Dialogue Between Christians*, p. 24. There is another statement of self-critique reported by Maurice Vidal in *Cette Église que je cherche a comprendre*, p. 39. In reference to his book *Lay People in the Church*, Congar said: 'It was much too systematized; get rid of that.'

13   Y. C., *Dialogue Between Christians*, p. 3.

14   Y. C., *Dialogue Between Christians*, p. 2.

15   Unity was already the topic of his lectorate thesis in 1928.

16   H. Legrand, 'Yves Congar (1904–1995): une passion pour l'unité', *Nouvelle Revue Théologique* 126/4 (2004), pp. 531–2. See also Y. C., *Dialogue Between Christians*, p. 5.

17   At that time Lallement was a sub-deacon. Ordained as a priest in 1919, he joined the faculty of philosophy at the Institut Catholique of Paris, and stayed there until 1963. Y. C., *Journal d'un théologien*, p. 30; and on the same page n. 66 by E. Fouilloux.

18 Y. C., *Journal d'un théologien*, p. 32.

19 Y. C., *Journal d'un théologien*, pp. 32–3 for all the quotations in this paragraph.

20 Y. C., *Journal d'un théologien*, p. 42.

21 Y. C., *Journal d'un théologien*, p. 42. Congar wrote elsewhere: 'One of the most serious limits of clerical formation in the nineteenth century was the absence of the historical dimension' (*Le Concile au jour le jour, Quatrième session* [Paris: Cerf, 1966], p. 172).

22 Y. C., *Journal d'un théologien*, pp. 42–3.

23 Y. C., *Lay People in the Church*, trans. Donald Attwater (Westminster, MD: The Newman Press, 1965), p. 258.

24 Jossua noted also 'his love of life, a taste for the things of the earth, a refusal of idealism, of evasion, of gnosis, of a disembodied spiritualism, of a supernaturalism which condemns (or at least suspects) the human' (*Yves Congar, Theology in the Service of God's People*, p. 41).

25 Jossua, *Yves Congar, Theology in the Service of God's People*, p. 127. See also Y. C., *Journal d'un théologien*, p. 70, where Congar indicates that he has been on this path since 1931.

26 This quotation comes from *Vraie et fausse réforme dans l'Église* (1950), p. 615. See also p. 45 in the same work. Paul Philibert's translation, *True and False Reform in the Church* (Collegeville, MN: Liturgical Press, 2011) which is based on the second edition, revised by Congar and published in 1968, does not include this passage, since Congar decided, as a gesture toward the 'traditionalists' of his day, to omit it in the revised version. The English translation used here is taken from Y. C., 'Attitudes toward Reform in the Church', trans. Bernard Gilligan, p. 85, which appeared in *Cross Currents* 4 (1951) and contains excerpts from *True and False Reform in the Church*. See also Y. C., *I Believe in the Holy Spirit*, Vol. II, trans. David Smith (New York: Seabury, 1983), p. 16: 'Individual persons, however, want to be the subjects of their actions.' See also *Fifty Years of Catholic Theology, Conversations with Yves Congar*, edited and introduced by Bernard Lauret, trans. John Bowden (Philadelphia: Fortress Press, 1988), p. 67: 'Today people no longer want to be objects but subjects […]. People want to be free and responsible subjects.' In a 1946 article that was published in *Études*, recalling that historicity and subjectivity characterize the modern world, Jean Daniélou wrote: 'These two abysses force theological thinking to be dilated' (quoted by Jean-Claude Petit, 'La compréhension de la théologie

française au XXe siècle', in *Laval théologique et philosophique*, 48 [October 1992], p. 418).

27 'Actualité de Kierkegaard' appeared in issue VI, 32 (1934) of *La vie intellectuelle*. Excerpts are also cited in *Istina* XVI (1996), pp. 17–21.

28 Y. C., 'Actualité de Kierkegaard', p. 34.

29 This does not make Congar, the son of St. Thomas, into a disciple of Kierkegaard. Congar rejected subjectivism and did not hide, throughout his work, the fact that he could not accept that which, for him, constituted the underlying principle of Barth's thought, and which he also believed Barth got from Kierkegaard: 'the absolute qualitative heterogeneity between the finite and the infinite' ('Actualité de Kierkegaard', p. 10n. 1). We can understand why Congar as a Thomist could not accept this idea. However, we can also understand how well he must have connected with other aspects of Kierkegaard's thought, especially when Kierkegaard denounced the fact that 'Christendom has turned Christianity into a system'. See J. Brun's article 'Kierkegaard' in *Encyclopaedia Universalis*, DVD 2008 edition.

30 Y. C., 'Actualité de Kierkegaard', p. 16.

31 Y. C., 'Actualité de Kierkegaard', p. 19.

32 Congar expressed regret that he had not received a better philosophical formation.

33 E. T. Groppe, *Yves Congar's Theology of the Holy Spirit* (New York: Oxford University Press, 2004), p. 86.

34 J. P. Jossua, *Yves Congar, Theology in the Service of God's People*, p. 48.

35 B. Dupuy, Art. 'Newman', in *Encyclopaedia Universalis*, DVD 2008 edition. See also J. Famerée, *L'ecclésiologie d'Yves Congar avant Vatican II* (Louvain: Bibliotheca Ephemeridum Theologicarum Lovaniensium CVII [1992]), p. 74.

36 Y. C., *The Mystery of the Church*, 2nd revised edition, trans. A. V. Littledale (Baltimore: Helicon, 1965), p. 145. A few lines later, in developing the same thought, Congar refers to Newman.

37 G. Martelet, *Deux mille ans d'Église en question*, vol. 2 (Paris: Cerf, 1990), p. 222.

38 J. Famerée, 'L'ecclésiologie du Père Yves Congar. Essai de synthèse critique', *Revue des Sciences philosophiques et théologiques* 76 (1992), pp. 377–418.

39 Congar wrote of Newman that he had 'a full blown Catholic sense

in a concrete and historical, not rigidly systematic, vision of things'
(*Le Concile au jour le jour, Quatrième session* [Paris: Cerf, 1966],
p. 27.) Jean Guitton wrote of Newman: 'He was so haunted by the
existence of singular things that he never took care to locate his
ideas and views within a system [...]' (*Œuvres Complètes de Jean
Guitton* [Paris: Desclée de Brouwer, 1968], p. 142.

40   Y. C., 'Attitudes toward Reform in the Church', p. 86.

41   Y. C., 'Attitudes toward Reform in the Church', p. 86.

42   Cited by B. Dupuy in his article 'Newman', in *Encyclopaedia
Universalis*, DVD 2008 edition.

43   Johann Adam Möhler, *Unity in the Church or the Principle of
Catholicism: Presented in the Spirit of the Church Fathers of the
First Three Centuries*, trans. Peter C. Erb (Washington: Catholic
University of America Press, 1995). Originally published in German
in 1825.

44   Johann Adam Möhler, *L'unité dans l'Église* (Paris: Cerf, *Unam
Sanctam* no. 2, 1938). A translation problem delayed its
publication, so *L'unité dans l'Église* actually became the second
volume in the series. Congar's wish underscores how much
Möhler's book influenced him.

45   Y. C., *L'Église de Saint Augustin à l'époque moderne* (Paris: Cerf,
1970), p. 418. Charles Taylor, *Sources of the Self: The Making of
the Modern Identity* (Cambridge, MA: Harvard University Press,
1989), p. 384: 'And so among the great aspirations which come
down to us from the Romantic era are those towards reunification:
bringing us back in contact with nature, healing the divisions within
between reason and sensibility, overcoming the divisions between
people, and creating community.'

46   Y. C., *L'Église de Saint Augustin à l'époque moderne*, p. 423.

47   Congar quoted this text in *L'Église de Saint Augustin à l'époque
moderne*, p. 420. Möhler's thought developed over time, as he
accorded a greater place to Christology, and consequently, to the
human principle. He 'preserves his ideas on spiritual interiority,
on the Trinitarian foundation of the Church, but he finds a more
satisfying formulation for the active relationship between the external
element, particularly the priesthood and the hierarchy, and the
intimate spiritual element' (*L'Église de Saint Augustin à l'époque
moderne*, pp. 421–2). Alain Nisus has written that Congar travelled
in the opposite direction: 'In his first writings the accent was mostly
Christological, even incarnationist; progressively he integrated
pneumatology into his ecclesiology' ('L'Esprit-Saint et l'Église dans

l'œuvre d'Yves Congar', *Transversalités* 98 [2006], p. 121). In the rest of his article Nisus adds all the necessary nuances.

48 Y. C., *L'Église de Saint Augustin à l'époque moderne*, p. 420.

49 Y. C., *L'Église de Saint Augustin à l'époque moderne*, p. 420. We can also add this remark by M.-D. Chenu on the Tübingen School – a remark that is all the more interesting when one realizes that it was Chenu who brought Möhler to the young Congar's attention: 'One of the characteristics of this school was the perfect coherence between the speculative renewal of theology and the reasoned observation of pastoral experiences at all levels, from fundamental catechesis to the practices of piety' ('Tradition et sociologie de la foi', in *Église et tradition*, J. Betz and H. Fries (eds) [Le Puy and Lyons: Éditions Xavier Mappus, 1963], p. 225).

50 Ignace de la Potterie, S. J. and Stanislaus (sic) Lyonnet, *The Christian Lives by the Spirit*, Preface by Yves Congar, trans. John Morriss (Staten Island, NY: Alba House, 1971).

51 Y. C., Preface to *The Christian Lives by the Spirit*, pp. v–vi.

52 Y. C., Preface to *The Christian Lives by the Spirit*, p. vi; tr. modified. This is a commentary on Hebrews 8:10. The word 'testament' is used here in the sense of 'covenant'. It is the gift of the Holy Spirit that really constitutes the new covenant.

53 Y. C., Preface to *The Christian Lives by the Spirit*, p. vii.

54 Y. C., Preface to *The Christian Lives by the Spirit*, p. viii; tr. modified.

55 Y. C., Preface to *The Christian Lives by the Spirit*, p. x; tr. modified.

56 Y. C., Preface to K. Delahaye, *Ecclesia Mater* (Paris: Cerf, 1964), p. 17.

57 Y. C., Preface to *Ecclesia Mater*, p. 17.

58 Y. C., Preface to *The Christian Lives by the Spirit*, p. ix.

59 *Lumen Gentium* II, 9. *Vatican Council II, The Conciliar and Post Conciliar Documents*, Austin Flannery, General Editor, Revised Edition (Boston: St. Paul Editions, 1988), pp. 359–60.

60 J.-P. Jossua, *Yves Congar, Theology in the Service of God's People*, p. 147.

61 *Jean Puyo interroge le Père Congar. Une vie pour la vérité* (Paris: Centurion, 1975), p. 43. This is a reproach addressed by Congar to Father Lallement: see Y. C., *Journal d'un théologien*, pp. 42–3. Jossua writes about the study of history: it 'corrodes simplistic attitudes, abstract reasoning, relative facts turned into absolutes,

fiction within which one can live' (*Yves Congar, Theology in the Service of God's People*, p. 89).

62 Y. C., 'Théologie historique', in *Initiation à la pratique de la théologie* (Paris: Cerf, 1982), p. 237.

63 *Jean Puyo interroge le Père Congar*, p. 43.

64 Y. C., *Église Catholique et France moderne*, p. 15.

65 Y. C., *Journal d'un théologien*, p. 57. See also the article by Michael Quisinsky, 'Congar avec Chenu et Féret au Saulchoir des années 1930', in *Transversalités* 98 (2006), pp. 3–35. This author writes, p. 5: 'Le Saulchoir between 1928 and 1938 was the place not only for "the decisive awakenings" which Congar mentions, but also for the implementation of a large part of the theological options which marked his entire œuvre.'

66 Y. C., 'Le Père M.-D. Chenu', in *Bilan de la théologie du XXe siècle*, vol. II (Paris-Tournai: Casterman, 1970), p. 773. All the quotations in this paragraph come from this article.

67 Not available in English. See reference to the French edition in preceding note.

68 Y. C., 'Le Père M.-D. Chenu', p. 777. Congar cites these words without saying where they come from. In June 1945, Vercors had written an article entitled 'La Vertu d'indignation'.

69 Y. C., 'Le Père M.-D. Chenu', p. 788.

70 Y. C., 'Le Père M.-D. Chenu', p. 789.

71 Y. C., 'Le Père M.-D. Chenu', pp. 789–90. In the epigraph of the first chapter of his *Église catholique et France moderne*, Congar placed the following text by the English writer Frederick Rolfe: 'This world is sick for the Church, but She would never confess it as long as the Church posed as her rival' (Baron Frederick Corvo, *Hadrien VII* [Montana: Kessinger Publishing, 2005], p. 128). By mistake Congar wrote 'Hadrien VI', in *Le Concile au jour le jour, Quatrième session*, p. 18.

72 Chapter 3 of *Une école de théologie. Le Saulchoir* was published again in M.-D. Chenu, O.P., *La Parole de Dieu*, Vol. I: *La foi dans l'intelligence* (Paris: Cerf, 1964), pp. 243–67. The quotation is from p. 247.

73 M.-D. Chenu, O.P., *Une école de théologie, La Parole de Dieu*, Vol. I: *La foi dans l'intelligence*, p. 257.

74 Y. C., *Journal d'un théologien*, p. 42.

75 M.-D. Chenu, *Une école de théologie*, p. 266.

76   M.-D. Chenu, *Une école de théologie*, p. 266.

77   M.-D. Chenu, *Une école de théologie*, p. 266.

78   Y. C., *Situation et tâches présentes de la théologie* (Paris: Cerf, 1967), p. 72. The first part of this text first appeared in *Informations Catholiques Internationales* 286 (15 April 1967). It was published again and gave its title to the Cerf volume during that same year.

79   Y. C., *Situation et tâches présentes de la théologie*, p. 72.

80   Y. C., 'Pour un sens vrai de l'Église', in *Cette Église que j'aime* (Paris: Cerf, 1968), p. 94.

81   This was P. Lecocq's expression, cited by Congar in *Situation et tâches présentes de la théologie*, p. 72, and in his article 'L'influence de la société et de l'histoire sur le développement de l'homme chrétien', *Nouvelle Revue Théologique* 96 (1974), p. 681.

82   Y. C., *I Believe in the Holy Spirit*, Vol. II, trans. David Smith (New York: Seabury, 1983), p. 35. On the same theme, see Y. C., 'L'Église, antique fontaine d'une eau jaillissante et fraîche' in *La Vie Spirituelle* 636 (1980), pp. 32–3.

83   Y. C., *The Mystery of the Church*, p. 103.

84   J. Famerée, 'Originalité de l'ecclésiologie du Père Congar', *Bulletin de Littérature ecclésiastique* CVI/1 (2005), p. 104. He saw this originality as Congar's ability to 'listen to concrete life and his theological interpretation of that life, connected with an impressive mastery of the ecclesial tradition's documents, starting with Scripture'.

85   Jossua, *Yves Congar, Theology in the Service of God's People*, trans. Sister Mary Jocelyn, O.P. (Chicago: The Priory Press, 1968).

86   Not available in English translation. The title can be translated as: 'The Theological Service in the Church'.

87   J.-J. Von Allmen, 'Note sur le ministère de docteur en ecclésiologie réformée', in *Le service théologique dans l'Église, Mélanges offerts à Yves Congar* (Paris: Cerf, 1974), p. 81.

88   *Jean Puyo interroge le Père Congar*, p. 45.

89   This happy turn of phrase comes from M. J. Le Guillou, 'Yves Congar', in *Bilan de la théologie du XXe siècle*, vol. II, Robert Van der Gucht and Herbert Vorgrimler (eds) (Paris: Casterman, 1970), p. 797.

90   In his recent book, on Congar, *La Relation de l'Esprit Saint au Christ* (Paris: Cerf, 2010), François-Marie Humann also underlines how Congar's captivity was a turning point in his life.

91   Y. C., *Journal d'un théologien*, p. 31. See n. 68 by E. Fouilloux.

92   Y. C., *La Traditions et les traditions*, vol. I *Essai historique* (Paris: Arthème Fayard, 1960). Published as the first part of *Tradition and Traditions: An Historical and a Theological Essay*, trans. Michael Naseby (New York: Macmilan, 1967).

93   E. Fouilloux, 'Un théologien dans l'Église du XXe siècle', *Bulletin de Littérature ecclésiastique* CVI/1 (2005), p. 22.

94   Y. C., *Journal d'un théologien*, p. 49; and *Dialogue Between Christians*, pp. 29–30.

95   *Jean Puyo interroge le Père Congar*, p. 94; and Y. C., *Journal d'un théologien*, p. 49.

96   This book, which was published in 1948, was presented as a 'Testimony by Yves Congar'. No publisher is mentioned, only 'En dépôt chez Albert Renault'. Not available in English translation.

97   Y. C., *Dialogue Between Christians*, pp. 29–30.

98   Quoted by Le Guillou, 'Yves Congar', p. 797.

99   Y. C., *Journal d'un théologien*, pp. 30–1.

100 *Jean Puyo interroge le Père Congar. Une vie pour la vérité* (Paris: Centurion, 1975). A book of interviews with Yves Congar. Not available in English translation.

101 *Jean Puyo interroge le Père Congar*, pp. 238–9. For the following quotation see p. 41.

102 Y. C., 'My Path-Findings in the Theology of Laity and Ministries', *The Jurist* 32 (1972), pp. 169–70.

103 Y. C., 'Tradition et ouverture', in *Fidelité et Ouverture*, ed. Gérard Soulages (Paris: Mame, 1972), pp. 55–6.

104 Y. C., *Je crois en l'Esprit Saint*, Vol. I, L'expérience de l'Esprit (Paris: Cerf, 1979); Vol. II, Il est Seigneur et Il donne la vie (Paris: Cerf, 1979); Vol. III, Le fleuve de vie (Paris: Cerf, 1980). English translation: *I Believe in the Holy Spirit*, 3 vol., trans. David Smith (New York: Seabury, 1983).

105 See 'Avant-propos' by André Vauchez, in *Cardinal Yves Congar (1904–1995)*, ed. A. Vauchez (Paris: Cerf, 1999), p. 7.

106 See *Jean Puyo interroge le Père Congar*, p. 171; Chapter 7 of this book is entitled 'Who is my God?' *Les voies du Dieu vivant* is the title chosen by Congar for a 1962 collection of studies on theology and the spiritual life. In English, the first two parts of this book were published under the title *The Revelation of God*, trans. A. Manson and L. C. Sheppard (London: Darton, Longman and Todd, 1968

and New York: Herder and Herder, 1968). The other chapters were published under the title *Faith and Spiritual Life*, trans. A. Manson and L. C. Sheppard (London: Darton, Longman and Todd, 1968).

107   Y. C., *I Believe in the Holy Spirit*, Vol. II, trans. David Smith (New York: Seabury, 1983), p. 16.

Notes to Chapter 2

1   Tradition is spelled with a capital letter for reasons that will become clear as the chapter progresses.

2   Congar is the author of three volumes entirely dedicated to the theme of Tradition. *La Tradition et la vie de l'Église* (Paris: Cerf, 1963) is addressed to a wider audience. It was republished in 1984 in French by Les Éditions du Cerf and includes a new preface in which Congar said how attached he was to this book. The English translation, *The Meaning of Tradition*, trans. A. N. Woodrow (San Francisco: Ignatius Press, 2004) does not include the new preface. With the help of J.-P. Jossua, *Yves Congar, Theology in the Service of God's People*, trans. John Bowden (Philadelphia: Fortress, 1988), p. 112, we can identify three main meanings to the word 'tradition' for Congar: 'as the *act* of transmitting or passing on something, as in a relay race; then (and at the same time), as the *content* communicated – what one passes on – the reality of Christianity; and finally, a more specific meaning according to which there is distinguished in this total content the ensemble of the Scriptures, the Bible as a book, and tradition in the sense of transmission by some means other than writing, whether by what is found in the Book, but in a living and personal way (this is essential), or by something else (which is possible but very secondary).'

3   Y. C., *The Meaning of Tradition*, p. 118; tr. modified. In this sense we can say, with F. Bousquet, 'In the Church, Tradition is mission!' See 'La dimension apostolique de la Tradition selon le P. Congar', *Transversalités* 98 (2006), p. 77.

4   Y. C., *The Meaning of Tradition*, trans. A. N. Woodrow (San Francisco: Ignatius Press, 2004), p. 1.

5   Y. C., *The Meaning of Tradition*, p. 1.

6   'I would not like very much to be labelled as a "conservative", but I do want and hope truly to be a man of Tradition' (Y. C., 'Tradition et Ouverture', *Fidélité et Ouverture*, ed. Gérard Soulages [Paris: Mame, 1972], p. 55).

7   Y. C., *La Tradition et les traditions*, vol 1: *Essai Historique* (Paris: Arthème Fayard, 1960). In English Volumes 1 and 2 are published together: *Tradition and Traditions*, Part 1 trans. Michael Naseby; Part 2 trans. Thomas Rainsborough (New York: Macmillan, 1967).

8   Jean-Georges Boeglin, *La question de la Tradition dans la théologie catholique contemporaine* (Paris: Cerf, 1998), p. 315. See also p. 323: 'The mission of the Word and that of the Spirit are connected. And it is because of this connection that traditionalism is impossible in Christianity.'

9   These words are from Henri Bouillard, *Conversion et grâce chez Saint Thomas d'Aquin* (Paris: Aubier, 1944), p. 219. We can also recall the words of the historian Jaroslav Pelikan: 'Tradition is the living faith of the dead, traditionalism is the dead faith of the living' (J. Pelikan, *The Vindication of Tradition* [New Haven: Yale University Press, 1984], p. 65).

10   Y. C., *The Meaning of Tradition*, pp. 77–8. See also Y. C., *Le Concile de Vatican II* (Paris: Beauchesne, 1984), pp. 89–90.

11   Y. C., *The Meaning of Tradition*, p. 157.

12   Y. C., *The Meaning of Tradition*, p. 158

13   Y. C., *The Meaning of Tradition*, p. 166; tr. modified. In *Vraie et fausse réforme dans l'Église*, p. 524, he also wrote: 'Tradition includes within itself all the expressions of the faith of the Church as it received them from the apostles and formulated them since, through space and time: this is what one might call the monuments of tradition. But tradition itself is even more profound than this, and also much more continuous. It does not consist only or even mainly in a certain number of ideas, of statements more or less attested by the texts, but in the continuous transmission and presence in the Church of its very principle, *of the reality of Christianity*.' This page is taken from a section of the book that is not included in Paul Philibert's recent translation *True and False Reform in Church* (Collegeville, MN: Liturgical Press, 2011).

14   Y. C., *The Meaning of Tradition*, p. 157. Using another word but expressing the same meaning, he wrote that Christianity is 'a transmitted message and reality [...]. It is not invented or founded. It is an "instituted" religion [...]. In its history there is a constitutive or institutive moment, from which all the other moments are constituted and instituted.' See Y. C., 'Le chrétien, son présent, son avenir et son passé', *Lumière et vie* 108 (1972), p. 73.

15   Y. C., *The Meaning of Tradition*, p. 157.

16 Y. C., 'Le chrétien, son présent, son avenir et son passé', p. 73.

17 Y. C., 'Institutionalized Religion,' in *The Word in History*, St. Francis Xavier Symposium, ed. Patrick Burke (New York: Sheed and Ward, 1966), p. 155.

18 Y. C., 'Tradition et Ouverture', 55. He used the same words in *Un peuple messianique* (Paris: Cerf, 1975), p. 8.

19 *Jean Puyo interroge le Père Congar*, p. 239. See Y. C., 'Le chrétien, son présent, son avenir et son passé', p. 75. We can cite here also another good formula on Tradition: 'It is the permanence of the past in the present, at the heart of which it prepares the future' (Jossua, *Yves Congar, Theology in the Service of God's People*, p. 113).

20 F. Bousquet, 'La dimension apostolique de la Tradition selon le P. Congar', *Transversalités* 98 (2006), p. 77. Michael J. Himes makes the same point: 'The primary Catholic meaning of tradition has shifted from *tradita* to *traditio*, i.e. from a body of truths to the corporate life which finds expression in the act of passing on the community's grasp of revelation in one generation to subsequent generations' ('The Ecclesiological Significance of the Reception of Doctrine', *The Heythrop Journal* 33/2 [1992], pp. 151–2).

21 Y. C., *The Meaning of Tradition*, p. 112; tr. modified.

22 Y. C., *The Meaning of Tradition*, p. 121.

23 Y. C., *The Meaning of Tradition*, p. 112. In *I Believe in the Holy Spirit*, vol. 2, trans. David Smith (New York: Seabury, 1983), p. 16, Congar recognized that in Catholicism 'in the modern era there has been a distrust of expressions of the personal principle'. He explained: 'excessive emphasis has been given in the Catholic Church to the role of authority and there has been a juridical tendency to reduce order to an observance of imposed rules, and unity to uniformity.' To underline the personal dimension in Christianity, Congar liked to recall that 'the liturgy celebrates the saints one at a time' (*Essais œcuméniques* [Paris: Centurion, 1984], p. 300 and p. 304).

24 This expression comes from the English poet Alfred Tennyson (1809–92).

25 Y. C., *Lay People in the Church*, trans. Donald Attwater (Westminster, MD: Newman Press, 1965), p. 327.

26 Y. C., *Situation et tâches présentes de la théologie* (Paris: Cerf, 1967), p. 72. In a conference paper delivered in Prague in 1967, Congar reacted to a Marxist analysis that argued that for Christians the concrete reality is not really a source of knowledge, and that 'history in the end is just the indefinite alteration of the identical that is repeated as it is deformed'. His paper was published in *Nouvelle Revue Théologique* 96 (1974) under the title: 'L'influence de la société et de l'histoire sur le développement de l'homme chrétien', p. 681.

27   Y. C., 'Le chrétien, son présent, son avenir et son passé', p. 73.

28   Y. C., *The Meaning of Tradition*, p. 114.

29   Y. C., *The Meaning of Tradition*, p. 114. There is no 'modernism' in Congar. For him, revelation is complete, but the unfolding of history is necessary for all of its riches to appear. We can recall here B. Sesboüé's good formulation of this: 'If revelation is complete from Christ's side of things, through the decisive event of his life among us, it is not complete from our side of things, in the sense that revelation is effective only when it is received. New things will always come to enrich the confession of Christ, as they have in the past' (*Jésus-Christ dans la tradition de l'Église* [Paris: Desclée, 1982], pp. 312–13).

30   Y. C., 'Changements et continuité dans l'Église', in *Notre foi* (Paris: Beauchesne, 1967), pp. 62–3.

31   Walter Kasper, *La théologie et l'Église* (Paris: Cerf, 1990), p. 203.

32   Henri de Lubac, *Catholicism: Christ and the Common Destiny of Man* (San Francisco: Ignatius Press, 1988), p. 323. When thinking about what was accomplished by the Church Fathers, de Lubac writes, pp. 321–2: 'For although the Church rests on eternal foundations, it is in a continual state of rebuilding, and since the Fathers' time it has undergone many changes in style; and without in any way considering ourselves better than our Fathers, what we in turn have to build for our own use must be built in our own style, that is, one that is adapted to our own needs and problems.'

33   Y. C., *The Meaning of Tradition*, p. 158.

34   I am paraphrasing various expressions used by Kasper.

35   Y. C., *The Meaning of Tradition*, p. 118; tr. modified.

36   Y. C., *The Meaning of Tradition*, p. 125. St. Irenaeus is for him a good example of the theologian of Tradition and apostolic succession, 'that is, precisely of the identity through that which changes' (Y. C., 'L'Église, antique fontaine d'une eau jaillissante et fraîche', *La Vie Spirituelle* 636 [1980], p. 32). The same idea has been eloquently expressed by Richard Lennan in his book, *The Ecclesiology of Karl Rahner* (Oxford: Clarendon Press, 1997), p. 4:

'In the last hundred years, [...] a new awareness of the implications of historical existence has made it possible to substantiate the paradoxical claim that change, far from being subversive of identity, is actually the precondition for maintaining intact what is essential to the authenticity of that identity.'

37 Hans Urs von Balthasar, *Presence and Thought: Essay on the Religious Philosophy of Gregory of Nyssa*, trans. Mark Sebanc (San Francisco: Ignatius Press, 1995), p. 12; quoted by Congar in *The Meaning of Tradition*, p. 117; tr. modified.

38 Y. C., *Lay People in the Church*, p. 328, and p. 310.

39 J. Moingt, 'Ouverture ou repli de la Tradition,' in *Études* 345 (1976), p. 546.

40 On the different meanings that Congar gave to this expression, see Y. C., *Lay People in the Church*, pp. 288–9 and in the same work, Appendix II: 'The *Sensus Fidelium* in the Fathers', pp. 465–7.

41 Y. C., *Lay People in the Church*, pp. 282–3 and Y. C., *Chrétiens en dialogue*, p. 275. Some of Congar's remarks on *sobornost'* were considered to be 'too highly specialized' and were omitted in the English translation *Dialogue Between Christians*; see translator's note p. 279n. 2.

42 Y. C., *Dialogue Between Christians*, p. 234; tr. modified.

43 Y. C., 'Autorité et liberté dans l'Église', in *À temps et à contretemps* (Paris: Cerf, 1969), p. 19 and p. 27.

44 J. Famerée, 'Originalité de l'ecclésiologie du Père Congar', *Bulletin de Littérature ecclésiastique* CVI/1 (2005), p. 104.

45 Y. C., 'Aspects ecclésiologiques de la querelle entre mendiants et séculiers dans la seconde moitié du XIIIe siècle et le début du XIVe', in *Archives d'histoire doctrinale et littéraire du Moyen Âge* 28 (1961), pp. 35–151. Not available in English translation. I am grateful to Dom Ghislain Lafont for drawing my attention to this important study by Congar, and to Helen Millet for giving me a copy of it.

46 'Aspects ecclésiologiques de la querelle entre mendiants et séculiers dans la seconde moitié du XIIIe siècle et le début du XIVe', p. 147.

47 'Aspects ecclésiologiques de la querelle entre mendiants et séculiers dans la seconde moitié du XIIIe siècle et le début du XIVe', p. 146. The expression reminds me of the famous word of Congar at the time of the condemnation of worker priests: 'One can condemn a solution if it is wrong, but one does not condemn a problem' ('L'avenir des prêtres-ouvriers' in *Témoignage chrétien* [25 September 1953]).

48 Y. C., 'Aspects ecclésiologiques de la querelle entre mendiants et
    séculiers dans la seconde moitié du XIIIe siècle et le début du XIVe',
    p. 146. He wrote also on p. 81: 'To think through a new reality is
    a difficult task for those who have at their disposal only received
    categories.'

49 Hans Urs Von Balthasar, *Presence and Thought*, trans. Mark
    Sebanc (San Francisco, CA: Ignatius Press, 1995), pp. 10–11.

50 Y. C., *The Meaning of Tradition*, p. 117.

51 Y. C., *Vraie et fausse réforme dans l'Église*, 1st edn (Paris: Cerf,
    1950), p. 525. This page is in a section of the book that is not
    included in Paul Philibert's recent translation *True and False
    Reform in Church*.

52 Y. C., *Laity, Church and World*, trans. Donald Attwater (Baltimore:
    Helicon Press, 1960), p. 35.

53 Y. C., *The Meaning of Tradition*, pp. 116–17. He also wrote:
    'The apostolic witness is not a pure material repetition of facts. It
    incorporates a penetration and an expression of the meaning of
    these facts' ('Pneumatologie dogmatique', in *Initiation à la pratique
    de la théologie*, Bernard Lauret and François Refoulé (eds), Volume
    II: Dogmatique I, [Paris: Cerf, 1982], p. 488).

54 J. Famerée and G. Routhier, *Yves Congar* (Paris: Cerf, 2008), p. 92.

55 Y. C., 'L'Église, antique fontaine', p. 34.

56 Y. C., 'Pneumatologie dogmatique', p. 488.

57 Y. C., 'Pneumatologie dogmatique', p. 496.

58 Y. C., 'Moving Towards a Pilgrim Church', in *Vatican II By
    Those Who Were There*, ed. Alberic Stacpoole (London: Geoffrey
    Chapman, 1986), p. 133.

59 Y. C., *The Word and the Spirit*, trans. David Smith (London:
    Geoffrey Chapman, and San Francisco: Harper and Row Publishers,
    1986), p. 80. From being a 'founder' situated only in the past,
    Christ becomes 'the ever present foundation'. According to Congar,
    this was St. Paul's vision (1 Corinthians 3:11). 'This does not rule
    out the fact that the institution has been achieved, but it prevents us
    from believing that it is no more than that' ('Pneumatology Today',
    The American Ecclesiastical Review 167 [1973], p. 442).

60 Y. C., *I Believe in the Holy Spirit*, vol. II, p. 34.

61 Y. C., 'Pneumatology Today', pp. 442–3; tr. modified.

62 These fine formulations are found in Congar's last theological
    work: *The Word and the Spirit*, pp. 71–2. Let us recall what

Congar saw ever more clearly as he progressed in his research: 'If, out of all my long studies on the Holy Spirit, I was able to keep just one conclusion, it would be: the good health of pneumatology is Christology' (Y. C., 'Actualité de la pneumatologie', p. 25).

63   Y. C., *The Meaning of Tradition*, p. 122.

64   Y. C., *The Meaning of Tradition*, p. 26.

65   Y. C., *The Meaning of Tradition*, p. 27.

66   Y. C., *Tradition and Traditions*, pp. 364–5; tr. modified.

67   Y. C., *The Meaning of Tradition*, p. 26.

68   Primarily his book *Senses of Tradition* (Oxford: Oxford University Press, 2000). See also his articles: 'The Analogy of Tradition: Method and Theological Judgment', in *Theological Studies* 66/2 (2005), pp. 358–80 and for a more accessible text, 'Faithfulness to Tradition', in *The Cresset* 69/4 (Easter 2006), pp. 18–27.

69   Y. C., 'La Réception comme réalité ecclésiologique', in *Revue des Sciences philosophiques et théologiques* 56 (1972), pp. 369–403; republished in Y. C., *Église et papauté*, pp. 229–66. In English: 'Reception as an Ecclesiological Reality', in *Election and Consensus in the Church*, Concilium 77, edited by Giuseppe Alberigo and Anton Weiler (New York: Herder and Herder, 1972), pp. 43–68.

70   For example, see Y. C., *The Word and the Spirit*. In underlining the role of the Spirit who makes it possible for us to recognize Christ's presence in history, Congar writes: 'He does so in history, that is, throughout the successive generations and in the conflict of ideas, the interweaving of events and the emergence not only of new methods, problems and errors [...]' (*The Word and the Spirit*, p. 28).

71   *Lettres intimes de Teilhard de Chardin* (Paris: Aubier Montaigne, 1974), p. 58.

72   See William L. Portier's review of *Senses of Tradition* in *Modern Theology* 18/1 (2002), pp. 136–7.

73   'This present moment, then, and not an idealized past *in illo tempore* imagined as a divine present, becomes the retrospective point of orientation in tradition's visual field. And as the present-day observer surveys the past of a developing tradition, continuity shows itself in retrospect, initially in the judgments of individual believers and eventually in the shared judgment of all together' (*Senses of Tradition*, p. 83).

74   John E. Thiel, 'Faithfulness to Tradition', *The Cresset*, p. 23. Also, p. 22: 'Even though a tradition can be conceived chronologically, from past to present, its sacred continuity is actually affirmed

in faith retrospectively, looking backward into the past.' The continuity he is writing about here is better understood by analogy with the plot of a novel: 'The traditional novel's twisting plot need not, and when well executed does not, vitiate narrative coherence as set out to the point of shocked expectations. The shocking eventuality, discovery, realization, conversion, or manifestation achieves its narrative power only against the backdrop of an established coherence. The appearance of the new does not discard that coherence but redefines it now in light of the new, enriching and extending the order of plot in ways that could not be anticipated before' (*Senses of Tradition*, p. 158).

75 Thiel, 'Faithfulness to Tradition', p. 25.

76 Y. C., *The Word and the Spirit*, p. 55; tr. modified.

77 J. Famerée and G. Routhier, *Yves Congar*, p. 147.

78 If Tradition is at the same time the act of transmitting and the content of what is transmitted, then catholicity – we will see this better in Chapter 4 – is this dynamism of unity and universality which dilates the content so it can germinate in all its fullness.

79 Y. C., *Esquisses du Mystère de l'Église* (Paris: Cerf, 1941). English translation: *The Mystery of the Church*, 2nd rev. edn, trans. A. V. Littledale (Baltimore and Dublin: Geoffrey Chapman Ltd and Helicon Press Inc., 1965).

80 Y. C., *The Mystery of the Church*, p. 101 and p. 104; tr. modified.

81 The last French edition was published in 1996: Heinrich Denzinger, *Symboles et définitions de la foi catholique*, under the direction of Peter Hünermann, for the original edition, and of J. Hoffmann for the French edition (Paris: Cerf, 1996). This edition took into account some of Congar's critiques in 1963. A new Latin-English edition has just been published, updated by Peter Hünermann: *Denzinger Enchiridion Symbolorum: A Compendium of Creeds, Definitions, and Declarations of the Catholic Church* (San Francisco: Ignatius Press, 2012).

82 Y. C., 'Du bon usage de "Denzinger"', in *Situation et tâches actuelles de la théologie*, p. 126.

83 The article 'Du bon usage du "Denzinger"' was first published in *L'ami du clergé* (23 May 1963), pp. 321–9; and then again in Congar, *Situation et tâches présentes de la théologie* (Paris: Cerf, 1967) which I am following for the page references. Not available in English translation.

84 Y. C., 'Du bon usage de "Denzinger"', p. 117.

85 Y. C., 'Du bon usage de "Denzinger"', p. 113.

86 For the meaning of this word, see the box on p. 115 in Ch. 5, and the glossary.

87 For some examples of this, see Y. C., 'Du bon usage de "Denzinger"', p. 117n. 9. What Congar expresses here corresponds to what Thiel called a 'dramatic development'. For this theme, see Thiel, *Senses of Tradition*, chapter 3.

88 Y. C., 'Du bon usage de "Denzinger"', pp. 120–1. These texts were included in later editions of *Denzinger*.

89 Y. C., *L'Épiscopat et l'Église Universelle* (Paris: Cerf, 1962). The declaration of the German bishops and the words of Pius IX can be found in the appendices (pp. 729–36) to the article by O. Rousseau, O.S.B, 'La vraie valeur de l'épiscopat dans l'Église d'après d'importants documents de 1875', pp. 709–29. The text by the German bishops is reproduced, along with the apostolic letter addressed by Pius IX to the German bishops and a part of the consistory allocution of 15 March 1875. The French translation of the German bishops' text is in the article by O. Rousseau. The signature 'Pius XI' (p. 725) is obviously a misprint: it was of course Pius IX.

90 Declaration by the German bishops, January 1875.

91 *L'Épiscopat et l'Église universelle*, p. 718.

92 Y. C., 'Du bon usage de "Denzinger"', p. 121.

93 Y. C., *The Meaning of Tradition*, p. 69.

94 Y. C., 'Du bon usage de "Denzinger"', p. 125.

95 Y. C., 'Du bon usage de "Denzinger"', p. 127.

96 Y. C., 'Du bon usage de "Denzinger"', p. 133.

97 On the meaning to give to this term, which is often used improperly, see Y. C., 'A Semantic History of the Term "Magisterium"', in *Readings in Moral Theology* No. 3: *The Magisterium and Morality*, (eds) C. Curran and R. McCormick (New York: Paulist Press, 1982), pp. 297–313.

98 Y. C., 'Du bon usage de "Denzinger"', p. 127. Similar and powerful remarks on the same question in *Divided Christendom*, p. 29.

99 Y. C., 'Du bon usage de "Denzinger"', p. 129. We know that 'one of the misfortunes of theology', as Congar put it, 'was the atomization into articles without an inner union with a living center' (Y. C., 'Christ in the Economy of Salvation and in Our Dogmatic Tracts', trans. Aimée Bourneuf, R.S.C.J., *Concilium* 11 [1966], p. 21).

100 Y. C., *The Meaning of Tradition*, p. 149; tr. modified.

101 Y. C., *The Meaning of Tradition*, p. 149.

102 For Congar, the post-Tridentine controversies were watershed moments when theology and spirituality became separated, like two separate domains in which each is self-sufficient. As a result, Tradition appears to be like the mechanical transmission of a deposit of faith already constituted.

103 See Y. C., *Tradition and Traditions*, p. 397; tr. modified.

104 Y. C., 'Du bon usage du "Denzinger"', p. 130.

105 'Yves Congar, un pionnier de l'unité': an unsigned editorial that appeared in *Istina* XLI/2 (1996), p. 113.

106 Y. C., *Le Concile au jour le jour, Quatrième session* (Paris: Cerf, 1966), p. 27.

107 We can admire the eloquence with which Urs Von Balthasar expressed this: 'Being faithful to tradition most definitely does not consist, therefore, of a literal repetition and transmission of the philosophical and theological theses that one imagines lie hidden in time and in the contingencies of history. Rather, being faithful to tradition consists much more of imitating our Fathers in the faith with respect to their attitude of intimate reflection and their effort of audacious creation, which are the necessary preludes to true spiritual fidelity' (Hans Urs von Balthasar, *Presence and Thought*, p. 12).

108 Y. C., 'Les Théologiens, Vatican II et la théologie', in Y. C. *Le Concile de Vatican II* (Paris: Beauchesne, 1984), pp. 89–90. See also Y. C., *Le Concile au jour le jour, Quatrième session*, p. 26: 'The future of the Church is to be present to the future of the world.'

109 For his great book which is known by the title of *Truth and Method*, Gadamer had initially thought of the title *Foundation for a Philosophical Hermeneutic*, but in 1959 (the book was published in German in 1960), even the German editor thought that 'the term "hermeneutic" was a bit exotic'. See the article 'Gadamer' by Jean Grondin in *Encyclopaedia Universalis*, DVD 2008 edition. In 1972, Congar wrote that even if the term 'hermeneutic' is used with some exaggeration it still 'fulfils multiple and necessary functions'.

110 Y. C. 'Le chrétien, son présent, son avenir et son passé', in *Lumière et Vie* 100 (1972), pp. 72–82. Not available in English translation.

111 Y. C., 'Le chrétien, son présent, son avenir et son passé', p. 75. Claude Geffré defined in a similar way the purpose of hermeneutics: 'The will to interpret the Christian message in function of our

historical experience' ('Profession théologien: retour sur plus de quarante ans de pratique', in *Laval théologique et philosophique* 62/1 [2006], pp. 7–21).

112 Y. C., 'Le chrétien, son présent, son avenir et son passé', p. 75.

113 Y. C., 'Le chrétien, son présent, son avenir et son passé', p. 75.

114 Y. C., *I Believe in the Holy Spirit*, Volume II 'He is Lord and Giver of Life', trans. David Smith (New York: Seabury, 1983), p. 39. Pannenberg's text, 'La signification de l'eschatologie pour la compréhension de l'apostolicité et de la catholicité de l'Église' was published in French in *Istina* 1 (1969), pp. 154–70. This is a revised version of a presentation made by Pannenberg to the working group of the Roman Catholic Church and the World Council of Churches. In *I Believe in the Holy Spirit*, Vol II, p. 69, Congar summarized Pannenberg's article. An English translation by Keith Crim of Pannenberg's text, 'The Significance of Eschatology for an Understanding of the Apostolicity and Catholicity of the Church', is available in a collection of Pannenberg's essays: *The Church* (Philadelphia: The Westminster Press, 1983).

115 Y. C., *I Believe in the Holy Spirit*, Vol II, p. 69; tr. modified.

116 Jean-Georges Boeglin, *La question de la Tradition*, p. 320.

117 This point is well made by Boeglin, *La question de la Tradition*, p. 321.

118 Y. C, *I Believe in the Holy Spirit*, Vol II, p. 41; tr. modified.

119 Woflhart Pannenberg, 'The Significance of Eschatology for an Understanding of the Apostolicity and Catholicity of the Church', trans. Keith Crim, *The Church* (Philadelphia: The Westminster Press, 1983), p. 53; tr. modified.

120 Y. C., *I Believe in the Holy Spirit*, Vol. II, p. 39; tr. modified.

121 Y. C., *I Believe in the Holy Spirit*, Vol. II, p. 41.

122 John O'Malley, 'Vatican II: Did Anything Happen?', *Theological Studies* 67 (2006), p. 9.

123 Y. C., *Église catholique et France moderne*, p. 53.

124 Y. C., *The Meaning of Tradition*, p. 117.

125 Y. C., *Situation et tâches présentes de la théologie*, p. 72.

126 Y. C., *Église catholique et France moderne* (Paris: Hachette, 1978). Not available in English translation. One can also admire the extraordinary intellectual openness and serenity of Congar in his conversations with Bernard Lauret in *Fifty Years of Catholic Theology: Conversations with Yves Congar*, trans. John Bowden

(Philadelphia: Fortress, 1988), ed. B. Lauret. Congar was 83 years old at the time.

127   Y. C., *Église catholique et France moderne*, p. 17.

128   Y. C., *Église catholique et France moderne*, p. 10.

Notes to Chapter 3

1   Jean-Pierre Jossua, *Yves Congar, Theology in the Service of God's People*, trans. Sister Mary Jocelyn, O.P. (Chicago: The Priory Press, 1968), p. 53.

2   Y. C., *Situation et tâches présentes de la théologie* (Paris: Cerf, 1967), p. 9.

3   H. de Lubac, *The Splendor of the Church*, trans. Michael Mason (San Francisco: Ignatius Press, 1999), p. 218; tr. modified. Originally published in French: *Méditation sur l'Église* (Paris: Aubier-Montaigne, 1953).

4   H. de Lubac, *The Splendor of the Church*, p. 279.

5   Y. C., *True and False Reform in the Church*, trans. Paul Philibert. O.P. (Collegille, MN: Liturgical Press, 2011). The original French edition was published under the title: *Vraie et fausse réforme dans l'Église* (Paris: Cerf, 1950). For even earlier reflections by Congar on the theme of reform, see 'True and False Reform in the Church', in *Orate Fratres* 23 (1948–9), pp. 252–9.

6   J. Famerée, 'Formation et ecclésiologie du "premier" Congar', in *Cardinal Yves Congar (1904–1995)*, ed. A. Vauchez (Paris: Cerf, 1999), p. 64.

7   J. Famerée and G. Routhier, *Yves Congar* (Paris: Cerf, 2008), p. 206.

8   Jean-Pierre Jossua, in Y. C., *Écrits Réformateurs* (Paris: Cerf, 1995), p. 171.

9   *Jean Puyo interroge le Père Congar. Une vie pour la vérité* (Paris: Centurion, 1975), p. 117.

10   Congar himself mentioned this in the second edition which has been used by Paul Philibert in his recent translation of *True and False Reform in the Church* (Collegeville, MN: Liturgical Press, 2011), p. 2.

11   Y. C., *Divided Christendom. A Catholic Study of the Problem of Reunion*, trans. M. A. Bousfield (London: Centenary Press, 1939),

p. 272; tr. modified. It is with this book that the *Unam Sanctam* series was opened. The Éditions du Cerf have taken the excellent initiative of making this book available on the Internet at http://www.editionsducerf.fr/site_congar/cadre_gal.htm and have included the corrections that in 1948 Congar had intended to make in a new edition that was never published. Congar cites this same passage in *True and False Reform in the Church*, p. 21. The Introduction to *True and False Reform*, p. 17, begins with these words: 'The Church has always tried to reform itself.' One recalls the words of Vatican II: 'Christ summons the Church to continual reformation as she sojourns here on earth. The Church is always in need of this [...]' (*Unitatis Redintegratio*, 6).

12 Congar quotes, among others, F. Mourret, who had written in 1937: 'It is a fact that the Church has never ceased to work at reforming itself' (*True and False Reform*, p. 52n. 1). See the anthology of texts on the theme of reform in Saverio Xeres and Matthias Wirz, *Una chiesa da riformare* (Bose: Edizione Quiqajon, 2009).

13 G. Ladner, *The Idea of Reform: Its Impact on Christian Thought and Action in the Age of the Fathers* (Cambridge: Harvard University Press, 1959). See Congar's article 'Comment l'Église doit se renouveler sans cesse', *Irénikon* 34 (1961), p. 342n. 2.

14 Y. C., 'Renewal of the Spirit and Reform of the Institution', trans. John Griffiths, *Concilium* 73 (1972), p. 42.

15 A. Vauchez, Foreword to *Cardinal Yves Congar 1904–1995*, ed. A. Vauchez (Paris: Cerf, 1999), p. 7. Congar wrote: 'Vatican II was set to be a council of reform' (*Le Concile de Vatican II* [Paris: Beauchesne, 1984], p. 58).

16 Paul VI was referring here to his encyclical *Ecclesiam Suam*.

17 Y. C., *True and False Reform*, p. 334; tr. modified.

18 Y. C., *True and False Reform*, p. 225.

19 Y. C., *True and False Reform*, p. 218.

20 Y. C., *True and False Reform*, pp. 229–30.

21 Y. C., *True and False Reform*, p. 298.

22 Y. C., *True and False Reform*, pp. 264–89.

23 Y. C., *Dialogue Between Christians*, p. 44 and Y. C., 'Autorité et liberté dans l'Église', in *À temps et à contretemps* (Paris: Cerf, 1969), p. 38.

24 Jossua, *Yves Congar, Theology in the Service of God's People*, p. 55; tr. modified.

25 Y. C., *True and False Reform*, p. 264. On p. 267, Congar writes: 'Only what's done in cooperation with the nature of time itself can conquer time.'

26 Y. C., *True and False Reform*, p. 266; tr. modified.

27 The complete text is in *Documentation Catholique* 1541 (June 1969), p. 506. We note that even the very serious *Documentation Catholique* does not cite accurately the title of Congar's book which is 'Vraie et fausse réforme *dans* l'Église' ['True and False Reform *in* the Church'], and not 'Vraie et fausse réforme *de* l'Église' ['True and False Reform *of* the Church']. This is a frequent mistake. Congar refers again to the audience of Paul VI, 'where he quoted my own book' in *I Believe in the Holy Spirit*, vol. II, trans. David Smith (New York: Seabury, 1983), p. 62n. 19.

28 Y. C., *True and False Reform*, p. 24. Later, in an article published in *Irénikon*, 'Comment l'Église Sainte doit se renouveler sans cesse', p. 324, Congar distinguished between the need for reform that was experienced for pastoral reasons in the period that followed the second world war, and the fifteen or twenty years of the modernist crisis, when the demands and the search for renovation came out of an intellectual critique.

29 François-Marie Humann, *La relation de l'Esprit-Saint au Christ, une relecture d'Yves Congar* (Paris: Cerf, 2010), p. 153.

30 Y. C., *True and False Reform*, p. 130.

31 Y. C., *True and False Reform*, p. 130.

32 Congar explained what he meant by 'reformism': 'I understand by it a tendency toward reform, and not so much the movement itself toward reform or the ensemble of activities which reform entails as what preceded these things and provides their context' (*True and False Reform*, p. 17, 'Remarks on Vocabulary').

33 Y. C., *True and False Reform*, p. 314.

34 See Jean-Pierre Jossua, *Signification de quelques retours sur le passé dans l'œuvre d'Yves Congar* in *Cardinal Yves Congar*, ed. A. Vauchez (Paris: Cerf, 1999), p. 95: 'When we speak of reforms, we do not do so from an abstract, ideological point of view. It is an undertaking that is born *from the reality of the living Church...*'

35 Y. C., *Journal d'un théologien* (Paris: Cerf, 2001), p. 295.

36 Y. C., *Journal d'un théologien*, p. 296.

37 Y. C., *Journal d'un théologien*, p. 303.

38 Congar will sometimes use the Greek word *ecclesia* instead of the

French translation 'Église' (Church) to avoid having his readers think too easily they know what it is about.

39   Y. C., *Journal d'un théologien*, p. 303.

40   Y. C., *True and False Reform*, p. 52.

41   Y. C., *True and False Reform*, p. 317; 'Attitudes Toward Reform', trans. Bernard Gilligan, *Cross Currents* 4 (1951), p. 89.

42   In the binomial 'structure and life', and at this stage of Congar's theology, J. Famerée discerns a certain dominance of the Christological principle, which Congar sought to complete later with a more developed pneumatology: 'L'ecclésiologie du Père Yves Congar', *Revue des Sciences philosophiques et théologiques* 76 (1992), p. 384. P. Guilmot, basing himself on the revised edition of *Jalons pour une théologie du laïcat* [*Lay People in the Church*] made by Congar in 1964, addenda p. 648f., writes that Congar 'was himself a victim' of the 'structure and life separation' (*Fin d'une Église cléricale?* [Paris: Cerf, 1969], p. 162). See also Rémi Chéno, 'Les *retractationes* d'Yves Congar sur le rôle de l'Esprit Saint dans les institutions ecclésiales', *Revue des Sciences philosophiques et théologiques* 91 (2007), pp. 265–84. Congar himself became more aware of the limitations of this 'structure and life' binomial when describing the Church, though he did not completely abandon it. See Y. C., *The Word and the Spirit*, trans. David Smith (San Francisco: Harper and Row, 1986), p. 81.

43   Y. C., 'Bulletin d'ecclésiologie', *Revue des Sciences philosophiques et théologiques* 54 (1970), p. 111, quoted by A. Nisus, 'L'Esprit Saint et l'Église dans l'œuvre d'Yves Congar', *Transversalités* 98 (2006), p. 110.

44   *Lay People in the Church*, p. 262; tr. modified.

45   Y. C., 'Renewal of the Spirit and Reform of the Institution', trans. John Griffiths, *Concilium* 73 (1972), p. 48.

46   Y. C., *Vraie et fausse réforme dans l'Église* (Paris: Cerf, 1950), p. 621. The passage on 'traditionalism' [Fr: *intégrisme*] was removed by Congar from the second revised edition of *Vraie et fausse réforme dans l'Église* published in 1969. Congar hoped that the suppression of these pages would be understood as a gesture of peace toward the various 'traditionalist' milieus of his day. A portion of the suppressed passage can be read in English in Y. C., 'Attitudes Towards Reform in the Church', trans. Bernard Gilligan, *Cross Currents* 4 (1951), pp. 85–7. 'Intégrisme' at the time was translated by 'integralism' whereas 'traditionalism' is more commonly used today.

47 Y. C., *Vraie et fausse réforme dans l'Église*, p. 621.

48 Y. C., *True and False Reform*, pp. 7–9, and in Y. C., *Écrits réformateurs*, p. 173.

49 J. Famerée and G. Routhier, *Yves Congar*, p. 180.

50 J. Famerée and G. Routhier, *Yves Congar*, p. 177.

51 Y. C., 'Attitudes Towards Reform in the Church', p. 82. Or in Paul Philibert's translation: 'Because they lack a backbone, certain animals have to be enveloped in a shell' (Y. C, *True and False Reform*, p. 313). Congar adds: 'In attitudes of defensiveness that above all avoid risk (and so also avoid what is new, if not vitality itself), there is a feeling of weakness and sometimes even of fear. It is because we are not sure of ourselves that we can feel eclipsed culturally and dynamically by a world that we know in only a distant way. Fright makes us put up barriers' (*True and False Reform*, p. 313).

52 Often attributed to Ozanam, this expression is actually much older. It is said to be the cry of the monk Salvien who took refuge in Marseille and witnessed the barbarian invasions of Gaul and the fall of the Roman Empire. He died around 480. Congar writes in *True and False Reform*, pp. 43–4: 'The accumulation of venerable old pieces of furniture in its cultural baggage creates an impossibility for the Church "to move on to the barbarians" according to the famous remark of Ozanam.' Tr. modified.

53 H. de Lubac, *The Splendor of the Church*, p. 282; tr. modified.

54 Congar is the author of the article entitled 'Apôtre et apostolat' ['Apostle and Apostolate'] in *Encyclopædia Universalis*, DVD 2008 edition.

55 Y. C., 'Comment l'Église doit se renouveler sans cesse', p. 341.

56 Y. C., *True and False Reform*, p. 240.

57 Jossua, *Yves Congar, Theology in the Service of God's People*, p. 127.

58 Y. C., *True and False Reform in the Church*, p. 42. To my knowledge Congar did not ever bring this project to completion.

59 See pages 16–17 above.

60 Y. C., 'Attitudes Towards Reform in the Church', p. 86; tr. modified.

61 Y. C., *Journal d'un théologien*, p. 59.

62 These words by Étienne Gilson, which are part of a letter from Gilson to de Lubac, are cited in Henri de Lubac, *At the Service of*

the Church, Henri de Lubac Lubac reflects on the Circumstances that Occasioned his Writings, trans. Anne Elizabeth Englund (San Francisco: Communio Books, Ignatius Press, 1993), p. 26. See also *Letters of Étienne Gilson to Henri de Lubac*, trans. Mary Emily Hamiton (San Francisco: Ignatius Press, 1988), pp. 94–5.

63   Article 'Modernisme' in *Encyclopædia Universalis*, DVD 2008 edition.

64   Y. C., *Tradition and Traditions, An historical and a theological essay*, trans. Michael Naseby, Part One, and Thomas Rainborough, Part Two (New York: Macmillan, 1967), p. 457.

65   M.-D. Chenu, *La foi dans l'intelligence*, Vol I (Paris: Cerf, 1964), p. 253. See also Congar's article entitled 'Théologie', in *Dictionnaire de Théologie Catholique*, Vol. 15 (Paris: Letouzey et Ané, 1943) published as a book in English: Y. C., *A History of Theology*, trans. H. Guthrie (Garden City, NY: Doubleday, 1996).

66   Y. C., *Journal d'un théologien*, p. 59.

67   *Fifty Years of Catholic Theology, Conversations with Yves Congar*, edited and introduced by Bernard Lauret, trans. John Bowden (Philadelphia: Fortress Press, 1988), p. 68.

68   Y. C., 'Authority, Initiative, Co-responsibility', p. 64.

69   Y. C., 'Authority, Initiative, Co-responsibility', p. 41; tr. modified. In a note Congar invites his audience to read *Lumen Gentium* 12 and 30, and the *Decree on the Apostolate of the Laity* 3 and 30.

70   Y. C., 'Pneumatology Today', *The American Ecclesiastical Review* 167 (1973), p. 443; tr. modified.

71   Y. C., *Journal d'un théologien*, p. 59.

72   Letter to the author, 26 October 2009.

73   Charles Taylor, *A Secular Age* (Cambridge, MA: The Belknap of Harvard University Press, 2007), p. 473. 'The Age of Authenticity' is the title of Chapter 13 of this book. See also Chantal Delsol, *Éloge de la singularité* (Paris: La Table Ronde, 2000). Delsol, p. 20, calls our period 'late modernity' and sees it 'inhabited by a common certitude, [...] perhaps the only one that remains anchored in its mental *habitus*: it believes in the dignity of the singular human being [...], autonomous individual, endowed with his/her own project and capable of intellectual independence'.

74   'We now have a widespread "expressive" individualism' (Charles Taylor, *A Secular Age*, p. 473).

75   Taylor, *A Secular Age*, p. 475.

76   Taylor, *A Secular Age*, p. 508.

77   Wade Clark Roof, *The Spiritual Marketplace: Baby Boomers and the Remaking of American Religion* (Princeton: Princeton University Press, 1999).

78   Wade Clark Roof, *The Spiritual Marketplace*, p. 41.

79   It is in this sense that Charles Taylor writes: 'Many people are not satisfied with a momentary sense of wow! They want to take it further, and they're looking for ways of doing so. That is what leads them into the practices which are their main access to traditional forms of faith' (*A Secular Age*, p. 518).

80   Taylor, *A Secular Age*, p. 509.

81   Y. C., *Le Concile au jour le jour, Troisième session* (Paris: Cerf, 1965), p. 157.

82   Y. C., *Le Concile au jour le jour, Troisième session*, p. 159.

83   E. T. Groppe, *Yves Congar's Theology of the Holy Spirit* (New York: Oxford University Press, 2004).

84   E. T. Groppe, *Yves Congar's Theology of the Holy Spirit*, p. 113.

85   J. Famerée and G. Routhier, *Yves Congar*, p. 179.

86   Y. C., 'Le monothéisme politique et le Dieu Trinité', *Nouvelle Revue Théologique* 103 (1981), pp. 3–17. Not available in English translation.

87   Y. C., 'La Tri-unité de Dieu et de l'Église', *La Vie Spirituelle*, 604 (1974), pp. 687–701. Not available in English translation.

88   Y. C., 'Pneumatologie dogmatique', in Bernard Lauret and François Refoulé (eds), *Initiation à la pratique de la théologie*, Vol. II: Dogmatique I (Paris: Cerf, 1982), pp. 493–516. Not available in English translation.

89   Y. C., *Diversity and Communion*, trans. John Bowden (London: SCM Press, 1984). Originally published as *Diversités et communion: Dossier historique et conclusion théologique* (Paris: Cerf, 1982).

90   Y. C., *I Believe in the Holy Spirit*, 3 vols, trans. David Smith (New York: Seabury, 1983). Originally published as *Je crois en l'Esprit Saint*, Vol. I, L'expérience de l'Esprit (Paris: Cerf, 1979); Vol. II, Il est Seigneur et Il donne la vie (Paris: Cerf, 1979); Vol. III, Le fleuve de vie (Paris: Cerf, 1980).

91   Y. C., 'Pneumatologie dogmatique', p. 500.

92   Y. C., 'Le monothéisme politique et le Dieu Trinité', *Nouvelle Revue Théologique* 103 (1981), p. 11. Congar notes also that 'the faithful

and the peoples have not always been treated like "subjects" possessing within themselves life, their own gifts and demands'. He discerned such a tendency that was particularly strong in the nineteenth century. We will come back to this later when we discuss the question of authority.

93 Y. C., 'Le monothéisme politique et le Dieu Trinité', p. 13.

94 Y. C., 'Authority, Initiative and Co-responsibility', in *Blessed Is the Peace of my Church*, trans. Salvator Attanasio (Denville, NJ: Dimension Books, 1973) p. 62.

95 Y. C., *Essais œcuméniques* (Paris: Centurion, 1984), pp. 303–4.

96 Y. C., *I Believe in the Holy Spirit*, vol. 2, p. 17.

97 Y. C., *Laity, Church and World*, trans. Donald Attwater (Baltimore: Helicon Press, 1960), p. 22. Donald Attwater has added a footnote to explain Congar's use of the terms 'object' and 'subject': '*Object* in the sense of a person (or thing) to whom something is done or about whom somebody acts or operates (passive), as opposed to the *subject* that thus acts or operates (active).'

98 Y. C., 'Pneumatology Today', p. 443; tr. modified.

99 Y. C., *The Mystery of the Church*, 2nd rev. edn, trans A. V. Littledale (Baltimore and Dublin: Helicon Press and Geoffrey Chapman, 1965), p. 172; tr. modified.

100 J. Famerée and G. Routhier, *Yves Congar*, p. 198. The quote within the quote is from Y. C., *Journal d'un théologien*, p. 288.

101 Georges Michonneau, *Pas de vie chrétienne sans communauté* (Paris: Cerf, 1960).

102 Y. C., Preface to *Pas de vie chrétienne sans communauté*, p. 16.

103 Y. C., Preface to *Pas de vie chrétienne sans communauté*, p. 6.

104 Y. C., Preface to *Pas de vie chrétienne sans communauté*, pp. 16–17.

105 Y. C., Preface to K. Delahaye, *Ecclesia Mater* (Paris: Cerf, 1964), pp. 17–18.

106 Y. C., *Essais œcuméniques*, p. 304.

107 Y. C., *True and Fasle Reform*, p. 42.

108 E. T. Groppe, *Yves Congar's Theology of the Holy Spirit*, p. 107.

109 Y. C., 'Renewal of the Spirit and Reform of the Institution', p. 47.

110 Y. C., *Le Concile de Vatican II*, p. 55: 'The novelty of Vatican II has been emphasized. This is undeniable, but it seems necessary to underline the desired reality of continuity.' He proved this by listing all the quotations Vatican II made of previous councils. We can

also recall what Congar confided to Jean Puyo: 'I am a rooted man. I detest rupture with what founds us. Is such a rupture necessary sometimes in order to create? I think that great creations are rooted in the cultural and spiritual ground from which they come forth in their newness' (*Jean Puyo interroge le Père Congar*, p. 185).

111 Y. C., 1984 Preface to *La Tradition et la vie de l'Église* (Paris: Cerf, 1984), p. 5.

112 Y. C., *True and False Reform*, p. 46.

113 Y. C., *True and False Reform*, p. 45.

114 Y. C., *True and False Reform*, p. 41.

115 Y. C., *True and False Reform*, p. 46.

116 *Jean Puyo interroge le Père Congar*, p. 220: 'The Council got rid of what I would call the unconditionality of the system.' Congar returned to the theme of liturgy and the personal principle in his article 'Autorité, initiative, coresponsabilité', pp. 53–7; this part of the article was not translated into English.

117 Y. C., 'Institutionalized Religion', in *The Word in History*, St. Francis Xavier Symposium, ed. Patrick Burke, p. 132; tr. modified.

118 Y. C., 'Institutionalized Religion', pp. 140–1.

119 *Jean Puyo interroge le Père Congar*, p. 220. E. Fouilloux rightly underlines how Congar, far from being a simplistic optimist, differed from several other theologians of his generation by his unchanged confidence in the work accomplished by the Council (Étienne Fouilloux, 'Friar Yves, Cardinal Congar, Dominican: Itinerary of a Theologian', *U.S. Catholic Historian* 17/2 [1999], pp. 84–5). Congar considered that it would take two generations to re-learn freedom. See also: *Jean Puyo interroge le Père Congar*, p. 159.

120 Y. C., 'At Last Look at the Council', in *Vatican II By Those Who Were There*, ed. A. Stacpoole (London: Geoffrey Chapman, 1986), p. 351; tr. modified.

121 Congar wrote that the book he would have liked to write, and which he welcomed into his *Unam Sanctam* series (no. 3 of the series, 1938) was Henri de Lubac's *Catholicism*. As for Henri de Lubac, he wrote the following about *Catholicism*: 'I owe the publication of the book to Father Yves Congar, O.P., who had just then launched the ecclesiological series *Unam Sanctam* at Éditions du Cerf. Having read several of the pieces that had already appeared, he gave me the idea for it and extracted, so to speak, the accomplishment of it from me.' See Henri de Lubac, *At the Service*

of the Church, Henri de Lubac Reflects on the Circumstances that Occasioned his Writings, p. 28.

122 H. de Lubac, *The Splendor of the Church*, pp. 282–3. All of the remaining quotations of this chapter are taken from these two pages.

Notes to Chapter 4

1 See Y. C., 'The Reasons for the Unbelief of Our Time', *Integration*, Part One: August-September 1938; Part Two: December 1938–January 1939. Originally published in *La vie intellectuelle* 37 (1935), pp. 214–49. See also Y. C., *The Mystery of the Church*, second revised edition, trans. V. Littledate (Baltimore: Helicon Press, 1965); originally published as *Esquisses du Mystère de l'Église* (Paris: Cerf, 1941).

2 To understand how ideology is on the opposite side of the spectrum from catholicity, let us recall the criterion used by Karl Rahner to distinguish between Christianity and fanaticism. He wrote: 'Christianity, however, by its very nature, is called to see itself in the other, and to trust that in the other it encounters itself again in a greater abundance.' See Karl Rahner, 'Christianity and Ideology', trans. Bernard E. Scott, in *Concilium* 6 (New York: Paulist Press, 1965), p. 57.

3 The Greek word *kath'olon* literally means 'according to the whole'. I use this word in a non-denominational fashion. Congar wrote: 'What characterizes a sect is its lack of reference to totality' (Y. C., *L'Église Une, Sainte, Catholique et Apostolique* [Paris: Cerf, 1970], p. 170).

4 J. Famerée and G. Routhier, *Yves Congar* (Paris: Cerf, 2008), pp. 92–3. Is it because of his unending search for truth that Congar never 'completed' the ecclesiological work he had set out to accomplish as a young man?

5 G. Flynn writes perceptively: 'The search for wholeness is, then, a defining feature of Congar's theology. It is the golden thread that helps to bind together all his theological projects' (*Yves Congar's Vision of the Church in a World of Unbelief* [Aldershot: Ashgate Publishing, 2004], p. 78).

6 Y. C., *Tradition and Traditions, An Historical and a Theological Essay*, trans. Michael Naseby for Part I and Thomas Rainborough for Part II (New York: Macmillan, 1967), p. 449. We should

recall that Congar had welcomed into his *Unam Sanctam* series A. Gratieux's book, *A. S. Khomiakov et le Mouvement Slavophile*, vol. 1 (Paris: Cerf, 1939), where these same words were quoted on p. 74.

7   In 1935, Congar was only 31 years old when he published 'Une Conclusion théologique à l'Enquête sur les raisons actuelles de l'incroyance' ['The Reasons for the Unbelief of Our Time', *Integration*, Part One: August–September 1938 Part Two: December 1938–January 1939]. See footnote 1.

8   Universality 'is obviously something that is always in need of being realized, since humanity never ceases to grow, and like the world, never ceases to reveal new dimensions and as yet unexplored depths' (Y. C., *L'Église Une, Sainte, Catholique et Apostolique*, p. 171).

9   '...when the Church is confronted with novelty, it is inclined first and foremost to distance itself and to turn in upon itself. As if leaving to the future the need to respond to its present challenges, the church focuses in upon itself and refuses to consider anything other than what it has always found familiar' (Y. C., *True and False Reform in the Chuch*, trans. Paul Philibert [Collegeville, MN: Liturgical Press, 2011], pp. 309–10).

10 Y. C., 'The Reasons for the Unbelief of Our Time', Part One, p. 21.

11 Y. C., 'The Reasons for the Unbelief of Our Time', Part One, p. 21; tr. modified.

12 Y. C., 'The Reasons for the Unbelief of Our Time', Part Two, p. 19; tr. modified.

13 Y. C., 'The Reasons for the Unbelief of Our Time', Part Two, p. 19.

14 Y. C., 'The Reasons for the Unbelief of Our Time', Part Two, p. 19.

15 Y. C., *Divided Christendom, A Catholic Study of the Problem of Reunion*, trans. M. A. Bousfield (London: Centenary Press, 1939), p. 271.

16 Y. C., 'The Reasons for the Unbelief of Our Time', Part Two, p. 21; tr. modified.

17 Y. C., 'The Reasons for the Unbelief of Our Time', Part Two, p. 21.

18 This was quoted by H. de Lubac in *Mémoire sur l'occasion de mes écrits*, Œuvres complètes XXXIII (Paris: Cerf, 2006), p. 337.

19 'The conservative character of the liturgy makes it possible for it to preserve and transmit intact the values whose importance one epoch may have forgotten, but which the next epoch is happy to find intact and preserved, so that it can live from them again. Where would we be if this liturgical conservatism had

not resisted the late medieval taste for sensory devotions, the eighteenth century's individualistic, rational, and moralizing imperatives, the nineteenth century's critique, or the modern period's subjective philosophies? Thanks to the liturgy everything has been retained and transmitted. Ah! Let us not expose ourselves to the reproach sixty years hence that we squandered and lost the sacred heritage of the Catholic communion as it is deployed in the slow flow of time. Let us keep a healthy awareness that we carry in ourselves only a moment, the tip of the iceberg in relation to a reality which is beyond us in every way' (Y. C., 'Autorité, initiative, coresponsabilité' in *La Maison Dieu* 97 [1969], p. 55). The quotation is taken from Part III of Congar's article which was left out when the article was republished in Congar's book *Au milieu des orages* (Paris: Cerf, 1969). The English translation of this book, *Blessed is the Peace of My Church* (Denville, NJ: Dimension Bookhas, 1973), is based on *Au milieu des orages* and therefore omits the same material.

20   Y. C., *Journal d'un théologien* (Paris: Cerf, 2001).

21   Y. C., *Journal d'un théologien*, p. 90.

22   Y. C., *True and False Reform in the Church*, p. 316; tr. modified.

23   Y. C., *True and False Reform in the Church*, Appendix II, 'Two Types of Fidelity', pp. 364–71.

24   Y. C., *True and False Reform in the Church*, Appendix II, p. 366.

25   Y. C., *True and False Reform in the Church*, Appendix II, p. 366.

26   Y. C., *Église Catholique et France moderne* (Paris: Hachette, 1978), p. 10.

27   Y. C., *Divided Christendom: A Catholic Study of the Problem of Reunion*, trans. M. A. Bousfield (London: Centenary Press, 1939). Originally published as *Chrétiens désunis: Principes d'un 'oecuménisme' catholique*, Unam Sanctam 1 (Paris: Cerf, 1937).

28   See M. J. Le Guillou and Ghislain Lafont, *L'Église en marche* (Cahiers de la Pierre-qui-Vire; Paris: Desclée de Brouwer, 1964), p. 39.

29   Y. C., *Divided Christendom*, Table of Contents, p. viii.

30   Y. C., *Divided Christendom*, p. 271; tr. modified.

31   J. Famerée and G. Routhier, *Yves Congar* (Paris: Cerf, 2008), p. 57.

32   H. Legrand, 'Yves Congar (1904–1995): une passion pour l'unité', *Nouvelle Revue Théologique* 126/4 (2004), p. 532. See also Thomas O'Meara, 'Ecumenist of our Times: Yves Congar', *Mid-Stream* 27/1 (1988), p. 69: 'His pioneering and tireless ecumenical vocation,

however, was not an avocation or one of his life's activities: it was a facet of the primal call to renew the Roman Catholic Church (and thereby to influence the other Christian churches) by a new perspective of the limits and dynamics of the Church's life in history.'

33 Y. C., *Une passion: l'unité*, p. 10.

34 H. Legrand, 'Yves Congar (1904–1995): Une passion pour l'unité', pp. 531–2.

35 'In the end, the ecumenical that was not intended, not on purpose; the ecumenical that was done by its own internal dimension or quality: that was the most efficaciously ecumenical' (Y. C., *Une passion: l'unité*, p. 42).

36 Y. C., *Divided Christendom*, p. 254. Congar's influence is easily recognizable in this text of Vatican II: 'The divisions among Christians prevent the Church from attaining the fullness of catholicity proper to her, in those of her sons who, though attached to her by Baptism, are yet separated from full communion with her. Furthermore, the Church herself finds it more difficult to express in actual life her full catholicity in all her bearings' (*Unitatis Redintegratio*, 4).

37 Congar read Martin Luther extensively and wrote about him a great deal. See Y. C., *Dialogue Between Christians*, pp. 289–434; *Diversity and Communion*, trans. John Bowden (London: SCM Press, 1984), pp. 107–14 and pp. 145–8; and above all his book *Martin Luther, sa foi, sa réforme* (Paris: Cerf, 1983), p. 35. See also A. Birmelé's interesting article entitled 'Yves-Marie Congar en dialogue avec la Réforme', *Bulletin de Littérature ecclésiastique* CVI/1 (2005), pp. 65–88. Birmelé has this to say about Congar: 'His erudition was such that he was appropriately considered in Protestant circles to be one of the best scholars of the Reformation' (p. 68). Birmelé also shows how Congar's understanding of Luther evolved over time.

38 *Jean Puyo interroge le Père Congar* (Paris: Centurion, 1975), p. 59.

39 On this period that followed the Council of Trent, see the article by Jean Delumeau, 'Contre-Réforme et Réforme catholique', in *Encyclopaedia Universalis*, DVD 2008 edition. For the terminology referring to this period, see Y. C., *L'Église de Saint Augustin à l'époque moderne* (Paris: Cerf, 1970), p. 380.

40 Y. C., *L'Église de Saint Augustin à l'époque moderne*, p. 381. One can be sceptical of the position that sees this view of the Counter-Reformation as outdated. Congar in no way denied what was positive about this period. He critiqued its *theoretical* ecclesiology.

41 Congar quoted de Lubac's words in a note written in 1948
    which he intended to add to a new edition of *Chrétiens désunis*
    [*Divided Christendom*], p. 34n. 1. See Éditions du Cerf:
    http://www.editionsducerf.fr/site_congar/cadre_gal.htm
42 Y. C., *Divided Christendom*, p. 29; tr. modified.
43 Y. C., *Divided Christendom*, p. 29; tr. modified.
44 Y. C., *Divided Christendom*, p. 257; tr. modified.
45 Y. C., *Divided Christendom*, p. 257.
46 Congar affirmed that the notion of 'a post-Tridentine Catholicism'
    corresponded to a reality, and he added: 'We find on the whole
    a hardening and concentration in the expression of the Catholic
    doctrines directly opposed to Protestant positions, and silence and
    reserve regarding those elements of the faith most nearly adaptable
    to the demands or protestations of the Reformers' (*Divided
    Christendom*, p. 30).
47 See the text by the Groupe des Dombes, which is especially
    remarkable for its historical analysis, in *Pour la conversion des
    Églises* (Paris: Centurion, 1991), p. 60. To describe the period
    that followed the Council of Trent and applied its decrees, Congar
    evoked the existence of a 'Roman Catholic system that externally
    was dynamic and conquering, but internally was closed in on itself,
    as if under siege' (Y. C., *L'Église de Saint Augustin à l'époque
    moderne*, p. 381).
48 Y. C., *Martin Luther, sa foi, sa réforme*, p. 9.
49 Y. C., *Essais œcuméniques* (Paris: Centurion, 1984), p. 226.
50 Y. C., *Divided Christendom*, p. 247; tr. modified.
51 An addition to *Chrétiens désunis* [*Divided Christendom*], p. 331 that
    is available at: http://www.editionsducerf.fr/site_congar_fal.htm
52 Y. C., *True and False Reform in the Church*, pp. 317–18.
53 Y. C., *Challenge to the Church, The Case of Archbishop Lefebvre*,
    trans. Paul Inwood (Huntington, IN: Our Sunday Visitor, 1976),
    p. 29.
54 Y. C., *True and False Reform in the Church*, p. 318; tr. modified.
55 Y. C., 'A Last Look at the Council', in *Vatican II By Those Who
    Were There*, ed. A. Stacpoole (London: Geoffrey Chapman, 1986),
    p. 343; tr. modified. *Divided Christendom* was already written in
    this spirit. We can cite this passage: 'It is not with the faintest desire
    to prove ourselves in the right, but only that we should all of us
    together be in the right, and that we should together realize the

necessity of each to the other and to the Catholicity of the whole' (*Divided Christendom*, p. 260).

56 Y. C., 'A Last Look at the Council', p. 343.

57 Y. C., *Divided Christendom*, p. 264; tr. modified.

58 Y. C., *Divided Christendom*, pp. 264–65.

59 This is what Dom Ghislain Lafont called Congar's Introduction. See Ghislain Lafont and M. J. Le Guillou, *L'Église en marche*, p. 44n. 1.

60 Y. C., *Divided Christendom*, p. 260; tr. modified.

61 He said in a conversation with Bernard Lauret: '... I began with solid affirmations. It was the idea of Catholicity which at the time seemed to me to encompass the diversities; today I am more aware of the diversities, as is evident in my book *Diversity and Communion*' (in *Fifty Years of Catholic Theology*, edited and introduced by Bernard Lauret, trans. John Bowden [Philadelphia: Fortress Press, 1988], p. 81).

62 Y. C., Preface to A. Feuillet, *Le Christ Sagesse de Dieu* (Paris: Gabalda, 1966), p. 14.

63 Y. C., Preface to A. Feuillet, *Le Christ Sagesse de Dieu*, p. 14.

64 See Pawel Pietrusiak, 'La catholicité de l'Église dans la pensée d'Yves Congar', *Roczniki Teologiczne* LIII–LIV (2006–7), pp. 39–60.

65 Y. C., *Divided Christendom*, p. 93.

66 Y. C., *Divided Christendom*, pp. 93–4.

67 Y. C., *Divided Christendom*, pp. 94–5; tr. modified.

68 Y. C., *Divided Christendom*, p. 227. 'The catholicity of the Church is the catholicity *of Christ*' (Y. C., *I Believe in the Holy Spirit*, Vol. II:, trans. David Smith [New York: Seabury, 1983], p. 35).

69 Y. C., *The Mystery of the Church*, second revised edition, trans. V. Littledate (Baltimore: Helicon Press, 1965), p. 24.

70 Y. C., *Essais œcuméniques*, pp. 288–9.

71 V. Lossky, 'Du troisième attribut de l'Église', in *Dieu Vivant* 10 (1948), p. 85.

72 V. Lossky, 'Du troisième attribut de l'Église', p. 85.

73 V. Lossky, 'Du troisième attribut de l'Église', p. 86.

74 See *Le Concile et les Conciles* (Paris: Cerf, 1960), p. 303. Among the contributions that make up this book, three (including the Conclusion) are from Congar.

75 In addition to the text that we have already quoted from *Fifty Years of Catholic Theology*, p. 81; see also G. Alberigo, 'Réforme et Unité de l'Église' in *Cardinal Yves Congar (1904–1995)*, ed. A. Vauchez (Paris: Cerf, 1999), p. 21. Alberigo agrees with Jossua (see his introduction to *Écrits réformateurs* [Paris: Cerf, 1995], pp. 252–3) and speaks of Congar's 'important evolution concerning the concept of unity'. Alberigo thought that Congar went from 'the centrality of the trait of "catholicity" to the valuing of "diversity" and "pluralism"'.

76 P. Pietrusiak, 'La catholicité de l'Église dans la pensée d'Yves Congar', p. 55.

77 Y. C., Preface to F. Dvornik's book *Le schisme de Photius* (Paris: Cerf, 1950), p. 9.

78 Y. C., Conclusion to *Le Concile et les Conciles*, p. 303. In the same article published in *Dieu vivant*, Lossky wrote the following, p. 86: 'Without personal diversity, natural unity would not be possible; it would be replaced by an external unity, one that is abstract, administrative, and endured blindly by the members of the collectivity.' And he concluded: 'Catholicity consists of the perfect accord between these two things: unity and diversity, nature and persons.'

79 Y. C., Conclusion to *Le Concile et les Conciles*, p. 303.

80 'The unity which does not depend upon the multitude is tyranny.' Congar is quoting Pascal (*Pensées*, fr. 871); see *Le Concile et les Conciles*, p. 303.

81 Y. C., *L'Église Une, Sainte, Catholique et Apostolique*, p. 165.

82 Y. C., 'Le monothéisme politique et le Dieu Trinité', *Nouvelle Revue Théologique* 103 (1981), pp. 3–17. Not available in English translation.

83 Y. C., 'Le monothéisme politique et le Dieu Trinité', p. 16. See also p. 13.

84 Congar quoted H. Legrand: 'Because the church is catholic, it must be particular' (Y. C., 'Le monothéisme politique et le Dieu Trinité', p. 17).

85 P. Pietrusiak, 'La catholicité de l'Église dans la pensée d'Yves Congar', p. 43. See also Lossky, 'Du troisième attribut de l'Église', p. 88.

86 J. Famerée and G. Routhier, *Yves Congar*, p. 73.

87 J. Famerée and G. Routhier, *Yves Congar*, p. 55.

88 Y. C., *Diversity and Communion*, p. 23.

89 Y. C., *Divided Christendom*, p. 99; tr. modified.

90 I am using the word 'ideology' in the pejorative sense given to it by Jean Lacroix in *Personnalisme comme anti-idéologie* (Paris: PUF, 1972), p. 12: 'In the pejorative sense, ideology becomes a more or less coherent system of ideas which a group presents as required by reason, but which is actually motivated by the need to satisfy and justify self-interested aspirations.'

91 Y. C., *The Mystery of the Church*, pp. 99, 101, 104. J.-P. Jossua has noted Congar's evolution between his way of framing the issues in 1937 and in 1982. On the topic of the later works where the Spirit occupies a greater place, Jossua writes: 'Henceforth unity is grasped as a mystery [Fr.: *mystériquement*], but this occurs from its root, as a *communion* of persons or of churches, with a pneumatological point of reference (implying unpredictability, liberty, the insistence on the transcendence of the Mystery that is not possessed), not just a Christological one' (in Y. C., *Écrits Réformateurs*, p. 252). We may note, however, that this 'unpredictability' was already present in *Esquisses du Mystère de l'Église*, written in 1941.

Notes to Chapter 5

1 Y. C., *Dialogue Between Christians*, trans. Philip Loretz, S.J. (Westminster, MD: The Newman Press, 1966), p. 23 and *Église catholique et France moderne* (Paris: Hachette, 1978), p. 31.

2 Y. C., *Dialogue Between Christians*, p. 23; tr. modified.

3 Y. C., *Dialogue Between Christians*, p. 7; tr. modified.

4 Y. C., *Dialogue Between Christians*, p. 6.

5 See Congar's article 'Authority, Initiative and Co-responsibility', in *Blessed Is the Peace of My Church*, trans. Salvator Attanasio (Denville, NJ: Dimension Books, 1973), p. 57, in which Congar establishes a link between the crisis of authority within the Church and the broader crisis of civilization.

6 These words were to be added to a new edition of *Chrétiens désunis*, which is available at http://www.editionsducerf.fr/site_congar/cadre_gal. htm

7 'Something prodigious takes place at the beginning of the seventeenth century. There is a shift in the role attributed to time: regarding the past, in the present, and in the future. How could people be unaware of it? How could there not be a depreciation of

what is ancient? How not to see in this one of the reasons – there are no doubt others – for calling the principle of authority into question, which is precisely a characteristic of modernity?' (Pierre Chaunu, *La modernité, qu'est-ce que c'est ? Introduction historique*. A lecture given by Chaunu in the reformed church at Auteuil, 20 February 1996, available in French at: http://www.erf-auteuil.org/conferences/la-modernite-qu-est-ce-que-c-est.html). Accessed 4 August 2013.

8   Y. C., *Église catholique et France moderne* (Paris: Hachette, 1978), p. 51 and p. 168: 'Every institution is seen as an enslavement; every authority is considered to be arbitrary.'

9   Congar sometimes gives different dates for the beginning of the modern world: 'The modern world – to which one may, depending on what aspect of it is being considered, assign a beginning anywhere from the end of the twelfth century to around 1680, covering the beginning of the fourteenth century, the Italian Renaissance, the great discoveries, the Reformation [...].' See Y. C., 'Attitudes toward Reform in the Church', trans. Bernard Gilligan, *Cross Currents* 4 (1951), p. 85. This is a translation from a chapter that is in the first edition of *Vraie et fausse réforme dans l'Église*, but that Congar left out of the second edition. Since Paul Philibert's recent translation of Congar's book, *True and False Reform in the Church* (Collegeville, MN: Liturgical Press, 2011) is based on the second edition, this passage does not appear in Philibert's translation.

10   Y. C., 'The Historical Development of Authority in the Church. Points for Christian Reflection' in *Problems of Authority*, ed. John M. Todd (Baltimore: The Helicon Press and London: DLT, 1962), p. 144. Same page for the indented quote above. Elsewhere he mentions the 'primacy of the future over the past and its legacy' (Y. C., *Église catholique et France moderne*, p. 50).

11   Y. C., *Église catholique et France moderne*, pp. 50–1.

12   Y. C., *Église catholique et France moderne*, p. 50.

13   Y. C., *Église catholique et France moderne*, p. 27. Congar knew that the attempt to establish precise dates for these changes is always debatable. He is trying to give a 'symbolic expression of an epoch in which a cultural, but also social and political world came into being outside of the Catholic world and even in opposition to it' (*Église catholique et France moderne*, p. 21). These dates were also used by Paul Hazard in his famous work, first published in 1935 *La Crise de la conscience européenne 1680–1715* (Paris: Livre de Poche, coll. Références, 1994); a new edition English is now available *The Crisis of the European Mind*, trans. Anthony Grafton (New York: NYRB Classics, 2013).

14 Y. C., *Église catholique et France moderne*, p. 27.

15 Émile Poulat, Art. 'Modernisme', in *Encyclopædia Universalis*, DVD 2008 edition.

16 Y. C., *Église catholique et France moderne*, pp. 28–9.

17 Y. C., *Église catholique et France moderne*, p. 31.

18 Y. C., *Église catholique et France moderne*, p. 53.

19 J. Moingt, 'Quaestiones. Actualité des ministères', in *Recherches de Science Religieuse* 90 (2002/2), p. 224.

20 Y. C., *Église catholique et France moderne*, pp. 30–1 and p. 47.

21 Y. C., *Église catholique et France moderne*, p. 33.

22 Y. C., *Église catholique et France moderne*, p. 37. Elsewhere, in his article 'Authority, Initiative, and Co-responsibility', Congar wrote, p. 81: 'In the nineteenth century, after the shock of the French Revolution, the Church lived with the obsession of constantly reaffirming authority, and everything that could be construed as personal evaluation or preference was eliminated as "rationalism" or "free inquiry".' Tr. modified.

23 Y. C., 'L'ecclésiologie, de la Révolution française au Concile du Vatican, sous le signe de l'affirmation de l'autorité', in *L'ecclésiologie au XIXe siècle*, Unam Sanctam 34 (Paris: Cerf, 1960), pp. 77–114. Not available in English translation.

24 Among other works, he published in the series *Unam Sanctam* the volume, *L'ecclésiologie au XIXe siècle*, 34 (Paris: Cerf, 1960). This book contains thirteen contributions from various experts, among them Congar's on ecclesiology under the banner of authority (pp. 77–114), that I have just alluded to.

25 Y. C., *Report from Rome II, On the Second Session of the Vatican Council*, trans. Lancelot Sheppard (London: Geoffrey Chapman, Christian Living Series, 1964), p. 181.

26 Y. C., 'Pneumatology Today', in *The American Ecclesiastical Review* 167 (1973), p. 436.

27 Congar's lecture 'The Historical Development of Authority in the Church. Points for Christian Reflection' and the other papers presented during this Anglo-French symposium on authority which took place at the Abbey of Notre-Dame du Bec in April 1961 can be found in *Problems of Authority*, ed. John M. Todd (Baltimore: The Helicon Press, and London: DLT, 1962), pp. 119–56 for Congar's text.

28 Congar's article, 'La hiérarchie comme service selon le Nouveau

Testament et les documents de la Tradition', is published in *L'Épiscopat et l'Église universelle* (Paris: Cerf, 1962), pp. 67–99. It is completed by another text published in the same volume: 'Quelques expressions traditionnelles du service chrétien', pp. 100–32. Part of the first text has been published in Y. C., *Power and Poverty in the Church*, trans. Jennifer Nicholson (Baltimore: Helicon, 1964), pp. 17–100. It includes material taken from *Problems of Authority* (pp. 40–79).

29 Y. C., 'Authority, Initiative, and Co-responsibility', p. 75; tr. modified.

30 Y. C., *Ministères et communion ecclésiale* (Paris: Cerf, 1971), p. 39. See the remarks made by J. Famerée in *L'ecclésiologie d'Yves Congar avant Vatican II*, Histoire et Église (Louvain: Bibliotheca Ephemeridum Theologicarum Lovaniensium CVII [1992], p. 112n. 305): 'The understanding of ordained ministries in *hierarchical* terms is in the long run unfortunate: theologically, the use of such vocabulary obscures the reality of "service" involved in the various "ministries" and instills a conception of these ministries that suggests a kind of ranking (from diaconate to episcopacy), whereas each of these ministries is a unique gift of the Spirit; pastorally, the ecclesial meaning given to the term "hierarchy" which appeared for the first time in the Neo-Platonic world of the Pseudo-Dionysius (sixth century) cannot be understood by the modern world, and the social connotations attached to it only further trouble the understanding of Christian ministry.'

31 Y. C., *Power and Poverty in the Church*, p. 83.

32 Quoted by Congar in *Power and Poverty in the Church*, p. 86 and in 'Authority, Initiative and Co-responsibility', p. 76.

33 Y. C., *Le Concile de Vatican II* (Paris: Beauchesne, 1984), p. 158.

34 G. Martelet, *Les idées maîtresses de Vatican II* (Paris: coll. Foi vivante 105, 1969), pp. 261–2.

35 G. Martelet, *Deux mille ans d'Église en question*, t. II (Paris: Cerf, 1990), p. 259.

36 Y. C., *Lay People in the Church, A Study for a Theology of the Laity*, trans. Donald Attwater (Westminster, MD: Newman Press, 1965), pp. 281–2.

37 Y. C., *Lay People in the Church*, p. 263; tr. modified.

38 Y. C., *Lay People in the Church*, p. 263; tr. modified.

39 Y. C., *Lay People in the Church*, p. 264; tr. modified.

40 Y. C., *Lay People in the Church*, p. 264; tr. modified.

41 Y. C., *Lay People in the Church*, p. 282; tr. modified.

42 Y. C., 'The *Ecclesia* or Christian Community as a Whole Celebrates the Liturgy', trans. Paul Philibert in *At the Heart of Christian Worship, Liturgical Essays of Yves Congar* (Collegeville, MN: Liturgical Press, 2010), pp. 15–68.

43 Y. C., 'The *Ecclesia* or Christian Community as a Whole', p. 16.

44 Y. C., 'The *Ecclesia* or Christian Community as a Whole', p. 16.

45 Y. C., 'The *Ecclesia* or Christian Community as a Whole', p. 20.

46 Y. C., 'The *Ecclesia* or Christian Community as a Whole', p. 37; tr. modified.

47 Y. C., Preface to K. Delahaye's, *Ecclesia mater* (Paris: Cerf, 1964), p. 12.

48 Y. C., 'The *Ecclesia* or Christian Community as a Whole', p. 37.

49 Y. C., 'The *Ecclesia* or Christian Community as a Whole', p. 38.

50 Other examples of this in Y. C., *Ministères et communion ecclésiale*, pp. 37–8.

51 Y. C., *L'ecclésiologie du haut moyen âge* (Paris: Cerf, 1968), p. 162.

52 Y. C., *L'ecclésiologie du haut moyen âge*, p. 162.

53 Y. C., *L'ecclésiologie du haut moyen âge*, pp. 162–3.

54 Y. C., *L'ecclésiologie du haut moyen âge* was written by Congar in 1954–5 and published for the first time in German in 1955 (Herder Verlag). A completely revised version was published later in French (Paris: Cerf, 1968).

55 See Gabriel Le Bras' review of the book published in *Archives des sciences sociales des religions* 27/1 (1969), pp. 168–70; he pointed out Congar's 'overwhelming erudition'. Pierre Nautin reviewing the same work in *Revue de l'histoire des religions* 179/2 (1971), pp. 221–2, wrote: 'A celebrated theologian can at the same time be a historian. This work is the proof of that.'

56 These two texts were published in French in *L'Épiscopat et L'Église Universelle* (Paris: Cerf, 1962). An English translation of 'The Hierarchy as Service' can be found in Y. C., *Power and Poverty in the Church*, trans. Jennifer Nicholson (Baltimore: Helicon, 1964), pp. 15–100.

57 *The Rule of Saint Benedict*, trans. Leonard Doyle (Collegeville, MN: The Liturgical Press, 2001), p. 141.

58 See 'L'ecclésiologie de Saint Bernard' in Y. C., *Église et papauté*, pp. 115–85.

59 Y. C., 'Quelques expressions traditionnelles du service chrétien', in *L'Épiscopat et l'Église universelle*, p. 104. In the French edition of *Wikipedia's* article on Wellesley College, the motto of the college which is 'non ministrari, sed ministrare' is mistranslated 'Not be governed but to govern'! One sees through this example how the Christian way of seeing authority can be surprising. See http://fr.wikipedia.org/wiki/Wellesley_College (accessed 11 November 2012).

60 See Y. C., *Église et Papauté*, p. 16n. 204 for the references in the writings of Augustine.

61 Y. C., 'Expressions traditionnelles du service chrétien', p. 110.

62 Y. C., 'Expressions traditionnelles du service chrétien', pp. 122–3.

63 Y. C., *Lay People in the Church*, p. 245. These words by Pope Celestine were used at the councils of Orléans (549) and Paris (557).

64 The Eastern Churches did not attempt to codify the notion of reception in legal categories. See the article 'Reception', in *Encyclopedia of Christianity* (Grand Rapids, MI: Eerdmans-Brill, 2005), vol. 4, p. 503.

65 Unless otherwise indicated, all the quotations inside this box are taken from Congar's article: 'Reception as an Ecclesiological Reality', trans. John Griffiths, *Concilium* 77 (1972), pp. 43–68.

66 'In the soundest Christian tradition, those *ministers exercising authority never act alone*'. According to Congar, this needs to be remembered if we are to respect 'certain aspects of the very nature of the Church, whose authenticity is indefeasible and which Vatican II rediscovered' ('Reception as an Ecclesiological Reality', trans. John Griffiths, *Concilium* 77 [1972], p. 64 and p. 63).

67 Y. C., 'Pneumatologie dogmatique' (Paris: Cerf, 1982), p. 500.

68 Y. C., *Lay People in the Church*, p. 269 and HDA, p. 134.

69 The same pope wrote to the bishops of the region of Narbonne: 'We should be distinguished from others, not by our dress but by our knowledge, by our conversation not by our manner of life' (quoted by Y. C., HDA, p. 135n. 4).

70 Sermon 340 and other references in HDA, p. 133n. 2.

71 Y. C., *Église et papauté*, p. 101. See also: 'Aspects ecclésiologiques de la querelle entre mendiants et séculiers dans la seconde moitié du XIIIe siècle et le début du XIVe', in *Archives d'histoire doctrinale et littéraire du Moyen Âge* 28 (1961), p. 148.

72 See also Congar's article 'Papauté' in the French *Encyclopædia*

Universalis, DVD 2008 edition. He writes on this period: 'We go from *primatus* to *papatus*'.

73 See also Y. C., *Église et papauté*, p. 100.

74 HDA, p. 138. Congar devoted an entire study to the use that was made of this text by the Roman pontiffs: 'Ecce constitui te super gentes et regna (Jer. 1:10)', republished in *Études d'ecclésiologie médiévale* (London: Variorum Reprints, 1983), pp. 671–96.

75 The text was first published in German: *Gott in Welt. Festgabe Karl Rahner* (Fribourg: Herder, 1963), pp. 865–95. An English translation was published in Y. C., *Report from Rome II, On the Second Session of the Vatican Council*, trans. Lancelot Sheppard (London: Geoffrey Chapman, 1964), pp. 173–97. All of the quotations of this paragraph are taken from pp. 189–90.

76 He would not deny that similar traits could be found in the early Middle Ages. He is attempting to capture a prevailing tendency.

77 The English translation of Congar's text has 'bodily mortification', which is not satisfactory. When Paul speaks of the 'flesh' he is not thinking of the body, but of human tendencies that are selfish and self-centred.

78 Jean Delumeau, 'Réforme Catholique', in *Encyclopædia Universalis*, DVD 2008 edition.

79 In addition to the reaction that I mention here, another aspect of this reaction was to revise the conception and the exercise of authority on a moral and pastoral level.

80 Y. C., *Power and Poverty*, p. 109; tr. modified.

81 HDA, p. 144. In addition to Congar's study on this theme ('L'ecclésiologie, de la Révolution française au Concile du Vatican, sous le signe de l'affirmation de l'autorité'), see also J.-F. Chiron's article, 'Une barrière éternelle – L'autorité de l'Église dans la définition du dogme au XIXe siècle', *Recherches de science religieuse* 94 (2006/1), pp. 29–52.

82 J.-F. Chiron, 'Une barrière éternelle', p. 30; he was quoting Agnès Antoine, *L'impensé de la démocratie. Tocqueville et la religion* (Paris: Fayard, 2003), p. 150.

83 On this question see G. Alberigo's article, 'Le Concile de Trente et le tridentinisme', *Irénikon* 54 (1981), pp. 92–220, and the remarkable document published by the Groupe des Dombes: *For the Conversion of the Churches*, trans. James Greig (Geneva: WCC publications, 1994).

84 See Y. C., *Le Concile au jour le jour, Troisième* and *Quatrième*

session, respectively (Paris: Cerf, 1965) and (Paris: Cerf, 1966). Not available in English translation.

85 The first Vatican Council, as is well known, was interrupted for political reasons (Rome was annexed to the kingdom of Italy), and this prevented the Council from taking up the many other items that were on its program. As a result, the Constitution on the infallibility of the pope, when detached from its context, inspired Congar to write the following: 'The fact that the Constitution *Pastor aeternus* on papal power was separated from a more encompassing *De Ecclesia* and that it wound up being proclaimed as an isolated document introduced into ecclesiology a gap and an imbalance that have often been criticized and deplored' (*L'Église de Saint Augustin à l'époque moderne*, 1970, p. 442). See also Y. C., 'A Last Look at the Council' in *Vatican II By Those Who Were There*, ed. A. Stacpoole (London: Geoffrey Chapman, 1986), p. 341, on the continuity desired by Pope Paul VI between Vatican I and Vatican II: '[...] the teaching of Vatican II about the episcopate and its collegiality is thought to have restored an equilibrium to the purely papal emphasis of Vatican I, as Paul VI declared on two occasions (29 September and 21 December 1963) that it ought to do. The continuity between the two councils was demonstrated by the evidence that the teaching of Vatican II had already been sketched out in the plans of Vatican I.'

86 *Jean Puyo interroge le Père Congar* (Paris: Centurion, 1975), p. 213.

87 Y. C., *Journal d'un théologien* (Paris: Cerf, 2001), p. 305. During the Council, his serene reaction to the addition of the *Nota praevia* to chapter 3 of *Lumen Gentium* should also be noted. See Y. C., *Le Concile au jour le jour, Troisième session*, pp. 115–29. On collegiality, see *Le Concile et les conciles* (Paris: Cerf, 1960), p. 301 and pp. 306–7; without defining collegiality as such, he sheds light on its status.

88 Y. C., *Le Concile au jour le jour, Quatrième session*, p. 33. See also *Jean Puyo interroge le Père Congar*, p. 210 and p. 150: 'But the conciliar life of the Church cannot be reduced to holding synods. It implies that from one end of the Church to the other, the Christian communities have a say in determining their life.' See also *Fifty Years of Catholic Theology*, p. 12.

89 In his article 'Papauté' [Papacy], which he wrote for the *Encyclopædia Universalis*, Congar explained: 'Conciliarism emerged because it had become impossible to resolve the crisis created by the rivalry between two, then three popes. The crisis characterized

the councils of Pisa (1409), Constance (1414–18), Basel (1431–49): an entire theological movement reduced the pope to a minister subordinate to the body of the faithful or to the Church, of which the Council was the "representative".'

90 See also Y. C., *Le Concile au jour le jour, Troisième session*, pp. 117–18 that reveals how remarkably balanced Congar's thought was: he never set primacy and collegiality in opposition to one another.

91 Y. C., *Le Concile au jour le jour, Troisième session*, p. 118. He returns to this point in his comments on the Fourth Session of the Council and liturgical reform: 'Neither the liturgical reform nor the rest of the Council's work proceeded from a system, from preconceived ideas, or from a thesis' (*Le Concile au jour le jour, Quatrième session*, p. 26). And p. 32: '[...] actions often preceded and opened the way to ideas.'

92 *Encyclopædia Universalis*, DVD 2008 edition.

93 *Jean Puyo interroge le Père Congar*, pp. 131–2 and p. 149.

94 Y. C., *Une passion: l'unité* (Paris: Foi Vivante 156, 1974), p. 90.

95 Congar would certainly have agreed with Cardinal Suenens: 'Within the conciliar texts there are formulas and statements whose role was to provide a balancing or rallying point. At times, they were arrived at like some stair landing on the way to the top' (Cardinal Léon-Joseph Suenens, *Coresponsibility in the Church*, trans. Francis Martin [New York: Herder and Herder, 1968], p. 21). Congar's realism during the Council is remarkable. Having bishops adopt *his* theology was not his aim. The 'all or nothing' attitude was foreign to him. He wrote in *Pourquoi j'aime l'Église*, p. 25: 'If we were to wait for a perfect Church before becoming involved, we would never begin. E. Mounier possibly gave us the golden rule when he wrote: "The human condition is one of creative ambiguity [...]".'

96 Cardinal Léon-Joseph Suenens, *Coresponsibility in the Church*, p. 13.

97 'Nothing is more significant in this respect than the sequence of chapters II and III of *Lumen Gentium*. There was a vote about this' (Y. C., 'Moving toward a Pilgrim Church', in *Vatican II By Those Who Were There*, ed. A. Stacpoole (London: Geoffrey Chapman, 1986), p. 141; tr. modified). See also Y. C., *Le Concile de Vatican II* (Paris: Beauchesne, 1984), pp. 109–10 and pp. 131–2 on the voting of the text.

98 Congar gave this account in *Le Concile de Vatican II*, p. 132.

99 Y. C., 'The Church: The People of God', trans. Kathryn Sullivan, R.S.C.J, *Concilium* 1 (New York: Paulist Press, 1965), p. 13.

100 Y. C., *Le Concile au jour le jour, Troisième session*, pp. 135–6.

101 'My Path-Findings', *The Jurist* 32 (1972), p. 176.

102 The wording here is taken from G. Martelet, *Deux mille ans d'Église en question*, t. I (Paris: Cerf, 1984), p. 94. The use of the concept 'people' is considered legitimate by Martelet. He writes that though the Church is not a democracy, it should not be prevented from integrating what is best in democracy. He stresses on the same page that 'without refusing anything that is good in the political structures of the world, the Church as the people of God is not enslaved to any of its structures because it finds nowhere an adequate model for its own mystery'.

103 It is useful to refer once more to G. Martelet's wording on this question: 'But the fact that all are equal in the eyes of love does not exclude within the people of God the distinction of roles and functions [...]' (G. Martelet, *Deux mille ans d'Église en question*, t. I, p. 94). In her book *Yves Congar's Theology of the Holy Spirit* (2004), E. T. Groppe, p. 143, writes that 'Congar's references to ecclesial hierarchy decrease sharply in frequency in his later works'.

104 Y. C., *Le Concile de Vatican II*, p. 114. See also Y. C., *Un peuple messianique* (Paris: Cerf, 1975), p. 134: 'Authority in Christianity is functional.'

105 In 1969, Congar could still write: 'Developing a theology of ministries is of utmost importance: *concretely*, in order to see the true reality of the Church; *ecclesiologically*, to declericalize our vision of the Church, because the Church is still *incredibly clerical*, and my knowledge of history allows me to see fairly clearly how we got there' (Y. C., 'Baptême, sacerdoce et vie religieuse', in *La vocation religieuse et sacerdotale* [Paris: Cerf, 1969], p. 34).

106 *Fifty Years of Catholic Theology*, p. 65.

107 Y. C., 'My Path-Findings', p. 174.

108 Y. C., 'My Path-Findings', p. 176; tr. modified. On this question see also J. Famerée, *L'ecclésiologie d'Yves Congar avant Vatican II*, Histoire et Église (Louvain: Bibliotheca Ephemeridum Theologicarum Lovaniensium CVII, 1992), p. 441. When he revised the first two editions of *Lay People in the Church*, Congar pointed out another weakness in his presentation of the relationship between the faithful and ministerial priesthood: '[...] in examining the Church's functions, we have looked at things too statically, concentrating more on the functions' structure than on their actual working in practice' (*Lay People in the Church*, Addenda

in 1964, p. xxi). Basically, ministry and authority can be properly understood only in the dynamic of mission and growth.

109 'Autorité, initiative, coresponsabilité' was published in *La Maison-Dieu* 97 (1969), pp. 34–57. The article's subtitle is 'Elements of reflection on the conditions in which the problem is discussed in the Church today'. For a partial translation in English see 'Authority, Initiative and Co-responsibility', in *Blessed Is the Peace of My Church*, trans. Salvator Attanasio (Denville, NJ: Dimension Books, 1973), pp. 57–90.

110 In *À temps et à contretemps* (Paris: Cerf, 1969). Not available in English translation. This book contains contributions by various authors, including Congar's 'Autorité et liberté dans l'Église'.

111 Y. C., 'Authority, Initiative, and Co-responsibility', p. 66.

112 Y. C., 'Authority, Initiative, and Co-responsibility', pp. 66–7; tr. modified.

113 Y. C., 'Authority, Initiative, and Co-responsibility', p. 67; tr. modified.

114 Y. C., 'Authority, Initiative, and Co-responsibility', p. 65; tr. modified.

115 Y. C., 'Authority, Initiative, and Co-responsibility', p. 65. See also 'Renewal of the Spirit and Reform of the Institution', trans. John Griffiths in *Concilium* 73 (1973), p. 46.

116 Y. C., 'Institutionalized Religion', in *The Word in History*, St. Francis Xavier Symposium, ed. Patrick Burke (New York: Sheed and Ward, 1966), p. 150; tr. modified.

117 Y. C., 'Institutionalized Religion', p. 139.

118 Y. C., 'Autorité et liberté', p. 14.

119 Y. C., 'Autorité et liberté', pp. 28–9 and p. 29 for the quotation that follows.

120 The article first appeared in *La Vie Spirituelle* 604 (1974) and was later republished in Congar's book of essays, *Essais œcuméniques*, pp. 297–312. Pagination used is that of *Essais oecuméniques*.

121 Y. C., *Essais œcuméniques*, p. 308.

122 Y. C., 'Le monothéisme politique et le Dieu Trinité', *Nouvelle Revue Théologique* 103 (1981), p. 13.

123 He does this when he recalls that 'the functional relation of inequality is nevertheless not destroyed' ('Authority, Initiative, and Co-responsibility', p. 74).

124 Y. C., 'Authority, Initiative, and Co-responsibility', p. 58.

125 Y. C., 'Authority, Initiative, and Co-responsibility', p. 63. See also Y. C., 'Institutionalized Religion', pp. 133–53.

126 Y. C., 'Authority, Initiative, and Co-responsibility', p. 78; tr. modified. Congar continues: 'If we go beyond the point of view of the single structure "*secundum sub et supra*", and of obedience as a simple means of the order to be maintained, and if we adopt instead the point of view of a mission to be advocated, of a responsibility to be honored, then authority and obedience are exercised in dialogue without thereby being reduced to equality in dialogue' (pp. 78–9; tr. modified).

127 In his conversations with Jean Puyo, Congar bemoans 'the apparent lack of interest for the Trinitarian mystery among theologians and Church leaders' (*Jean Puyo interroge le Père Congar*, p. 195).

128 Y. C., 'Pneumatologie Dogmatique', p. 500.

129 Groupe des Dombes, *Towards a Reconciliation of Ministries*, trans. Pamela Gaughan no. 24. See *Modern Ecumenical Documents on the Ministry*, ed. H. R. McAdoo (London: SPCK, 1975), p. 98. Recently reprinted in *For the Communion of the Churches*, ed. C. E. Clifford (Grand Rapids, MI: Wm. B. Eerdmans, 2010), p. 29.

130 Y. C., *Essais œcuméniques*, p. 309.

131 This term that Cardinal Suenens was fond of was taken up recently by Pope Benedict XVI at the opening of the 'Pastoral Convention of the Diocese of Rome' on the theme, 'Church Membership and Pastoral Co-responsiblity' (26 May 2009). In his address, Pope Benedict invited participants 'to understand ever better what this Church is, this People of God in the Body of Christ'. He continued: 'At the same time, it is necessary to improve pastoral structures in such a way that the co-responsibility of all the members of the People of God in their entirety is gradually promoted, with respect for vocations and for the respective roles of the consecrated and of lay people. This demands a change in mindset, particularly concerning lay people. They must no longer be viewed as "collaborators" of the clergy but truly recognized as "co-responsible" for the Church's being and action, thereby fostering the consolidation of a mature and committed laity. This common awareness of being Church of all the baptized in no way diminishes the responsibility of parish priests. It is precisely your task, dear parish priests, to nurture the spiritual and apostolic growth of those who are already committed to working hard in the parishes. They form the core of the community that will act as a leaven for the others.' The complete address is available at: http://www.vatican.va/holy_father/benedict_xvi/speeches/2009/may/

documents/hf_ben-xvi_spe_20090526_convegno-diocesi-rm_en.html (accessed 20 November 2012).

132 Y. C., 'Autorité et liberté dans l'Église', p. 19 and p. 27.

133 *Jean Puyo interroge le Père Congar*, p. 196.

134 Y. C., 'Autorité et liberté dans l'Église', p. 19.

135 Y. C., 'Autorité et liberté dans l'Église', pp. 28–30.

136 Quoted by Y. C. in *The Mystery of the Church*, Second revised edition, trans. A. V. Littledale (Baltimore and Dublin: Helicon Press and Geoffrey Chapman, revised translation, 1965), p. 103; tr. modified.

Notes to the Conclusion

1 Y. C., *Faith and Spiritual Life*, trans. A. Mason and L. C. Sheppard (New York: Herder and Herder, 1968) contains three texts on Lacordaire, pp. 94–121. Congar said to Jean Puyo: 'Father Lacordaire is for us French Dominicans like a second founder' (*Jean Puyo interroge le Père Congar* [Paris: Centurion, 1975], p. 34). See also Y. C., *True and False Reform in the Church*, trans. Paul Philibert (Collegeville, MN: Liturgical Press, 2011), pp. 329–34.

2 Y. C., *True and False Reform*, p. 334. 'Congar admired St. Thomas Aquinas and his will to be "a servant of the truth", but increasingly, he found confirmation for his goals in the model of Henri-Dominique Lacordaire and his will to bring the Gospel to the world born of the French Revolution' (Michael Quisinsky, 'Congar avec Chenu et Féret au Saulchoir des années 1930', p. 8).

3 Y. C., *True and False Reform*, p. 217.

4 Y. C., 'Father Lacordaire, Minister of the Word of God', *Faith and Spiritual Life*, p. 106.

5 Y. C., 'Freedom in the Life of Henry Dominic Lacordaire', *Faith and Spiritual Life*, p. 106; tr. modified.

6 Y. C., *Lay People in the Church: A Study for a Theology of the Laity*, trans. Donald Attwater (Westminster, MD: Newman Press, 1965), p. xix.

7 Y. C., *I Believe in the Holy Spirit*, vol. 2, trans. David Smith (New York: Seabury, 1983), p. 34.

8 Y. C., *I Believe in the Holy Spirit*, vol. 2, p. 35.

9 Y. C., *I Believe in the Holy Spirit*, vol. 2, p. 35.

10   *Fifty Years of Catholic Theology, Conversations with Yves Congar*,
     edited and introduced by Bernard Lauret, trans. John Bowden
     (Philadelphia: Fortress Press, 1988), p. 72.

11   Cardinal Walter Kasper, 'La théologie oecuménique d'Yves-Marie
     Congar et la situation actuelle de l'oecuménisme', *Bulletin de
     Littérature ecclésiastique* CVI/1 (2005), p. 5 and p. 8.

12   Y. C., *True and False Reform*, p. 368.

13   Y. C., 'Ecumenical Experience and Conversion', in *The Sufficiency
     of God*, Robert C. Mackie and Charles C. West (eds) (London:
     SCM Press, 1963), p. 75.

14   Y. C., 'Ecumenical Experience and Conversion', p. 75.

15   Y. C., 'Ecumenical Experience and Conversion', p. 75.

16   *Jean Puyo interroge le Père Congar* (1975), pp. 191–2.

17   Y. C., *True and False Reform*, p. 369; tr. modified.

18   Y. C., *True and False Reform*, p. 369; tr. modified.

19   Y. C., 'L'influence de la société et de l'histoire sur le développement
     de l'homme chrétien', *Nouvelle Revue Théologique* 96 (1974),
     p. 677.

WORKS QUOTED

I. Works by Yves Congar

This section includes books and other writings by Yves Congar.
The editions quoted are specified. Works are cited chronologically
in order of the date of the original French publication.

A. Books

Divided Christendom: A Catholic Study of the Problem of Reunion (trans.
M.A. Bousfield; London: Centenary Press, 1939). Originally published
as *Chrétiens désunis: Principes d'un 'œcuménisme' catholique* (Unam
Sanctam 1, Paris: Les Éditions de Cerf, 1937). A French edition of this
book, which includes the corrections Congar had prepared in 1948 for
a new edition, is available on the web at: http://www.editionsducerf.fr/
site_congar/cadre_gal.htm (accessed 30 July 2013).

The Mystery of the Church (trans. A. V. Littledale; Baltimore: Helicon,
2nd edn, 1965). Originally published as *Esquisses du Mystère de
l'Église* (Unam Sanctam 8, Paris: Cerf, 1941; 2nd edn, 1953; 3rd edn,
1963; and *La Pentecôte—Chartres*, Paris: Cerf, 1956).

*Leur résistance, Mémorial des évadés anciens de Colditz et de Lübeck
morts pour la France*, Témoignage d'Yves Congar, 1948. No publisher
is mentioned, only 'En dépôt chez Albert Renault'.

True and False Reform in the Church (trans. Paul Philibert O.P.;
Collegeville, MN: Liturgical Press, 2011). Originally published as
Vraie et fausse réforme dans l'Église (Unam Sanctam, 20; Paris:
Cerf, 1950; 2nd rev. edn, Unam Sanctam, 72, 1968). Paul Philibert's
translation is based on the second revised edition and does not include
the third part of *Vraie et fausse réforme dans l'Église* nor does it
include Appendix III that Congar chose to omit from the second
edition of *Vraie et fausse réforme dans l'Église*. See below 'Attitudes
toward Reform in the Church' in section D: 'Articles'.

Lay People in the Church: A Study for a Theology of the Laity (trans. Donald Attwater; Westminster, MD: Newman Press, 1965). Originally published as *Jalons pour une théologie du laïcat* (Unam Sanctam, 23; Paris: Cerf, 1953; 2nd edn, 1954; 3rd rev. edn, 1964).

La Pentecôte—Chartres 1956 (Paris: Cerf, 1956). See above *The Mystery of the Church*.

Laity, Church, World (trans. Donald Attwater; Baltimore, MD: Helicon, 1960). Originally published as *Si vous êtes mes témoins: Trois conférences sur laïcat, Église et monde* (Paris: Cerf, 1959).

Tradition and Traditions: An Historical and a Theological Essay (trans. Michael Naseby and Thomas Rainborough; New York: Macmilan, 1967). Originally published as *La Tradition et les traditions: Essai historique* (Paris: Fayard, 1960) and *La Tradition et les traditions: Essai théologique* (Paris: Fayard, 1963).

Faith and Spiritual Life (trans. A. Manson and L. C. Sheppard; New York: Herder and Herder, 1968). Originally published as Part II of *Les Voies du Dieu vivant: Théologie et vie spirituelle* (Cogitatio Fidei, 3; Paris: Cerf, 1962).

Priest and Layman (London, Darton, Longman & Todd, 1967). Originally published as *Sacerdoce et laïcat devant leurs tâches d'évangélisation et de civilisation* (Cogitatio Fidei, 4; Paris: Cerf, 1962).

The Meaning of Tradition (trans. A. N. Woodrow; San Francisco: Ignatius Press, 2004). Originally published as *La Tradition et la vie de l'Église* (Je sais–Je crois; Paris: Cerf, 1963; 2nd edn, 1984), the 2nd edition includes a new preface by Congar, which has not been translated into English.

Power and Poverty in the Church (trans. Jennifer Nicholson; London and Dublin: Geoffrey Chapman, 1965). Originally published as *Pour une Église servante et pauvre* (Paris: Cerf, 1963).

Report from Rome, On the First Session of the Vatican Council (trans. A. Manson; London: Geoffrey Chapman, 1963). Originally published as *Le Concile au jour le jour, Première session* (L'Église aux cent visages; Paris: Cerf, 1963).

Dialogue Between Christians (trans. Philip Loretz, S.J.; Westminster, MD: Newman Press, 1966). Originally published as *Chrétiens en dialogue: Contributions catholiques à l'œcuménisme* (Unam Sanctam, 50; Paris: Cerf, 1964).

Report from Rome II, On the Second Session of the Vatican Council (trans. Lancelot Sheppard; London: Geoffrey Chapman, 1964). Originally published as *Le Concile au jour le jour, Deuxième session* (L'Église aux cent visages; Paris: Cerf, 1964).

Le Concile au jour le jour, Troisième session (L'Église aux cent visages; Paris: Cerf, 1965).

Le Concile au jour le jour, Quatrième session (L'Église aux cent visages; Paris: Cerf, 1966).

Situation et tâches présentes de la théologie (Cogitatio Fidei, 27; Paris: Cerf, 1967).

L'ecclésiologie du haut moyen âge (Paris: Cerf, 1968).

This Church That I Love (trans. Lucien Delafuente; Denville, NJ: Dimension Books, 1969). Originally published as *Cette Église que j'aime* (Foi Vivante, 70; Paris: Cerf, 1968).

Blessed Is the Peace of My Church (trans. Salvator Attanasio; Denville, NJ: Dimension Books, 1973). Originally published as *Au milieu des orages: L'Église affronte aujourd'hui son avenir* (Paris: Cerf, 1969).

L'Église Une, Sainte, Catholique et Apostolique (Mysterium Salutis, 15; Paris: Cerf, 1970).

L'Église de Saint Augustin à l'époque moderne (Histoire des Dogmes; Paris: Cerf, 1970).

Ministères et communion ecclésiale (Paris: Cerf, 1971).

Une passion: l'unité. Réflexions et souvenirs 1929–1973 (Foi Vivante, 156; Paris: Cerf, 1974).

Un peuple messianique, Salut et libération (Cogitatio Fidei, 85; Paris: Cerf, 1975).

Challenge to the Church: The Case of Archbishop Lefebvre (trans. Paul Inwood; Huntington, IN: Our Sunday Visitor, 1976). Originally published as *La Crise dans l'Église et Mgr. Lefebvre* (Paris: Cerf, 1976).

Église Catholique et France moderne (Paris: Hachette, 1978).

I Believe in the Holy Spirit (trans. David Smith; 3 vols; New York: Seabury, 1983). Originally published as *Je crois en l'Esprit Saint* (Vol. I, L'expérience de l'Esprit; Paris: Cerf, 1979; Vol. II, Il est Seigneur et Il donne la vie; Paris: Cerf, 1979; Vol. III, Le fleuve de vie; Paris: Cerf, 1980).

Diversity and Communion (trans. John Bowden; London: SCM Press, 1984). Originally published as *Diversités et communion: Dossier historique et conclusion théologique* (Cogitatio Fidei, 112; Paris: Cerf, 1982).

Martin Luther, sa foi, sa réforme (Cogitatio Fidei, 119; Paris: Cerf, 1983).

Études d'ecclésiologie médiévale (London: Variorum Reprints, 1983).

Essais œcuméniques: Les hommes, le mouvement, les problèmes (Paris: Le Centurion, 1984).

The Word and the Spirit (trans. David Smith; San Francisco: Harper and Row, 1986).Originally published as *La Parole et le Souffle* (Jésus et Jésus-Christ; Paris: Éditions Desclée de Brouwer, 1984); the 2nd edn includes a presentation by Rémi Chéno (Paris: Mame-Desclée, 2010).

Le Concile de Vatican II, Son Église, Peuple de Dieu et Corps du Christ
(Théologie Historique, 71; Paris: Éditions Beauchesne, 1984).
Église et papauté (Paris: Cerf, 1994; 2nd edn, 2002.
Écrits Réformateurs, Selected texts presented by Jean-Pierre Jossua
(Textes en main; Paris: Cerf, 1995).
Journal de la Guerre, 1914–1918 (Stéphane Audoin-Rouzeau and
Dominique Congar (eds); Paris: Cerf, 1997).
Journal d'un théologien (ed. Étienne Fouilloux; Paris: Cerf, 2001).
My Journal of the Council (trans. Mary John Ronayne, O.P. and Mary
Cecily Boulding O.P.; Collegeville, MN: Liturgical Press, 2012).
Originally published as *Mon Journal du Concile*, Vol. 1, 1960–3;
Vol. 2, 1964–6 (presented and annotated by Éric Mahieu; Paris: Cerf,
2002).

B. Two Books of Conversations with Yves Congar

Jean Puyo interroge le Père Congar: Une vie pour la vérité (Les
interviews; Paris: Centurion, 1975).
Fifty Years of Catholic Theology: Conversations with Yves Congar (ed.
Bernard Lauret; trans. John Bowden; Philadelphia: Fortress, 1988).
Originally published as *Entretiens d'automne* (Théologies, presented
by B. Lauret; Paris: Cerf, 1987).

C. Contributions

A History of Theology (trans. Hunter Guthrie; Garden City, NY:
Doubleday, 1968). Originally published as 'Théologie', in
Dictionnaire de Théologie Catholique, 15, Letouzey et Ané (1943),
pp. 342–502.
'L'ecclésiologie de la Révolution française au Concile du Vatican, sous le
signe de l'affirmation de l'autorité', in *L'ecclésiologie au XIXe siècle*
(Unam Sanctam, 34; Paris: Cerf, 1960), pp. 77–114.
'Conclusion' to *Le Concile et les Conciles, Contribution à l'histoire de la
vie conciliaire de l'Église* (Paris: Cerf, 1960), pp. 285–334.
'The Historical Development of Authority in the Church: Points for
Christian Reflection', ed. John M. Todd, *Problems of Authority*
(Baltimore: The Helicon Press and London: DLT, 1962), pp. 119–56.
Originally published as 'Le développement historique de l'autorité

dans l'Église: Éléments pour la réflexion chrétienne' in *Problèmes de l'autorité* (Unam Sanctam, 38; Paris: Cerf, 1962), pp. 145–81.

'Quelques expressions traditionnelles du service chrétien', in *L'Épiscopat et L'Église Universelle* (Unam Sanctam, 39; Paris: Cerf, 1962), pp. 101–32.

'The Hierarchy as Service', in *Power and Poverty in the Church* (trans. Jennifer Nicholson; London and Dublin: Geoffrey Chapman, 1965), pp. 15–39. Originally published as 'La hiérarchie comme service' in *L'Épiscopat et L'Église Universelle* (Unam Sanctam, 39; Paris: Cerf, 1962), pp. 67–99.

Traités anti-donatistes, by St. Augustine, Introduction by Yves Congar, *Œuvres de Saint Augustin*, 28, Quatrième série, Vol. 1, Paris, Desclée de Brouwer (1963), pp. 9–133.

'The Ecclesia or Christian Community as a Whole Celebrates the Liturgy', in *At the Heart of Christian Worship: Liturgical Essays of Yves Congar* (trans. Paul Philibert; Collegeville, MN: Liturgical Press, 2010), pp. 15–68. Originally published as 'L'Ecclesia ou communauté chrétienne, sujet intégral de l'action liturgique' in *La Liturgie après Vatican II* (Unam Sanctam, 66; Paris: Cerf, 1967), pp. 241–82.

'Changements et continuité dans l'Église', in *Notre foi* (Paris: Beauchesne, 1967), pp. 55–73.

'Baptême, sacerdoce et vie religieuse', in *La vocation religieuse et sacerdotale* (Paris: Cerf, 1969), pp. 23–34.

'Autorité et liberté dans l'Église', in Yves Congar, René Voillaume and Jacques Loew, *À temps et à contretemps: Retrouver dans l'Église le visage de Jésus-Christ* (Paris: Cerf, 1969), pp. 7–39.

'Le Père M.-D. Chenu', in Robert Van der Gucht and Herbert Vorgrimler (eds), *Bilan de la théologie du XXe siècle*, Vol. II (Paris-Tournai: Casterman, 1970), pp. 772–90.

'Tradition et Ouverture', in Gérard Soulages ed. *Fidélité et Ouverture* (Paris: Mame-Desclée, 1972), pp. 55–68.

'Ecumenical Experience and Conversion', in Robert C. Mackie and Charles C. West (eds), *The Sufficiency of God* (London: SCM Press, 1963), pp. 71–87.

'Pneumatologie dogmatique', in Bernard Lauret and François Refoulé (eds), *Initiation à la pratique de la théologie*, Vol. II: Dogmatique I (Paris: Cerf, 1982), pp. 493–516.

'Théologie historique', in Bernard Lauret and François Refoulé (eds), *Initiation à la pratique de la théologie*, Vol. I: Introduction (Paris: Cerf, 1982), pp. 233–62.

'A Last Look at the Council', in A. Stacpoole, ed. *Vatican II By Those Who Were There* (London: Geoffrey Chapman, 1986), pp. 337–53.

'Moving Toward a Pilgrim Church', in A. Stacpoole, ed., *Vatican II*

By Those Who Were There (London: Geoffrey Chapman, 1986), pp. 129–52.

D. Articles

'Actualité de Kierkegaard', *La vie intellectuelle* (vol. 32; 1934), pp. 9–36.

'The Reasons for the Unbelief of Our Time', *Integration* (August–September 1938 and December 1938–January 1939), pp. 13–21 and pp. 10–26. Originally published as 'Une conclusion théologique à l'enquête sur les raisons actuelles de l'incroyance', *La vie intellectuelle* (vol. 37; 1935), pp. 214–49.

'"Real" Liturgy, "Real" Preaching' in *At the Heart of Christian Worship: Liturgical Essays of Yves Congar* (trans. Paul Philibert: Collegeville, MN: Liturgical Press, 2010), 1–13. First published as 'Pour une prédication et une liturgie réelles', *La Maison-Dieu* (vol. 16; 1948, pp. 75–87).

'True and False Reform in the Church', *Orate Fratres* (vol. 23; 1948–49), pp. 252–9. Abbreviated version of an article published as 'Pourquoi le Peuple de Dieu doit-il sans cesse se réformer?', *Irénikon* (vol. 21, no. 4; 1948), pp. 365–94.

'Attitudes toward Reform in the Church' (trans. Bernard Gilligan; *Cross Currents* vol. 4; 1951), pp. 80–102. Originally published as 'Part A' of the Conclusion to *Vraie et fausse réforme dans l'Église* (Unam Sanctam, 20; Paris: Cerf, 1950), pp. 539–69. 'Attitudes toward Reform in the Church', pp. 83–7, includes also part of Appendix III, 'Mentalité 'de droite' et Intégrisme en France', pp. 605–11 and pp. 612–18, that was part of the first edition of *Vraie et fausse réforme dans l'Église*, but that Congar chose to omit in the second edition in 1968.

'Comment l'Église doit se renouveler sans cesse', *Irénikon* (vol. 34; 1961), pp. 322–45.

'Aspects ecclésiologiques de la querelle entre mendiants et séculiers dans la seconde moitié du XIIIe siècle et le début du XIVe', *Archives d'histoire doctrinale et littéraire du Moyen Âge* (vol. 28, 1961), pp. 35–151.

'Du bon usage de "Denzinger"', *L'Ami du Clergé* (21 mai 1963), pp. 321–9, republished in *Situation et tâches présentes de la théologie* (Cogitatio Fidei, 27; Paris: Cerf, 1967), pp. 111–13. Pagination follows the book.

'The Church: People of God' (trans. Kathryn Sullivan; *Concilium* 1, Karl Rahner and Edward Schillebeeckx (eds); New York: Paulist Press,

1965), pp. 11–37. Originally published as 'L'Église comme peuple de Dieu', *Concilium* (vol. 1; 1965), pp. 5–32.

'Christ in the Economy of Salvation and in Our Dogmatic Tracts' (trans. Aimée Bourneuf, R.S.C.J.; *Concilium*, vol. 1, 1966), pp. 4–15. Originally published as 'Le Christ dans l'Économie salutaire et dans nos traités dogmatiques' *Concilium* (vol. 11, 1966), pp. 11–26.

'Institutionalized Religion' in Patrick Burke ed. *The Word in History* (St. Francis Xavier Symposium; New York: Sheed and Ward, 1966), pp. 133–53. Originally published as 'Religion et institution', *Théologie d'aujourd'hui et de demain* (Cogitatio Fidei, 23: Paris: Cerf, 1967), pp. 81–97.

'Authority, Initiative and Co-responsibility', in *Blessed Is the Peace of my Church* (trans. Salvator Attanasio; Denville, NJ: Dimension Books, 1973), pp. 57–90. This is a partial translation of 'Autorité, initiative, coresponsabilité', that appeared in *La Maison-Dieu* (vol. 97; 1969), pp. 34–57, and a complete translation of the version that appeared in *Au milieu des orages* (Paris: Cerf, 1969), pp. 65–103.

'Pourquoi j'aime l'Église', *Verbum Caro* (vol. 95; 1970), pp. 23–30.

'My Path-Findings in the Theology of Laity and Ministries', *The Jurist* (vol. 32; 1972), pp. 169–88. Originally published as 'Mon cheminement dans la théologie du laïcat et des ministères', in *Ministères et communion ecclésiale* (Théologie sans frontières; Paris: Cerf, 1971), pp. 9–30.

'Le chrétien, son présent, son avenir et son passé', *Lumière et vie* (vol. 108; 1972), pp. 72–82.

'Reception as an Ecclesiological Reality' in Giuseppe Alberigo and Anton Weiler (eds), *Concilium: Election and Consensus in the Church* (Vol. 77; New York: Herder and Herder, 1972), pp. 43–68. Originally published as 'La "Reception" comme réalité ecclésiologique,' *Revue des Sciences philosophiques et théologiques* (vol. 56; 1972), pp. 369–403, republished in *Église et papauté* (Paris: Cerf, 2002), pp. 369–403.

'Pneumatology Today', *The American Ecclesiastical Review* (vol. 167; 1973), pp. 435–41. Originally published as 'Actualité d'une pneumatologie', *Proche Orient chrétien* (vol. 23; 1973), pp. 126–32.

'Renewal of the Spirit and Reform of the Institution' (trans. John Griffiths; *Concilium*, vol. 73; 1973), pp. 39–49. Originally published as 'Renouvellement de l'Esprit et réforme de l'institution', *Concilium* (vol. 73; 1973), pp. 37–45.

'La Tri-unité de Dieu et l'Église', *La Vie Spirituelle* (vol. 604; 1974), pp. 687–701 and republished in *Essais œcuméniques* (Paris: Centurion, 1984), pp. 297–312. Pagination follows the book.

'L'influence de la société et de l'histoire sur le développement de l'homme chrétien', *Nouvelle Revue Théologique* (vol. 96; 1974), pp. 673–92.

'A Semantic History of the Term "Magisterium"', *Readings in Moral Theology* No. 3: *The Magisterium and Morality* (C. Curran and R. McCormick (eds); New York: Paulist Press, 1982), pp. 297–313. Originally published as 'Bref historique des formes du "magistère" et de ses relations avec les docteurs', *Revue des Sciences philosophiques et théologiques* (vol. 60; 1976), pp. 99–112. Republished in Yves Congar, *Église et papauté* (Paris: Cerf, 2002), pp. 299–315.

'L'Église, antique fontaine d'une eau jaillissante et fraîche', *La Vie Spirituelle* (vol. 636; 1980), pp. 31–40.

'Le monothéisme politique et le Dieu Trinité', *Nouvelle Revue Théologique* (vol. 103; 1981), pp. 3–17.

'Actualité de la pneumatologie', in *Credo in Spiritum Sanctum* (Atti del congresso teologico internazionale di pneumatologia; Rome: Libreria Editrice Vaticana, 1982), pp. 15–28.

'Papauté' in *Encyclopædia Universalis* (DVD 2008 edition).

'Apôtres et Apostolat' in *Encyclopædia Universalis* (DVD 2008 edition).

E. Prefaces by Yves Congar to works by other authors

Dvornik, François, *Le schisme de Photius* (Unam Sanctam, 19; Paris: Cerf, 1950). Preface by Congar.

Michonneau, G., *Pas de vie chrétienne sans communauté* (Rencontres, 58; Paris: Cerf, 1960). Preface-Letter by Congar.

Delahaye, K., *Ecclesia Mater* (Unam Sanctam, 46; Paris: Cerf, 1964). Preface by Congar.

Feuillet, André, *Le Christ Sagesse de Dieu* (Paris: Les Éditions Gabalda, 1966). Preface by Congar.

de la Potterie, Ignace and Lyonnet Stanislas, *The Christian Lives by the Spirit* (trans. John Morriss; Staten Island, NY: Alba House, 1971). Originally published as *La vie selon l'Esprit* (Unam Sanctam, 55; Paris: Cerf, 1965). Preface by Congar.

II. Works on Congar

Alberigo, G., 'Réforme et unité de l'Église', in A. Vauchez, ed. *Cardinal Yves Congar 1904–1995* (Acts of the Colloquium of Rome 3–4 June 1996; Paris: Cerf, 1999), pp. 9–25.

Birmelé, André, 'Yves-Marie Congar en dialogue avec la Réforme', *Bulletin de Littérature ecclésiastique* (CVI/1; 2005), pp. 65–88.

Bousquet, François, 'La dimension apostolique de la Tradition selon le P. Congar', *Transversalités* (vol. 98; 2006), pp. 77–88.

Chéno Remi, 'Les *retractationes* d'Yves Congar sur le rôle de l'Esprit Saint dans les institutions ecclésiales', *Revue des Sciences philosophiques et théologiques* (vol. 91; 2007), pp. 265–84.

—Presentation of a new edition of *La Parole et le Souffle* (Jésus et Jésus-Christ; Paris: Mame-Desclée, 2010), pp. 207–21.

Humann, François-Marie, *La relation de l'Esprit-Saint au Christ, une relecture d'Yves Congar* (Cogitatio Fidei, 274; Paris: Cerf, 2010).

Famerée, J., 'L'ecclésiologie du Père Yves Congar: Essai de synthèse critique', *Revue des Sciences philosophiques et théologiques* (vol. 76; Paris: Vrin, 1992), pp. 377–418.

—'Originalité de l'ecclésiologie du Père Congar', *Bulletin de Littérature ecclésiastique* (CVI/1; Toulouse, 2005), pp. 89–112.

—'Formation et ecclésiologie du "premier" Congar', in A. Vauchez, ed. *Cardinal Yves Congar (1904–1995)* (Acts of the Colloquium of Rome 3–4 June 1996; Paris: Cerf, 1999), pp. 51–70.

—*L'ecclésiologie d'Yves Congar avant Vatican II* (Histoire et Église; Louvain: Bibliotheca Ephemeridum Theologicarum Lovaniensium, CVII, 1992).

—'Y. M.-J. Congar, Théologien de la catholicité', *Cahiers œcuméniques* (33; Fribourg, 1998), pp. 15–31.

—'Orthodox influence on the Roman Catholic Theologian Yves Congar, O.P.: A Sketch', *St Vladimir's Theological Quarterly* (vol. 39; 1995), pp. 409–16.

Famerée J. and Routhier Gilles, *Yves Congar* (Initiations aux théologiens; Paris: Cerf, 2008).

Flynn, Gabriel, *Yves Congar's Vision of the Church in a World of Unbelief* (Aldershot: Ashgate Publishing, 2004).

Fouilloux, Étienne, 'Friar Yves, Cardinal Congar, Dominican: Itinerary of a Theologian', *U.S. Catholic Historian* 17/2 (1999), pp. 62–90. Originally published as 'Yves Congar, Itinéraire d'un théologien', *Revue des Sciences philosophiques et théologiques* (vol. 79; 1995), pp. 379–404.

—'Congar, témoin de l'Église de son temps (1930–1960)', in A. Vauchez ed. *Cardinal Yves Congar (1904–1995)* (Acts of the Colloquium of Rome 3–4 June 1996; Paris: Cerf, 1999), pp. 71–91.

—'Un théologien dans l'Église du XXe siècle', *Bulletin de Littérature ecclésiastique* (CVI/1; 2005), pp. 21–38.

—Introduction and Notes to Yves Congar, *Journal d'un théologien* (Paris: Cerf, 2001).

Groppe, Elizabeth Teresa, *Yves Congar's Theology of the Holy Spirit* (New York: Oxford University Press, 2004).

Guilmot, P., *Fin d'une Église cléricale?* (Paris: Cerf, 1969). Chapter 3, pp. 151–249, is devoted entirely to Congar.

ISTINA, 1996, XL1, Editorial (unsigned): 'Yves Congar, pionnier de l'unité': pp. 113–16.

Jossua, Jean-Pierre, *Fifty Years of Catholic Theology: Conversations with Yves Congar* (ed. Bernard Lauret; trans. John Bowden; Philadelphia: Fortress, 1988). Originally published as *Entretiens d'automne* (Présentés par B. Lauret; Théologies; Paris: Cerf, 1987).

—'Signification théologique de quelques retours sur le passé dans l'œuvre d'Yves Congar', in A. Vauchez ed. *Cardinal Yves Congar (1904–1995)* (Acts of the Colloquium of Rome 3–4 June 1996; Paris: Cerf, 1999), pp. 93–103.

—'L'œuvre œcuménique du Père Congar', *Études* (vol. 357, 1982), pp. 543–55.

—Avant-propos (Foreword) to selected texts of Congar: *Écrits Réformateurs* (Textes en main; Paris: Cerf, 1995) and introduction to each of the five parts of this selection.

Kasper, Walter Cardinal, 'La théologie œcuménique d'Yves-Marie Congar et la situation actuelle de l'œcuménisme', *Bulletin de Littérature ecclésiastique* (CVI/1; 2005), pp. 5–20.

Legrand, Hervé, 'Yves Congar (1904–1995): une passion pour l'unité', *Nouvelle Revue Théologique* (vol. 126/4; 2004), pp. 529–54.

Le Guillou, M. J., 'Yves Congar', in Robert Van der Gucht and Herbert Vorgrimler (eds), *Bilan de la théologie du XXe siècle*, Vol. II (Paris-Tournai: Casterman, 1970), pp. 791–805.

McBrien, Richard P., 'I Believe in the Holy Spirit: The Role of Pneumatology in Yves Congar's Theology', in G. Flynn, ed., *Yves Congar Theologian of the Church* (Louvain Theological Pastoral Monographs 32; Louvain: Peeters, 2005), pp. 303–28.

Nisus, Alain, 'L'Esprit-Saint et l'Église dans l'œuvre d'Yves Congar', *Transversalités* (vol. 98; 2006), pp. 109–55.

O'Meara, Thomas, 'Ecumenist of our Times: Yves Congar', *Mid-Stream* (vol. 27, no. 1; 1988), pp. 67–76.

Pietrusiak, Pawel, 'La catholicité de l'Église dans la pensée d'Yves Congar', *Roczniki Teologiczne* (LIII-LIV; 2006–7), pp. 39–60.

Quisinsky, Michael, 'Congar avec Chenu et Féret au Saulchoir des années 1930', *Transversalités* (vol. 98; 2006), pp. 3–35.

Rigal, Jean, 'L'évolution ecclésiologique d'Yves Congar', in *L'ecclésiologie de communion* (Cogitatio Fidei, 202; Paris: Cerf, 1997), pp. 149–73.

Le service théologique dans l'Église, Mélanges offerts à Yves Congar pour ses soixante-dix ans (Cogitatio Fidei, 76; Paris: Cerf, 1974).

Vauchez A., Foreword to A. Vauchez, ed. *Cardinal Yves Congar (1904–1995)* (Acts of the Colloquium of Rome 3–4 June 1996; Paris: Cerf, 1999).

GLOSSARY

Anti-Donatist Writings: These are the writings of St. Augustine (354–430) against the Donatists. Donatism is a schism that began in the Church in the fourth century and takes its name from the schismatic bishop Donatus, bishop of Carthage. In his Anti-Donatist writings, Augustine expresses himself forcefully on the unity and catholicity of the Church.

Catholicity: From the Greek *kath'olon*, meaning 'according to the whole', this term expresses the original genius of the Christian faith. Christians believe that the event that took place in Jesus Christ concerns the whole of reality, all humans individually and humanity as a whole. In this sense 'Catholicity' is used by several Christian confessions. Its opposite is the sectarianism characterized by an absence of reference to totality.

Collegiality: Congar himself defined this word: 'This means that the bishops are jointly responsible for the Church in union with the pope.' The 'rediscovery' of collegiality at Vatican II is related to a certain rediscovery of the particular Churches. One can also give this term a broader meaning. See the term *Sobornost'* below.

Conciliarity: The Church is 'conciliar' by nature because it is founded on the belief that all its members have received the Holy Spirit and need each other to be the Church. Conciliarity is not limited to periods during which the Church is officially gathered in Council, as was the case during the last Council, Vatican II (1962–1965), or even during local synods. The life of the Church is permanently conciliar: this means paying attention to what each person and each community can bring to the life of the Church.

Conciliarism: Conciliarism argues that the supreme authority in the Church is located in the Council. It thinks of the relation of the Pope to the Council in terms of opposition. Particularly strong in the fifteenth century, with the councils of Constance and Basel, this trend has its theoretical roots in the thirteenth century.

Council of Trent: This is the Council that met in the city of Trento in northern Italy beginning in December 1545 and that, after several lengthy interruptions, was completed 18 years later in December 1563. Its purpose was to work towards the reform of the Catholic Church.

Ecclesia: This Greek word, which passed into Latin, means 'assembly' and is usually translated as 'church'. Congar uses this term without translation to mean the Church as the people of God in all its components, and not only the hierarchy, as many of his contemporaries were inclined to think.

Ecclesiology: A theological discipline that deals with the theology of the Church, ecclesiology does not come into its own until the twentieth century.

Eschatology: This term comes from the Greek *eschaton*, 'that which pertains to the end'. Congar is committed to an eschatological perspective on reality, since 'biblically, the truth of a thing is what it is called to become' (Congar).

Extrinsicism: Extrinsicism exists when the relation of God to human nature is conceived in a purely external fashion, as foreign to the human and as having no point of contact with human desire. It gives rise to a dualism, and sometimes an opposition between the natural and the supernatural.

Gregorian Reform: Name given to the reform movement begun in the second half of the eleventh century by Pope Gregory VII (1073–1085).

Lumen Gentium: The name of an important Vatican II document on the Church, voted on and approved 21 November 1964.

Ontology: Ontology is a doctrine or theory of being. When Congar describes the ontology of the Church or of the people of God, he affirms that it is an ontology of service, in order to say that the whole being of the Church is service.

Pneumatology: From the Greek *pneuma* (spirit), pneumatology for Congar is more than a study of the third Person of the Trinity. For him, it is 'the impact, in the vision we have of the Church, of the fact that the Spirit distributes his gifts as he wants, and thus builds the Church' (Congar). An ecclesiology that is insufficiently pneumatological promotes a certain legalism in the Church. Many theologians of the twentieth century, among them Congar, were sensitive to the accusation of legalism that was often brought by Orthodox theologians against Western Christianity.

Post-Tridentine: Referring to the era following the Council of Trent, this period extends almost to the Second Vatican Council. See 'Tridentinism' for its characteristics.

Reception: This is the process by which the people of God takes as its own the decision of a council or hierarchy. The consensus of the people of God in this case is seen as a sign of the presence of the Holy

Spirit. Reception is considered essential in a communion ecclesiology, where the free adherence of consciences to the same truth is valued. It is minimized in a pyramidal ecclesiology.

Sensus fidelium ('sense of the faithful'): It has been presented as the fruit, in each believer, of the *sensus fidei* ('sense of faith'). It can be compared to a sort of flair, an instinct, a spiritual sense that allows those who participate in the deep reality of the ecclesial body to intuit what is in harmony with the authentic meaning of faith or what constitutes a deviation from it. This sense is not exercised alone, but in communion with the whole Church, whence the plural 'sense of the faithful'. The sense of the faithful is the expression of the conscience of the Body of Christ; among other things, it anticipates how to best live faithfulness to the Gospel in new contexts.

Sobornost': This term is derived from the Slavic word *soborny*, which is used in the Creed to signify the Catholicity of the Church. In Russian *sobor* is the equivalent of 'assembly' or 'council'. Sobornost' is a neologism used in the sense of 'catholicity' and 'collegiality' (see above for definitions of these terms). The English translation 'togetherness' has been suggested, but it is a togetherness that describes both the unity within a communion and respect for the integrity of each person. This is a notion that is difficult to understand (and is often said to be untranslatable) in a culture of individualism and uniformity, because it assumes that we become truly ourselves in communion with others. It articulates freedom and community, unity and difference, and implies that truth is preserved by the whole Body of Christ.

Soteriology: This refers to the doctrine of salvation and of the God that saves. It comes from the Greek word *Soter*, meaning 'saviour'.

Tridentinism: The city of Trento is called *Tridentum* in Latin. Tridentinism is a pejorative term that refers not to the Council of Trent (1545–63), but to the way the Council was applied in favour of a Roman centralism which was quite reductive with respect to the great Catholic tradition and the Council of Trent itself. Faced with the struggle against the Protestant Reformation, Catholic theology in the Tridentinist mould was legalistic. It was driven to abandon or to be suspicious of elements that are part of the Catholic tradition but which it did not affirm because they were emphasized by the Reformers. Other elements, less central in the Catholic faith, were, in contrast, given greater prominence.

Vatican I: This Council was convened by Pope Pius IX, and met from December 1869 to 20 October 1870. Because it was interrupted by the annexation of Rome to the kingdom of Italy, it was not able to fulfil its original programme.

Vatican II: This Council was convened by Pope John XXIII and announced by him on 25 January 1959. The opening speech pronounced by John XXIII on 11 October 1962 caused a sensation. The pope assigned three tasks to the Council: 1) the updating of the Church in its structures, its language, and its orientations (John XXIII employed the Italian word *aggiornamento* in this sense); 2) ecumenism; 3) openness to the world. The four sessions of this Council extended from 1962 to 1965. A pastoral council, it was characterized by its refusal to pronounce anathemas. Its 'reception' is still in progress.

INDEX